Department of Health and Social Security
Development Group-Social Work Service

Violence

Edited by Norman Tutt

London   Her Majesty's Stationery Office

14

This book is to be returned on

Other publications of the Development Group are:

Care and Treatment in a Planned Environment, 1970, HMSO
Community Homes Design Guide, 1971, HMSO
Intermediate Treatment, 1973, HMSO
Hostels for Young People, 1975, HMSO

Further titles are in preparation in the HMSO series and a number of unpublished reports and studies are available on application to the

Development Group (Room B1104)
Social Work Service,
Department of Health & Social Security,
Alexander Fleming House,
London SE1

The Prologue

Violence – Just An Ordinary Word

What is violence?

I don't think anybody really thinks about the word violence, to everyday people it's just a word like fire, people, house; just an ordinary word.

If you were to stop and ask people what the word violence meant they'd probably say fighting, war, killing, etc, because people haven't given it much thought.

Violence is not just fighting with guns, you are violent towards people when you swear at them, and call them things. I don't like fighting of any description. Nowadays there is fighting going on all over the world, it really frightens me. I wish all this violence would come to an END! I'd like to see some of the heads of the different governments all over the world, and ask them why they fight? Why they're so violent WHY? If they don't intend being violent why do they make all these bombs. If all these bombs, guns, etc were destroyed there wouldn't be so much violence, I don't think so anyway

Annette . . . aged 13 years

'A bit of violence never hurt anybody."
Graffiti in a London Underground Station

Contents

Foreword
Barbara Kahan

In May 1970 the Chief Inspector[1] of the Home Office Children's Department received a request from the National Association of Approved Schools Staff for 'guidance' in the problem of dealing with 'acts of aggression' by some of the boys and girls with whom they worked. During the previous year a small survey of incidents of violence occurring during the recovery of girls who had absconded from their approved schools had been carried out on behalf of the Approved School Managers' Association and in their letter to the Chief Inspector, the Staff Association referred particularly to 'the problem of violence in girls' schools' expressing the view that violence was an immediate problem for them and a cause of fear and anxiety to their members.

The Children & Young Persons Act 1969 was just beginning to be implemented at this time and previous traditional methods in approved schools for boys and girls were being challenged and reviewed in the light of changing attitudes to young offenders and children in trouble resultant upon the development of child care services since 1948. The changes which the new legislation was to promote were controversial, and in anticipation of change The Home Office Children's Department in 1968 had established a Development Group[2] to provide a resource for exploration of ideas and methods in conjunction with field agencies, government departments, universities, training bodies and others. Its broad aims were to build 'models' to assist development of services and produce publications to stimulate discussion and debate.

It was to the Development Group that the National Association of Approved Schools Staff's request was referred by the Under Secretary for the Children's Department and the Chief Inspector, who in replying to the Association said that the problem of violence ('as a shorthand for many forms of behaviour') should not be regarded as exclusive to approved schools but 'if it is studied in any way then it should be looked at over a wide range of residential establishments for children and young people . . . The Development Group would be prepared to try to help in this matter provided it is understood that they would not want to work at it purely from a theoretical standpoint, but would need the full cooperation of a number of institutions from various parts of the field prepared to discuss their problem and to consider structure and practice'. The National Association of Approved Schools Staff had suggested that the establishment of Youth Treatment Centres, a new form of secure accommodation organised to combine a medical and social work

1

approach to the care and containment of certain exceptionally violent and aggressive children and young persons, might eventually provide the solution. The Chief Inspector's view, however, was that although specialised provision might help 'it remains important to increase the ability of staff working in a great variety of establishments to handle a difficult behaviour with competence. It is this which the Development Group would be the more concerned with'.

During the summer of 1970 a working party was established, chaired by the Deputy Chief Inspector[3] responsible for the Development Group and representative of social work, medical, research and administrative interests within the Home Office, residential work in field agencies and the Staff Association whose request had given rise to it. Twelve meetings in all were held over the course of about a year and a number of proposals for offering help and guidance to social work practitioners were considered. Amongst them were proposals for comparative research studies on violence in institutions and a study of absconding. The first did not proceed though one of the chapters in this book draws on other research studies of residential establishments for the same purpose. The second was also not undertaken as a consequence of the Development Group's work but a member of the working party has since published a study of absconding[4]. A survey of literature on aggression was carried out on behalf of the working party by two of its members[5] and is referred to in Chapter 8; in addition the National Association of Approved Schools Staff was provided with information and advice on behalf of its members concerning compensation rights and insurance against risk of injury or loss.

The major task undertaken in response to their request, however, was the provision of a series of residential seminars on the subject of violence, the purpose of which was to explore with those in the field of social work and related services the problem, its nature and causes, and possible ways of helping staff who faced it. It was hoped that this method might offer help and guidance reasonably quickly and might, through drawing together wide experience and knowledge, provide indicators of further work which might be done in the future. From the outset it was planned that the seminars should contribute to a publication so that not only those present might benefit from an experience-sharing and cooperative exercise between central government and field agencies but that by broadening perception and stimulating discussion, a contribution might be made to policy in the social services, staff development and problem solving. This book is the direct result of that intention.

Before planning the seminars the Development Group sought not only the advice and help of the working party, but also other parts of the Home Office concerned with institutional management of aggressive young people, the prisons, borstals and detention centres. The view expressed on their behalf, based on their experience, was that violence amongst women prisoners was a desperate call for attention and help, or an expression of frustration and misery, and in the long run should be treated as such. The inability of many of these prisoners to express their feelings adequately in words often led to aggression being worked out in violent action. Young men had similar problems and in general it was said that more unstable and disturbed young people than formerly were being committed to prison department establishments. Staff training, regularly and at all levels, was seen to be essential if the handling of situations which could lead to violence was to be effective. Prison department staff also drew attention to the importance of men working with women and to their own rule that no more force than necessary should be used to restrain the violent, while any suggestion of retaliation was out of the question.

With these considerations in mind the planning of a pilot series of seminars took place. As a matter of basic structure it was decided to combine opportunities for considering broad intellectual concepts and information with methods of increasing self-awareness and providing experiential learning. The difficulties of achieving this in relatively short periods of time had to be accepted and as far as possible overcome, and the practical problems of releasing very busy social workers and other professionals from residential work and allied services had to be understood and taken into account. Nevertheless it was firmly held that if the experiment were to yield the maximum results, some definite commitment of time and interest throughout the course of the seminars would be required from each participant whose own experience and others' would be enriched and facilitated in large part by shared learning and exchange of ideas and feelings. Thus it became a rule that unless an individual could undertake to be present throughout a series of seminars, he could not participate in part. Inevitably a very few members of each series who had initially accepted this requirement were unable to complete the experience for reasons ranging from unavoidable and unexpected official commitments such as illness or serious staff problems, to withdrawal for personal reasons and difficulties. Nevertheless of the five hundred or so people from many different settings and services, and at levels from very senior to relatively junior staff who became participants, over ninety per cent participated fully, making a personal contribution to the experience of the others and to the material contained in this book. At the time of publication the Development Group had run eight series of

3

seminars, one pilot series, and seven others in different regions, including Wales. Two more were being planned for regions not yet covered and meanwhile as a result of invitations to participate in the English seminars extended to members of the Social Work Services Group in the Scottish Home and Health Department and the Social Work Advisory Group, Northern Ireland Department of Health and Social Security, a series had been held in Scotland and another in Northern Ireland.

The first experimental series was held at Chichester in the late autumn of 1971 and the early spring of 1972 and was by invitation, mainly to heads and other staff of approved schools, (now community homes with education on the premises), remand homes and reception homes (now observation and assessment centres), and hostels for adolescents. A representative of the British Association of Social Workers was invited to this series, but otherwise, apart from members of the Social Work Service[6] and of the Social Work Services Group in the Scottish Home and Health Department, the participants were entirely drawn from residential work in child care services. This series, when evaluated, led to a decision to run a series in each region of England and Wales, and for a time, particularly during the series in the North West and West Midlands, the emphasis on children's services continued. It was not long, however, before it was clear that, if examination of the problem and experience sharing were to be as adequate as possible, field as well as residential staff needed to be included, and staff from other services such as probation and education. Inevitably the influence of changes in organisation of social services resulting from the Local Authority Social Services Act 1970, led to consideration of widening participation still further to those who worked with adults as well as children, and involvement of prison service and police personnel amongst speakers had suggested that their involvement in the whole exercise was important. With the reorganisation of the National Health Service, the emphasis placed on co-operation and joint work between health and social services and the recognition of common problems led to inclusion of health service personnel in the last three series before this book was published. Finally the close connection between child care problems at home and in school made day, as well as residential teachers another significant group to include. Members of HM Inspectorate of Schools participated in a number of seminars and representatives of the Central Council for Education and Training in Social Work were also involved whenever possible.

Prior to the pilot series of seminars a collection of readings on violence [7] was arranged to provide participants with an oppor-

4

tunity to begin thinking about the problem in a wider context than their own work setting or personal experience. This collection ranged through excerpts from psycho-analytic writings and research studies to first hand accounts of violence, news items, advice to nurses in handling mentally ill patients and a variety of other material and mirrored the intention of the seminars to broaden perpectives and knowledge and share experience and skill.

The pilot series of seminars was held in three parts, two residential weeks in September and October 1971 and a shorter period in January 1972. Subsequently various methods of timing were used, sometimes five separate day conferences at weekly intervals followed by a residential week, or two residential weeks with a period of two to five weeks in between. The latter pattern prevailed, partly because in spite of difficulties in releasing staff, it proved more convenient in practice to release them for a block period than a series of separate days, and partly because the time available in a residential week is considerably greater than the equivalent number of day conferences. The speed with which relationships were formed, ability to communicate developed and learning achieved was much greater too in a residential experience.

An outline of the seminars' content sent to intending participants proposed lecture topics which included personality structure; heredity and environment; behaviour difficulties, problems, causes and symptoms; basic human needs and their fulfilment; aggression in animals; human aggression in society; small children, adolescents, old people, the mentally sick etc.; social psychology; human environments; the balance between individual freedom and necessary controls; and living and working in groups.

Over the course of eight series of seminars a large number of nationally and internationally known speakers contributed and participants had opportunities to discuss with them many facets of human behaviour theory, historical perceptions, sociological interpretations, and the relevance of animal behaviour to human beings. Football violence, vandalism, murder, corporal punishment, the deterrent value of imprisonment, psychiatric treatment of mental illness and crime, the importance of early childhood nurturing practice on adult mature behaviour, matrimonial and parental violence and much more formed part of the seminar material. 'Problem' films and commercially produced films featuring various forms of violence, including verbal violence, were also part of each programme and bookstalls were available throughout with an extensive range of publications. A major objective of the more formal inputs was to provide tangible evidence of the need for a sense of proportion in considering the problem of violence, and a recognition that though we have a problem and one which must be tackled, we are better off than many societies and periods of history and certainly no worse off than many others. Our football hooligans are a nuisance to us but the Elizabethans had their problems too! Sir Thomas Elyot 1400–1546, friend of Sir Thomas Moore JP for Oxfordshire in 1522 and Clerk to the Privy Council in 1523–30, for example spoke of 'Foote balle, wherein is nothinge but beastlie furie and exstreme violence'. It may not solve our problems to know that others had them, but it may help us not to take them more seriously than they deserve. Small groups' discussion formed a major part of the programme and role playing, intergroup exercises and other methods of increasing awareness of human interaction were employed. Panels of practitioners drawn from a wide spectrum of services in which violence was a common problem were also invited to discuss and share their experience and further broaden the spectrum.

The Development Group recruited, to assist them in these seminars, a number of people whose experience and training provided the skill required to lead groups which were to be neither functional task groups nor T-groups. Each participant became a member of a small group of about eight to ten members and remained in that group with the same leader throughout the whole series of seminars he attended. The objective was to provide a setting in which experience, feeling and concern could be freely shared, and greater awareness and sensitivity developed but not to attempt the degree of self revelation and interpretation characteristic of the T-group method. This was a deliberate decision and one which was not modified in the light of experience. The groups did not therefore, fit clearly into any one theory of group work, but nevertheless in practice enabled most people to develop their thinking and share experience and learning in a way most had not been able to do before. Tom Douglas's chapter on his use of group exercises and socio-drama may illuminate this part of the seminars for readers, and it is unlikely that the socio-drama could have been the valuable experience it was for most participants if they had not had the small group experience in which to make relationships and gain confidence. It is of interest and relevance to the provision of services to troubled human beings that although the great majority of participants in these seminars were people who in their working lives had great influence, many great power, over the lives of other people, their almost universal reaction to coming to the seminars was anxiety, a degree of agitation and suspicion and consequent need to hold back initially, to demonstrate aggression in some cases to the organisers, and to be ready prey for rumours, fantasy, rivalry and gossip within the larger group and between small groups. Resentment of small domestic details in the setting, suspicion of organisers' intentions towards them and in the provision of seminars in general, the setting up of stereotypes and other well known indications of anxiety and feelings of inadequacy or powerlessness occurred regularly in each series of seminars. Plenary sessions in which the organisers exposed themselves to comment of whatever kind participants wished to make were used as a safety valve and later the whole 'institutional' experience was examined in an attempt to see its relevance to the work situation of participants. The overall impression of this aspect of the seminars was that it is very difficult for those who provide services to put themselves in the place of those who are receiving them and that sensitivity is not something which is easily acquired, either by training or by any of the usual methods of preparation for working in public services.

In consequence of the objectives outlined above and the common human traits exhibited under the pressures of anxiety and uncertainty, the task of group leaders was demanding and difficult. During the course of a series, small groups sessions would occupy twenty to twenty-five hours in all and group leaders, as Tom Douglas explains, were also asked to drop their role for a time and assume the role of observer for a period of approximately two days in the final week of each series. A number of skilled and interesting people from a wide range of professional settings worked as group leaders in these seminars; psychiatrists, psychologists, senior residential social workers, senior social workers from many other settings, social work tutors, teachers from residential establishments for the maladjusted, and many others.

Under their leadership, usually exercised in a relatively undirective manner, groups not only discussed the material arising from lectures, films, and individuals' practical experience but a range of inter-related subjects demonstrating the capacity available to see a problem in wider perspectives given an appropriate stimulus and opportunity. Rapporteurs were appointed in each group to keep a note of the more significant points discussed and these notes, unattributed to any individual speaker or group were then summarized and analysed and fed back to the total seminar at the end of each residential period. The demand for these summaries seemed to be related, not only to their usefulness in providing a basis for a report to employing authorities, but to the satisfaction participants felt in having the unrelated parts of their own and other groups' discussions put together into a related whole. It was interesting to see how in the relatively supportive

7

atmosphere and the intimacy of small groups people felt able to view their experience and their own actions in a more objective light than can have been customary for most of them. It was even possible in the accounts of violent incidents, they provided, (referred to later) for many of the writers to explain that they realised on looking back that the incident might never have happened but for the lack of sensitivity or skill or tolerance that they themselves had shown. To be able to write this down and then discuss it in detail with a group of other people seems to provide evidence that during the course of the seminars some people reached a point of self-criticism which might be of lasting value in their work with, and management of, people.

It was a common experience on all the seminars for participants to arrive with expectations, in spite of pre-seminar material and implicit indications to the contrary, of short-cut 'answers' to the problems of violence; perhaps a set of rules to follow, or a recipe for effective management. When these did not materialize sceptism and irritation followed in some cases, and it was important to have time and opportunity available, as well as techniques of group discussion and interaction to catch the interest, make the links between information, feeling and experience, to extend and deepen understanding beyond the trite response and cliché answer which tend to be a first response. Group leaders gave a great deal to their groups and claimed to have gained a great deal in return. A number of them worked on several series of seminars and in consequence became closely involved with the Development Group. One of these was Norman Tutt, who was a group leader on the pilot series at Chichester and subsequently on several other series. In addition, he lectured to one series, assisted Tom Douglas in his work with the groups on another, and carried out a consumer reaction study with the first group of participants. He was, therefore, steeped in the experiences of the Seminars on Violence and when it became possible, accepted an invitation from the Development Group to be the editor for this book. A group of writers were selected, all except one of whom had presented papers to the seminars and worked with them. The wealth of material which might have been presented could have filled much more than one book, but the present selection has aimed at providing a sequence of ideas and knowledge which is very similar to the pattern developed in the seminars, with the addition of some description of the experiential learning (the large group work and socio-drama) and a selection of accounts of incidents of violence contributed by participants.

During all but one of the series of seminars, participants were asked to prepare during the interval between the first and second weeks, a description of a violent incident in which they had participated or which they had witnessed and, if possible, to get another person involved or witnessing it, to write his or her account in addition. These descriptive accounts were then brought to the second week and used as discussion material in small groups and subsequently collected together for use in a publication at a later date. From the many vivid and fascinating studies produced, Norman Tutt has selected a few which he has arranged to form the last chapter in this book. They cannot fail to move the reader and many more, unable to be used here, are equally valuable and may, if opportunity presents, be used by the Development Group in another publication. The anonymous writers of these accounts gave generously of their personal experience and generously agreed to allow them to be used at the discretion of the Development Group in the publication of a book. They ranged from bitter personal experiences to accounts of fear, violence, anger, anguish and suffering of a kind which fortunately only a minority of people have to endure. In some respects they are the most important material in the book because they demonstrate so clearly the nature of many problems of violence.

The intention of the seminars was to broaden individual perceptions and knowledge, but also to use the experience and knowledge of people providing services to help a wide variety of other people carrying out the same or similar tasks and roles. Those who attended the seminars knew that their contribution would be assisting in achieving this objective and the Development Group is glad to have been able, with the help of Norman Tutt, to carry out this undertaking.

References
(1) Miss Joan Cooper CB Director of the Social Work Service, Department of Health and Social Security in 1971.
(2) The Development Group as part of the Home Office Children's Department was amalgamated with the Department of Health and Social Security in 1971.
(3) Mrs. B. J. Kahan who became Assistant Director, Social Work Service, Department of Health and Social Security in 1971.
(4) R. V. G. Clarke and D. N. Martin (1971) *Absconding,* HMSO, London.
(5) I. A. C. Sinclair and R. V. Clarke.
(6) Social Work Service was the name chosen for the group formed by joining together the Social Work Advisory Service of the Department of Health and Social Security and the Children's Inspectorate of the Home Office in 1971.
(7) Available on request from the Development Group.

The Contributors

NORMAN TUTT (EDITOR) Graduated from the University of Keele in Psychology and Politics, undertook a Masters degree in Clinical Psychology at Leeds University and a Doctoral degree at Nottingham University. He has worked in a range of clinical settings including both child and adult psychiatry. For some time he was resident psychologist at a boys' approved school, and this experience formed the basis for his first book 'Care or Custody' published in London by Darton, Longman and Todd. Since then he has held a number of advisory posts in the fields of delinquency and Social Services. He is currently a Principal Social Work Service Officer with the Department of Health and Social Security.

COLIN CAMPBELL Professor Campbell, born in Aberdeen, was educated at Robert Gordon's College and Aberdeen University. From 1967–1969 he was Lecturer in Jurisprudence at the University of Dundee and then Lecturer in the Department of Public Law at the University of Edinburgh from 1969–1973. Since 1974 he has been Professor of the Jurisprudence Law Faculty at Queens University Belfast.

JOHN ROBOTTOM was born and educated in Birmingham. He served two years as a national serviceman before reading history at Birmingham University. Nine years as a teacher in secondary modern schools was followed by work in teacher training, latterly as Head of the History Department at Crewe College of Education. Since September 1974 he has worked for the BBC as the School Broadcasting Council's education officer in the Midlands. Interested in many aspects of recent history, he has written books for secondary schools on Asian, European and British topics. He is married with three children.

HEIDI SWANSON was born in Copenhagen. She travelled widely as a child finally settling in Canada, where she completed her education with a Doctoral degree from McGill University, Montreal. She has held a number of research and teaching posts both in North America and Europe. She is currently Senior Lecturer in Anatomy, at the University of Birmingham; her fields of particular interest are the influence of hormones during development on sexual and social behaviour and mechanisms controlling population density. She is a member of several leading learned societies and a founder member of the European Brain and Behaviour Society. She is married with two children.

VLADIMIR KAHAN was educated at Cambridge University and trained at the London Hospital.

After some years in general practice in London he served in the RAMC in the Middle and Far East. On returning to the UK he worked in adult psychiatry and subsequently specialised in child and adolescent psychiatry. He was Medical Director of Child Guidance Services in Oxfordshire and Hampshire, Consultant to various approved schools and remand homes and worked closely with a number of Children's Departments. From 1959–72 he was in charge of a hospital unit for psychotic and severely disturbed children and his book 'Mental Illness in Childhood', describes the special environmental care used to counteract overactivity and violent behaviour.

Currently he is Staff Consultant to a Social Services Department in the London area and to two residental establishments for disturbed adolescent boys.

JOHN and ELIZABETH NEWSON John Newson was educated at Bancrofts School, South-West Essex Technical College, and University College, London, reading first physics and mathematics and later psychology. He has been lecturing and doing research at the University of Nottingham since 1951, specialising in child psychology and statistics.

ELIZABETH NEWSON was educated at the Mary Datchelor School and University College, London, where she read psychology. After teaching infants for a year in Nottingham, she joined the Nottingham University psychology department as a research student in 1952, and has been doing research ever since.

JOHN and ELIZABETH NEWSON met at University College and were married in 1951. Their first book was *Patterns of Infant Care in an Urban Community* (published in Pelicans). They have three children and regard the experience of parenthood as an almost indispensable professional qualification, a necessary and effective counterbalance to the study of child development as they encounter it in learned journals. They founded and jointly direct the Child Development Research Unit at Nottingham University, which is now well known for its interest in parents as a research resource. Their conviction that parents are the richest source of information about their own children is illustrated by their books on 'ordinary' children; but they are equally interested in parents problems in coping with a child's handicap. They are actively researching ways of using parents' individual knowledge to devise tailor-made remedial programmes for handicapped children, and to put tools for remediation into the hands of the parents themselves.

The Newsons' other research concern, the function of play in early child development, spills over into their main recreational pursuit, the design of toys. They take an active interest in a family-

11

run craft gallery and specialist toyshop in Enfield.

Books by John and Elizabeth Newson:

Infant Care in an Urban Community, Allen & Unwin (London) and International Universities Press, 1963; Penguin Books, 1965; Aldine (Chicago), 1968; Translated into Spanish: Matronas Revista Profesional, Madrid, 1965; Variously extracted, including Studies in English Society (J. A. Banks ed).

Four years Old in an Urban Community, Allen & Unwin (London) and Aldine (Chicago), 1968; Penguin Books, 1970.

With Sheila Hewett: *The Family and the Handicapped Child,* Allen & Unwin (London), 1970.

John Newson and Michael Matthews: *The Language of Basic Statistics,* Longmans.

In preparation:

All three books to be published by Allen & Unwin (London).

Seven Years Old in the Home Environment (published Spring 1976).

Perspectives On School at Seven Years Old.

Play and Playthings in Early Childhood.

RAY CASTLE, a social worker for 14 years, joined the original NSPCC Battered Child Research Project in 1968 and became head of that department in 1971.

In October, 1974 he was appointed as the Executive responsible for the Society's new National Advisory Centre on the Battered Child.

In addition to directing the work of the Centre, he is one of a small number of specialists who form an international working party on the problems of non-accidental injury to children and has published several papers on the subject. He is also a member of the Tunbridge Wells Study Group.

Prior to taking up his present appointment, Mr Castle spent a period of time working in the United States where he acted as a Consultant in the setting-up of two projects concerned with the prevention of child abuse and worked closely with Professor C. M. Kempe at the University of Colorado Medical Centre, Denver.

SPENCER MILLHAM, ROGER BULLOCK and KENNETH HOSIE are members of the Social Research Unit at Dartington Hall, Devon.

Until 1968 the Unit worked at Kings College, Cambridge on a Department of Education sponsored survey of boarding education for ordinary children. The Unit moved to Dartington in 1968 and began a study of boys' approved schools for the Home Office and later the DHSS. Since 1973 research has been undertaken in association with the Department of Social Administration at the University of Bristol under the direction of Professor Roy Parker. Current projects include studies of secure provision for adolescents and training for residential social work.

Spencer Millham taught in boarding schools for ten years before joining the team in 1966.

Roger Bullock graduated in social sciences before moving to Cambridge in 1965.

Kenneth Hosie worked for Dr Barnardo's and directed a school leavers' project in an educational priority area before joining the Unit in 1974.

Publications of the Unit are:

The State and Boarding Education: 1965. Methuen

The Hothouse Society: 1968. Weidenfeld & Nicholson

New Wine in Old Bottles: 1969. George Bell

A manual – To the Sociology of the School: 1970. Weidenfeld & Nicholson

The Chance of a Lifetime?: 1975. Weidenfeld & Nicholson

After Grace – Teeth: 1975. Chaucer Publishing Company

as well as many articles and research reports.

JOHN HARRINGTON received his early education at Bedford School proceeding to Christ College, Cambridge where he read Natural Sciences. After Clinical training at St Thomas' Hospital, London he did his war service in the medical branch of the RAF and on demobilization spent a year studying Public Health and Industrial Medicine at the London School of Hygiene. After two years as a research epidemiologist with the Medical Research Council, his interests turned to psychiatry and he completed his training at the Maudsley and Bethlem Royal Hospitals. He is currently Director of the Uffculme Clinic, a Regional Centre for Psychotherapy, which specializes in group psychotherapeutic techniques for the treatment of mainly young people. As a Senior Clinical Lecturer at the University of Birmingham he is actively involved in post-graduate training programmes in psychiatry and psychotherapy in the Midlands.

In 1968, at the suggestion of Mr Dennis Howells, Minister for Sport, he established a research group at Birmingham University which carried out a preliminary investigation of the problem of soccer hooliganism which emphasized in particular the group aspects of misbehaviour associated with football matches. More recent researches have been linked with the problem of vandalism and aspects of social psychiatry.

GEOFFREY PEARSON is Lecturer in Sociology in the School of Applied Social Studies, University of Bradford. He moved there in 1975 from University College, Cardiff where he developed and taught a course in Human Socialisation for four years, and before that held a teaching post at Sheffield Polytechnic. He therefore has an active interest in teaching social workers and has worked as a social worker himself for a number of years, having qualified as a psychiatric social worker in 1968. He has written on a number of the moral and political aspects of social work, psychiatry, criminology and the welfare state. His first book, *The Deviant Imagination*, is published by Macmillan, and he has edited another book (with Geoff Mungham) *Working Class Youth Culture* which is published by Routledge and Kegan Paul.

STUART HALL is Director of the Centre for Cultural Studies at the University of Birmingham. He was born in Kingston, Jamaica where he spent his early years. He was educated at Merton College, Oxford. On leaving Oxford he took up a teaching post in a seconday school in London. From 1959–61 he was the editor of the *New Left Review*. In 1961 he joined the teaching staff of the Chelsea College of Science (University of London) where he stayed until 1964 when he moved to the Centre for Cultural Studies, originally as Assistant Director and latterly in his present post as Director.

TOM DOUGLAS is Senior Lecturer in Social Work in the Department of Sociology, University of Keele. During the 1950s he worked in Deva Hospital, Chester in a social therapy programme. He then moved to Blackpool as a duly authorised officer in the Mental Health Service eventually becoming casework consultant and psychiatric social worker in the Child Guidance Clinic. He later became Tutor in Child Care, Harris College, Preston for two years and has been teaching social work at Keele since 1966.

Publications:

Decade of Small Group Theory: 1970. Bookstall Publications, Bristol.

Groupwork Practice: 1976. Tavistock, London.

Chapter I **Introduction**
Norman Tutt

The aim of this book is to put violence, particularly violence amongst children and young people, into perspective; to provide a broad based view of violence as an historical phenomenon, an adaptive piece of animal behaviour and in many instances a positive, or at least, inevitable human attribute.

It highlights for teachers, social workers, magistrates, politicians and general readers the many and varied forms violence can take including personal abuse, mental cruelty, physical attack and what is sometimes described in the studies of violence contributed to the seminars as the 'indirect' violence of 'the system'. The book questions which, if any, of these possible forms and others is more acceptable or justifiable. It questions and examines many contemporary myths about violence; are its perpetrators mentally ill, is the violence of soccer hooligans wanton and mindless, is the media to blame for increased violence? It enquires into how society treats the violent in institutions, and how the staff of institutions may present as much violence as the inmates. Its aim, in short, is not merely to provide some alternative to current sensational and negative views of violence, but also to offer a greater understanding of how the potential for violence is within us all. If only we can understand this our ability to contain and control violence in our society may be greatly enhanced.

It became clear in this book that a major problem in any detailed study of violence is how to define the word. There are many and varied forms of violence. There is also the problem of violence being legitimate or illegitimate. Today's violence may often, through the passage of time, become tomorrow's heroism or martyrdom. The problem of legitimate or illegitimate violence is extremely complex as Colin Campbell shows in the following chapter. For example, a declared war in which many thousands or even millions of men, women and children are slaughtered is regarded as legitimate violence. Yet undeclared acts of war such as the recent IRA bombings in England are regarded as illegitimate violence, although many fewer people are injured, maimed or killed. The fact that the action is regarded as terrorism rather than the action of one nation state against another means that the violence is regarded as illegitimate and unacceptable. Even this distinction is not clear since it often depends on the perception of the observer.

During the Second World War resistance movements carried out violent actions against the enemy occupying armies and were applauded by the population and regarded as heroes. Action of a similar nature now against their own governments would be regarded as murder and treason. The distinction between legitimate and illegitimate violence may be related to political and partisan perceptions and not to clear principles. Similar issues arise when lesser forms of violence in terms of physical contact are examined. In a game of rugby football a good deal of physical contact takes places, sometimes of a very brutal nature, in which punches, kicks or vicious tackles may be aimed by one member of a team against a member of another team. This is regarded as legitimate as long as it takes place during the hour and a half of play, and on the playing field. If the same behaviour took place in a club room or pub afterwards it would become a brawl and illegitimate, it is then open to police prosecution, and the whole of society's mechanisms begins to operate against the perpetrator.

Similar areas of uncertainty operate in the behaviour between parents or adults and children. Corporal punishment is allowed within schools, and an adult may inflict six strokes of the cane on a child's posterior; in some areas, even a leather tawse is used to inflict punishment on children. At the same time we live in a society that is particularly conscious and concerned about the problem of baby battering, and the parent who abuses his child by excessive physical punishment. Bruising, battering or damaging a child may be a reason for being taken before a court and charged with a criminal offence which will shock society.

The issues raised in trying to draw a dividing line between legitimate and illegitimate violence do not even depend on the extent of the damage done to the violated person. For example, an unrelated adult who clips a child on the ear in the street could well be taken to court for assault; yet, within some classroom situations this may be regarded as reasonable discipline, although it is contrary to the Education Act.

This confusion over the way in which our culture uses violence or aggressive behaviour makes it extremely difficult for any social scientist to study it as a piece of behaviour. Violence could be defined as a piece of behaviour that inflicts injury on another. The throwing of a punch is a simple straightforward behavioural act, which could be interpreted as violent; but it depends whether the punch is thrown within a boxing ring, in which case it is regarded as legitimate and therefore not an act of violence but a sporting activity, or alternatively if the punch is thrown in a public house or within a man's own home against his wife; then it becomes an act of violence. However, the situation is further confused since the similar behavioural activity, namely the punch, may be thumped on a table as an angry gesture in a speech; is it then an act of violence? Or if a punch is thrown by a psychiatric patient or a disturbed adolescent at a window, which is then broken, or against furniture which is damaged, is that an act of violence? Or is violence only behaviour inflicted on another individual or human being? If so what should we think about the 'hero' of Peter Schaffer's play 'Equus', a disturbed adolescent boy whose disturbance manifested itself in putting out the eyes of horses and blinding them. Was that violence or not?

The technology which Western society has developed adds further confusion. The punch is a piece of behaviour with obvious intent, but what about the throwing of a switch? If it is a light switch then that is not violent behaviour, but if it is the switch which precipitates a nuclear attack in which thousands of people are totally annihilated, is that violent behaviour? If the switch were operated by the leader of a nation he would presumably not be condemned as violent; he would have acted in a dispassionate and, to some extent, rational way; he might, in fact, be applauded for his courage and wisdom in acting at that time and in that way. However, the outcome of his action would be far more detrimental in terms of human suffering than the breaking of a few windows. We can add to this confusion by considering the possibility of verbal violence, when two people denigrate and abuse each other in an angry exchange, is this violence? Anyone who has seen the film 'Who's Afraid of Virginia Woolf' will recognise that violence can be perpetrated through the spoken word. In the same context the label 'black bastard' may have particular significance to a coloured child, and be seen by him as a violent attack on him personally.

A further form of violence, emotional violence, can be the opposite of verbal violence, the emotional violence of strictly observed silence within a home, in which a father and mother refuse to talk to one another, the pregnant pause, these can be a form of violence to the emotions and the senses. Writers of the case studies later in the book even saw the destruction of homes and communities to build motorways, the pollution of rivers and waterways as forms of violence.

A further complication, is how violence is perceived. Much youthful activity is regarded as merely high spirits or excitement by the participants, but older onlookers may interpret it as violent. A good example of this difference of view can be seen in the opening scene of 'The Wild Ones', a film issued in the middle fifties, but banned in England for many years as being too provocative. It described the activities of a group of Hell's Angels in a

17

middle-American town. The opening scenes show a number of very powerful motorbikes roaring down a road. The noise and menacing appearance of the bikes create an atmosphere of violence, or potential violence; yet the machines in themselves were harmless aggregates of hardware.

Similar interpretations can be made of events at football matches or pop concerts in which youthful crowds begin clapping and chanting in rythmic abuse, creating fears of violence although no actual injury is incurred.

So, the first and most important point about violence as behaviour, is that it is not a homogenous concept. It lumps together a whole range of behaviour, and simple explanations therefore cannot be expected since it is unlikely that such hetero-geneous behaviour could arise from one single cause.

The second important factor to consider in a study of violence is whether, as the media is continually telling us, violence is increasing and we now live in a violent age. Has violence increased? There is a good deal of evidence to suggest it has not, some of which is explored in the first two chapters of this book. However, in this introduction it may be useful to give some brief examples of how the media can create an impression of increasing violence although in reality little change has taken place. Over the last two or three years interest in the problem of 'battered wives' has greatly increased and rightly so. It is an appalling blot on our society that a number of women are savagely beaten by their husbands and partners, and are unable to do anything about it because of their emotional or financial dependence.

The report of the Select Committee on Violence in Marriage was given comprehensive press and television coverage[1]. Yet, it is a salutary experience to remember that this Committee sitting in 1975 reported on the centenary anniversary of a previous Committee. The prevalence of crimes of violence, especially of men against their wives in the notorious 'kicking' district of Liver-pool caused much concern. There were 3,000 such cases in 1874 and 160 wives were found dead. In 1875 a Government Commis-sion of eminent lawyers favoured flogging as an appropriate punishment for such offences although most women who had drawn attention to the problem feared that it would bring further retribution against wives without solving the fundamental prob-lem, i.e. that women without independent incomes could not support themselves and their children if they left their husbands. They could not afford to sue for assault and would have found the courts unsympathetic if they had. They had no refuge but the degrading workhouse and little hope of remedy against a cruel husband.[2] The problem of battered wives was, therefore, nothing new in the middle or late twentieth century. It has been with us for a long time and like many of the so-called modern problems of violence is deep rooted in the culture of our community, though it has not always previously been regarded as a problem.

A clear illustration of this is over the matter of baby 'battering' which is now regarded as a major social problem, and yet in the past one hundred and fifty years infant mortality was much greater, and the treatment of children often brutal (See Chapter III), but because the relationship between parent and children was regarded differently and the state's right of intervention into family affairs was limited, to most people it was not a cause for great concern.

The above argument is not to defend violence, much of which in any society is to be condemned; but, it is important to recognise that our society is capable now of much greater tolerance than ever before; we live in what the sociologists call a pluralistic society. By this they mean that society consists of a range of groups, different life styles, different attitudes, different norms of behaviour, the whole heterogeneous mass being welded and held together by a very loose structure of Government. The range of life styles and tolerance offered to them is comparatively recent. In England it is now possible to belong to a range of Buddhist sects, advertisements for temples and obscure gurus appear in tube stations and elsewhere. Yet both in this country and in Europe suffering or martyrdom for religious or political beliefs, and ethnic persecutions have been common until very recently. Religious and political tolerance is now part of our culture, but because it is comparatively recent it is not surprising in face of the range of behaviour which we try to accept that tolerance does not produce total harmony and when disharmony occurs violence is often there to be exploited.

Violence is normally part of a repertoire of behaviour within a pre-existing relationship and is usually taking place between people who know each other, not in consequence of attacks by unknown thugs or assassins. This is an extremely important fact because the media project an image of violence as something which arises 'out of the blue'; the mugger, the random, vicious knife attack or pub brawl are given large coverage. However, the majority of violence takes place either within the family or within other existing relationships; this fact is rarely given adequate coverage by the media mainly perhaps because it reflects adversely on some very deeply held attitudes about family life within this country. If violence is part of inter-personal relationships then our society may well have an increase in violence because, over the past fifty years, our culture had placed more and more emphasis on the importance of inter-personal relationships. This can be clearly seen in the sphere of the so-called helping professions. During the past fifty years, for example, the relationship between therapist and patient has assumed great importance in psychiatry, and in residential social work with children it is the relationship between the adult and the child which is seen as important. The range and development of encounter groups, T-groups and sensitivity training, are further examples of the importance our culture places on inter-personal relationships. If it is accepted that violence is often connected with personal relationships and that the emphasis on such relationships has greatly increased in recent years – it could be argued that there has been a slight increase in violence or perceived violence.

It is important to examine further the violence in personal relationships. It may be that any relationship must have within it a certain conflict of power. This point has been made elsewhere;[3] but briefly, any close personal relationship is potentially a threatening situation for one or both partners; the temptation to influence and constrain a partner, within a personal relationship, is very strong and perhaps inevitable because the partner is not a mirror image of one's self.

The Newsons, in Chapter VI of this book, show quite clearly the relationship between parent and child and the dependency on the threat of physical violence or actual physical violence in ensuring that the child follows the wishes of his parents. Similarly in Chapter VIII Spencer Millham and his research unit demonstrate the extent to which physical violence is used by residential workers in their care of children. The violence in both situations is part of the authority relationship that exists between the adult and the child. At a societal level a similar situation was seen in the filmed reports of the Red Lion Square disturbances. These reports were presented before the Scarman Commission which was examining the possibility of police brutality. A large, aggressive, and possibly violent mob was assembled in Red Lion Square. Mounted Police were deployed to maintain order and although 'the horses never reached a pace faster than a walk, and the pressure on the crowd was moderate and reasonable'[4] it was also 'firm' and was a symbol of the fact that the State is prepared to use physical force if necessary to ensure that order is maintained. Thus we have a society that operates from the basic level of the family right through to the Government on the belief that physical force is permissible within an authority relationship. If this is accepted then how can we accept that violence must always be condemned?

Given that violence is not an homogeneous concept and that changes in society may be reflected in changes in the level of violent behaviour, it is not surprising therefore that when an explanation is sought, no one explanation is sufficient. Any theory to explain human or social behaviour merely attempts to give the best description of the facts available and such a theory is always open to change as society's view of the behaviour changes. The reader of this book will find different and occasionally conflicting views on the causes of violence. This does not mean that one view is correct while another is incorrect; both may be correct or incorrect depending on different stages in society's development and how cultural attitudes have changed within the intervening period.

A further complication is that many theories put forward to explain violent behaviour, are more relevant to aggressive behaviour though the difference between aggression and violence is often difficult to define. It may well be that they describe similar behaviour in different people. Because aggression is a socially accepted and indeed a positive social attribute, people like successful executives, football players and politicians are expected to be aggressive and to fight for their opportunities. The same behaviour amongst disaffected blacks in an urban area of high unemployment would be regarded as violence. Perhaps aggression is something 'we' have and violence characterizes 'them'.

In the remainder of this chapter there is no attempt to differentiate between theories of aggression and theories of violence. The differentiation seems at best to be ill-founded and consequently possibly irrelevant.

Theories of violence

Theories of violent behaviour range widely. A selection is briefly summarized below as an introduction to the main body of the book which examines some of them in much greater detail. The first and perhaps most popular view of violence in the past has been that it is an inherited quality. Certain animal species have been bred for their aggressive or violent behaviour, for example terrier dogs and hounds which excel in tenacity and aggression. Similarly it has been believed in the past that certain cultures or races have perpetuated violence through inheritance; for example the Spartans were held to be particularly brave and aggressive warriors and during the latter end of the nineteenth and the twentieth centuries the German nation has been regarded as militaristic and aggressive. It is quite possible that certain personality characteristics, including a potentiality for violence, are passed on from parent to child. However it is interesting that in the chapter offered by Dr Kahan he describes the way in which even our view of animal behaviour has changed, showing that originally the cow was regarded as an aggressive animal.

An extension of the inheritance theories are the theories of transmission of abnormalities from chromosomal sources. In certain males, for example, XYY chromosomes have been found to be more common amongst individuals in special security hospitals than within the normal population and it may well be that a small percentage of violent offenders are the result of chromosomal abnormalities[5]. In a recent celebrated French case a man was acquitted of an offence of murder on the basis of a chromosomal abnormality.

Certain other abnormalities are also often linked with violence; these are usually abnormalities of the brain structure in some form either due to illness, such as meningitis, or to physical trauma resulting in brain damage. Brain damage reduces an individual's ability to inhibit certain behaviour; his behaviour therefore tends to be uncontrolled and being uncontrolled, if he becomes angry with other people he is more likely to lash out and be violent. This explanation obviously accounts for a very small number of violent cases appearing before the courts or occurring in society generally. Further theories of violence attribute it, or aggression, to a drive like hunger or sex, which builds up until it explodes into behaviour. Alternatively the Freudian view attributes violence to an instinct laid deep within the id of the individual and occasionally rising to the surface and being expressed in behaviour.

More recent theories have argued the frustration/aggression approach to violence; animal studies have shown that an animal which is frustrated from achieving a particular objective may react by becoming aggressive and direct its energies into violent attacks on the frustrating object. Anyone who has failed to start their car on a cold wet morning will soon appreciate the validity of this theory. The frustration/aggression theory could be seen in anthropological terms as one of the major causes for violence in our society today. We produce a cultural norm which involves sexual frustration of young people by delaying mating. This frustration in turn may lead to aggressive behaviour.

More appropriate may be the theory of displacement, in which an individual who has been abused by others displaces his violence either on to inanimate objects or on to people below him in status who in turn he can abuse. This interaction has been shown to exist in residential establishments in particular. Polsky's book on 'Cottage Six'[6] showed clearly the way in which the authoritarian

22

regime of a boys' institution was mimicked within the boys' sub culture, and 'violence' shown by adults to the boys was displaced from the recipients of the violence to other boys. This chain effect has been illustrated in the well known cartoon where the boss reprimands an employee who goes home and shouts at his wife, who turns on her children, and the smallest child then kicks the cat. Interpreted into societal terms the chain effect might be from a faceless government or monolithic bureaucracy which orders and manipulates individual people producing aggression and violence within those individuals who, unable to place it on to the responsible agent, displace their violence on to their families or harmless bystanders.

Other explanations of the causation of violence arise from studies of the family in which modelling seems to be a significant part. The child models his behaviour on the parent; if part of the parents behaviour is violence and aggression, the child picks it up in the modelling process, and when an adult himself, displays the same sort of behaviour. However, the modelling may be not quite so straightforward. Many subtle messages are passed on to children ensuring the transmission of the cultural norms across generations; these messages are transmitted by both action (including corporal punishment) and words. It is of interest that in the later part of the twentieth century we should be passing on to our children the following two rhymes – the messages of which they cannot ignore:

'There was an old woman who lived in a shoe
she had so many children she didn't know what to do,
so she gave them some broth without any bread,
and whipped them all soundly and put them to bed'.

A mixed message about family planning and the abuse of unwanted children can be seen in this. Alternatively, it is often claimed that parents' concern over material goods to the detriment of their children is a modern phenomenon, yet the following nursery rhyme shows that it is long standing:

'Little Polly Flinders
sat amongst the cinders
warming her pretty little toes,
her mother came and caught her and whipped her little daughter
for spoiling her nice new clothes'.

Such a line recounted many times to a child in his cot may pass on a significant message about parent/child relationships and the behaviour expected of young children.

Recent increases in communication between cultures, and with it the rise of sociology as a serious discipline, have produced

23

different explanations for violence and explanations which are based partly on cultural differences. Why, for example, is the homicide rate in the United States much greater than in the United Kingdom, which in turn is greater than in Japan. There must be reasons to explain these differences. The opportunity for violence given by the liberal gun laws in the United States may have some connection with these statistics. In fact homicide statistics run counter to some of the popular stereotypes of the countries concerned. For example, the Japanese are held to have little regard for human life, as evidenced by their suicide flights during the Second World War and their practice of hara-kiri. Their disregard for human life might suggest that the homicide rate in Japan would be higher than elsewhere, particularly in view of the overcrowding of their cities. However, this is not so and therefore more complex explanations must be sought.

Cultural differences occur not only between nations but within an individual nation. In the United Kingdom much stress has been put on the violence of the 'working class' culture in which a man is not a man unless he is aggressive, forceful and violent, particularly to his women folk. Similarly, 'middle class' people have been held to be rational, logical and open to verbal exchanges rather than physical violence. Some recent studies on wife battering, however, suggest that as a piece of behaviour it is evenly distributed throughout the social classes, and that wives may be beaten by consultant physicians as well as by labourers. Alternatively, different cultures can exist within the same age group, at the same time or at slightly different times. In this context one youthful sub-culture, the 'Hells Angels', makes a fetish of violence while the hippy, or 'freak' sub-culture decries violence and is epitomized by the slogan 'make love not war'. Why adolescents should be differentially attracted to these sub-groups must presumably be significant in any study of violence.

A more recent theoretical framework for examining violence is the 'social interactionist' approach which suggests that it may be as important to study the attacked as the attacker and that there may be subtle causes in the attacked person's behaviour or performance which provokes or precipitates the attack. This interactionist approach is discussed in some of the later chapters in this book.

One other important factor which looms large in any contemporary study of violence must be the media. It has been estimated that children in England watch television up to fifteen hours or more every week; many of the programmes they watch contain violence in one form or another, whether real and actual violence as transmitted through news programmes or fantasy violence in cartoon programmes and westerns. As yet, very little is known about the effect such viewing may have on children, either by influencing them to copy the behaviour they see on the television or the long term effect of a continual bombardment by frightening, and at times seriously alarming material. It may be that amongst the long term effects will be a race of adults no longer sensitive to the suffering that violence causes. However, at present this must remain a speculation.

This brief survey attempts to give some idea of the range of possible explanations. The purpose of this book is to provide, in the words of John Harrington in Chapter VIII 'a theory of multi-factorial aetiology of violence'. To do this a multi-disciplinary team of writers has contributed. Violence is not solely explicable in terms of psychiatry, psychology, social work, sociology, animal behaviour or history. Each plays a part, and the contributions which follow look at violence from many angles and through the eyes of many different professions.

The book starts with a Chapter by Colin Campbell in which he sets the stage historically and conceptually for a study of violence. In the next Chapter John Robottom examines the historical background of violence in more detail particularly over the last century and a half. Heidi Swanson then discusses the range of aggressive behaviour demonstrated in animal studies and the relevancy these may have for human behaviour. A psychiatrist, Vladimir Kahan examines one possible explanation of human violence and the ways in which it is instilled into children. His view of violent behaviour is supported by the work of the Newsons who present a very detailed study of the relationship that exists between young children and adults within normal families. Ray Castle, in Chapter VII, examines, through studies of 'battered' children, how normal behaviour can degenerate into pathological or abnormal behaviour.

Spencer Millham and the other members of the Dartington Research Team follow by showing that even when the child is removed from parents into residential care, violence may still exist and may be a problem of relationships between adults and children no matter what the setting or the blood relationship.

John Harrington's Chapter then takes the reader outside the realm of residential or family settings, and looks at the problem of group violence, whether in small groups, larger crowds or mobs. He offers some explanation and clarification of why violence can occur in these situations. Geoff Pearson, a sociologist looks at a similar area of study, but his view, as suggested in the title of his Chapter is that hooliganism is, in fact, not mindless and wanton, but that there are very good reasons why it should occur. Stuart Hall's Chapter explains the effect the media may have on an existing social phenomenon and how by giving violent events maximum coverage and exposure, the media may actually increase the possibility of the event recurring or escalating in violence.

Tom Douglas, a teacher of social work, then makes a specific contribution outlining ways in which people can be made more aware of the violence within themselves. Calling on his experience in conducting socio-drama exercises with large groups of social workers and other helping professions, he shows how self awareness can enable individuals to cope with novel, threatening situations.

The final Chapter is an edited selection of case studies of violence which have arisen during the lives, both professional and personal, of participants in the Development Group's Seminars on Violence. They give illuminating insights into the range of violent behaviour that can occur, and the suffering that its produces for both the guilty and the innocent parties.

In conclusion, the purpose of this book is not to outline any definitive theory of violence. It aims to provide some insights into the range of causation and manifestations of violence and thereby to broaden understanding and develop ability both to deal with it when provoked and to avoid unnecessary provocation; to show how it is both a positive and negative force in individuals, and in society, and an inevitable part of life in groups and in personal relationships; and finally to encourage readers to continue their own thinking and to seek further material on this important subject.

References
(1) VIOLENCE IN MARRIAGE (1975). *Report from the Select Committee on Violence in Marriage,* Vol. 1. HMSO, London. House of Commons Paper 553/1.
(2) NEW SOCIETY (1975). *Observations, 33,* 676, 18 September.
(3) TUTT N. S. (1974). *Nature of Authority in a Residential Setting* Part I. Residential Social Work 14, 6 June.
(4) Report on Inquiry by the Rt Hon Lord Justice Scarman OBE. *The Red Lion Square Disorders* of 15 June 1974, Cmnd 5919. Paragraph 74. HMSO.
(5) CASEY M. D., SEGALL L. J., STREET D. R. and BLANK C. E. (1966). *Sex Chromosome abnormalities in two state hospitals for patients requiring special security* Nature, 209, 641-662.
(6) POLSKY H. W. (1962). *Cottage Six,* John Wiley and Sons, New York.

Chapter II **Perspectives of violence**
Colin Campbell

At the best of times we find it difficult to make sense of present day society. The confusion and complexity of social, industrial, political and economic change, conspire against our efforts to comprehend what is really happening around us. Yet all too frequently even our attempts to understand are feeble and half-hearted. Whether statements about social problems or developments are accurate or truthful is too often decided by the acclamation which greets the statement, or its repetition, rather than by reference to available evidence, proof or demonstration. If some viewpoint is only repeated often enough then . . . 'it must be true'. Thereafter people act on and act out the 'truth'. Firmly within this category of truths, it seems, is the idea that we live in an increasingly violent world, that we live in a society in which violence is on the increase. As an idea it is popular, and it is affirmed and confirmed almost daily in the media's coverage of acts of brutality, aggression and violence. Press reports often sensationalize, chastise, moralize and blame. Their message is clear – violence is bad, abnormal, irrational and mindless. Its prevalence today is symptomatic of the ills of our society; senseless actions in a sick society; something must be done.

In this essay my purpose is neither to argue that such an attitude is entirely without basis in fact, nor that it is other than a natural reaction; but I will suggest it is partial, inadequate and unhelpful. My concern is to try to take violence out of the immediate and alarmed context of day to day incidents and press coverage, and place it and our reactions to it in a broader perspective. In doing so I will not dwell on specific acts of violence, on individualistic violence or aggression as such; instead I will touch on aspects of recurring or recurrent violence, on 'group' or collective violence. My aim will be to regard such violence from more than one point of view and thus avoid any insistence that violence is inherently bad, abnormal, irrational or senseless; indeed much of my argument goes the other way and I will conjecture where and why violence makes sense (or is sensible) may be rational and certainly is usual and normal. My view is the same as Bienen's that to 'treat violence as a phenomenon outside of a 'normal' social process . . . hinders analysis'.[1]

'Modernism is but provincialism transferred from the map to the calendar' said Macaulay, and our understanding of violence is modernist in that sense. What history teaches us, if we are prepared to learn, is that violence is not atypical or anomalous; on the contrary it is usual and endemic in the historical development of all nations; virtually every study points to the fact that violence has been pervasive, and sometimes chronic, as far as history records. In an early study Sorokin surveyed the history of eleven nations over twenty five centuries and concluded 'disturbances occur much oftener than is usually realized . . . On the average of from four to seven years, as a rule, one considerable social disturbance may be expected. The fact that these phenomena occur so frequently confirms our conclusions that they are inseparable from the very existence and functioning of social bodies'.[2]

Students of violence and civil strife in different countries have in more recent times confirmed Sorokin's general conclusions; three hundred and sixty-three revolutions occurred between 1900 and 1961 says Calvert[3]; of 82 countries included for study all except one experienced violent anti-government action between 1948 and 1961 report the Feierabends[4]; from 1961 to 1967 there was serious civil strife in 114 countries out of the 121 studied, says Gurr[5]. There are of course numerous interpretations as to the causes, type and nature of the violence found in different societies, but it is the continuity and pervasiveness of violence and of civil strife that is the most striking factor to emerge from these studies. The conclusion Sorokin reached after his study is seldom opposed. It is worth noting therefore that as a result of the data he analysed, Sorokin also felt he had been able to explode such myths as the belief that history exhibits a trend towards peacefulness, towards 'civilization' and that violence is thus atavistic, that only some countries are violent and disorderly and not others, that outbreaks of violence occur only in cases of decay and decline and not 'in periods of blossoming and healthy growth'[2].

In parenthesis it should be added that to emphasise the usualness, the normality and the continuity of violence is not to imply that it is desirable. But surely it might be? We tend, in thinking of violence, to conjure up notions of badness, evil and destruction; of riots, mobs and terrorism. But tyrants have been banished and despots deposed by violent methods – by the use of violence. The assassinations of the Kennedys and of Martin Luther King, and the attempts on President Ford's life, were violent acts that outraged us – but the attempts to kill Hitler are not similarly notorious, and the violence allegedly done to the Birmingham IRA bombers caused no public outcry. Slavery in America and elsewhere was only abolished after considerable turmoil and violence; civil rights have on occasion only been gained after violent protest; many of the rights and privileges of men, women and children (in the home, at work, in the political community) have been achieved through violent action – rights which today we value highly or take for granted. Some years ago in America the black leader du Bois said 'war is hell but there are things worse than hell as every Negro knows.' In such a way did he justify violence by blacks. It is unnecessary to pass judgement on the black movement to understand that for many people there are things 'worse than hell' that justify use of violence. Perhaps for most people there is some value or aspiration, some political belief or some love, that if infringed upon or attacked would prompt (consideration of) the use of violence.

We seem to be reluctant to learn from history and to keep today's events in perspective. Possibly we are still wedded to the notion that history represents a long and peaceful evolution to the present state of things. It may be our belief in progress that allows us to discard unpleasant memories. A more serious reason is that writers of history themselves have not assisted as they might. The suggestion has been made that this is because historians have tended, until recently, to 'do history from the top'[6]. Historians have (admittedly for obvious reasons) concentrated on leaders, emperors and governments, and on events which have proved significant or cathartic to political development. The effect has been that where violence is mentioned it tends to be that which, more or less, was successful in replacing or re-arranging major political and social relationships – the composition of the government or the nature of the constitution, etc. This has resulted in both an underestimation of the amount and pervasiveness of violence in different historical periods, and an unfortunate bias in 'recognising' violence, one that is unduly dependent on the victor's version of events. Of course the type of data and records available to the historian often constrain his studies, but an awareness of these biases has increased in recent years and histories of the people as such (rather than merely as auxiliaries to political strategy) have been written. These works (e.g. by E. P. Thompson) provide markedly different interpretations of historical development, persuading one historian to conclude 'the chief moments at which ordinary people appeared unmistakably on the European historical scene before the industrial age were moments of revolt'[7].

The relevance of such an appreciation has been illustrated and underlined in a discussion of workers' protests in English history:
'In feudal England peasants of Essex and Kent angered by
high taxes and attempts to re-establish old feudal practices
. . . marched on London in 1381 to demand redress . . . They
asked for a charter of freedom . . . (but) little or nothing was

immediately gained from the revolt which was bloodily suppressed . . . During the next century the Wars of the Roses kept the country in a continuous state of civil conflict . . . when the Tudors came to power in 1485 they were able by firm govenment . . . to create a stable society . . . (through harsh measures) they curbed any disposition of the poor to seek the improvement of working conditions through revolt . . . Between the death of Elizabeth I in 1603 and the death of Anne in 1714 England went through a major transformation . . . It was after the Civil War and the restoration of the Stuarts in 1660 that gatherings of unruly mobs from the poorer classes, called 'the mobile' – or simply 'the mob' – became a recurrent feature of city life. There was no single cause for the many riotous assemblies that occurred during this period. Poor harvests, high food prices, customs and excise duties, all gave rise to the manifestations of popular discontent . . . Most of the riots were spontaneous 'excited by some local or temporary grievance' . . . there was no common aim other than that of immediate revenge upon the personification of the people's enemies . . . In 1768 the London mob 'whose presence is continually felt in the political history of the eighteenth century' found a hero in John Wilkes . . . The crowd . . . was cleared . . . by a volley from the rifles of a Scottish regiment. This 'massacre' changed the temper of the mob . . . The Gordon Riots of 1780 . . . were inspired by a revival of the deep suspicions of Catholic plots to sieze power . . . During the next few years the urban mob recruited from the squalid, over-crowded and decaying areas of the rapidly growing cities were adroitly directed . . . against the doctrines of the French Revolution . . . (at the same time) there were many outbreaks of unrest and disturbance directed against the loss of old rights and the degradation of life brought about by the advance of industrialism . . . the essence of the Luddite disturbances was the smashing of (weaving and knitting) machinery in Notting-hamshire, Yorkshire, Lancashire and Cheshire . . . The alarm which they aroused . . . can be gauged by the fact that twelve thousand soldiers were used for their suppression . . . the Prime Minister abolished the old custom of billeting troops in people's homes for fear they might become contaminated by Radicalism . . . By the end of the War with France in 1815, there were 163,000 men in 200 barracks up and down the country'[8].

In similar vein John Robottom indicates (see Chap. III) that the nineteenth century was scarcely free of strife and violence. The relevance of such discussions, however, at least for my argument, is not that the *myth* of peaceful evolution ought to be replaced with another myth – that no change is possible without violent struggle. Rather, simply, they remind us of the usualness of violence in our history. It is interesting in this respect to note that after the urban racial riots in the 1960s the United States Government established a National Commission to inquire into the causes and prevention of violence[9]. One point the Commission emphasized – and had to repeat again and again – was that America's history was a violent one, and that the black riots were not atypical, far less unique[10]. The feuds with the Indians, the Revolution against Britain, the Civil War, the ethnic conflicts in the North, the labour strikes and riots, all contributed a respectable pedigree to the racial riots of the 60s. Yet in America this had been forgotten – just as we are wont to forget the violence of our own past.

So far what I understand violence to be has been implied rather than made explicit. Clearly something ought to be said about the meaning of the term but it seemed better to postpone any precise stipulation of meaning for two reasons. Firstly because the use of the word violence seems in many way more instructive than its definition. Few people bother to define 'violence' and even those who do frequently use the word – or see it come to be used – in a particularized and distorted way. As a term or epithet 'violent' is pejorative; we commonly use it to label an action of which we disapprove, we use it to stigmatize or discredit the act. It is a term which expresses emotion, and carries connotations of destruction and of badness; it is seldom used of acts which are welcomed, endorsed or seen as good. Secondly, arising from this, in proposing any definition care must be taken *both* to avoid being enmeshed in spurious semantic disputes that are totally divorced from what is significant and worth discussing about violence, *and* if the definition is not controversial, of having prematurely decided on the essential nature of violence, in what ways it is important and how it should be studied. Some definitions are more likely to avoid these dangers than others and a glance at some examples should be sufficient for present purposes.

Graham and Gurr[5] say that violence 'is behaviour designed to inflict personal injury to people or damage to property'. Skolnick[10] says it is 'the intentional use of force to injure, kill or to destroy property'. Macfarlane[11] states it is 'the capacity to impose, or the act of imposing, one's will upon another, where the position is held to be illegitimate. Force is the capacity to impose, or the act of imposing, one's will upon another where the imposition is held to be legitimate.' Walter[12] suggests it is 'destructive harm . . . including not only physical assaults that damage the

31

body, but also . . . the many techniques of inflicting harm by mental or emotional means.'

The first two definitions, by Graham and Gurr and by Skolnick, are instructive in that they properly avoid emotional terms and are neutral in themselves; no judgement as to the goodness or badness, justifiability or otherwise of a violent action flows from these definitions. Macfarlane is more explicit in referring to force and distinguishing it from violence on the grounds of legitimacy. If we see an action as wanting or desirable we will tend to avoid calling it violent but instead talk of force. Macfarlane thus recognises the way we commonly ascribe to actions some particular quality that they do not in themselves possess; our judgement of the actions is contained in the words we select to 'describe' them. Violent is one such word – insurgent, terrorist, are others. Here we may understand one difficulty with many discussions of violence in history or violence in our own society. We all of us 'see' violence according to our cultural, social and political values: there is often partiality and bias. Thus the notion of violence if juxtaposed to other words like legal, official, legitimate, can seem out of place. Commonly we will talk of legal force or coercion, or legal punishment – rather than legal violence. In the Vietnam war the Viet Cong regarded American military activity as violent aggression – even though the US Chiefs of Staff explained it as a show of force. Depending on who is watching, police seeking to break up a meeting may be seen to use necessary force (necessary because of the actions of the crowd, to maintain order) or to indulge in a calculated violent attack (calculated to repress freedom of speech, to maintain the crumbling capitalist regime). Bombings in Ulster, war in the Sinai desert, hijacking and kidnapping world-wide, can be understood or represented in different ways. But Walter's definition is even more helpful insofar as the violence of which he speaks need not be individualistic physical violence – 'destructive harm' may be accomplished by 'many techniques . . . by mental or emotional means.' There may be violence even if its manifestation is not dramatic, obvious or particularly directed against some individual. Thus some critics of western societies see capitalism as utilizing economic exploitation as an instrument of terror, and, no doubt the deviant poets in the Soviet Union see violence to them, or their rights, as a *leit motif* of the socialist state.

Criminologists have recently, and not before time, realized the necessity in constructing any adequate understanding of criminality, of locating the relevant acts and actors in the context of the norms and enforcement processes that define the act as criminal,

32

and that label the perpetrator of the act as a deviant or a criminal. Adapting one 'model' from such literature[13] we may, rather simply, illustrate different perspectives on violence.

Figure A: Defining Violence in terms of Authority

	Against Authority	Not Against Authority
Goal Oriented	1 Enemy	2 Supporter/ Official
Non-Goal Oriented	3 Cynic	4 Sick

Figure B: Defining Violence in terms of 'The Cause'

	Against The Cause	Not Against The Cause
Goal Oriented	1 Enemy	2 Supporter/ Official
Non-Goal Oriented	3 Cynic	4 Sick

Accepting that the Figures are of heuristic value only (they do not describe reality nor imply that specific acts of violence fall neatly into one category only) they do nevertheless highlight two important dimensions of much violence: firstly violence may be for or against some social or political grouping and its values, and, secondly, the action may be directed or oriented to that group and its norms – constituting a threat or offering support – or not. According to Figure A we may interpret or define violence in terms of prevailing authority (e.g. the Government in power and its policies), and we can also decide whether the activity is motivated by aims relevent to that authority, or prompted by unrelated or extraneous considerations.

In Box 1 we place – we categorize – our enemies; a clear example would be terrorist activity. Into Box 2 we put the supporters and officials of authority, for example actions by the police and army and sometimes citizens supporting authority. Box 3 contains cynical or instrumental perpetrators of violence – people who carry out acts of violence but not (necessarily) because of the norms that authority stands for – for example protection racketeers and professional or organized criminals. Activity in this category constitutes an exploitation of the situation, frequently for monetary gain, rather than because of any particular normative or political aspiration. Box 4 is reserved for the 'sick' people — persons who seem to us to be irrational — who do not have a good explanation or justification (or one that makes sense to us) for their activity.

This much is unremarkable but if we delete 'authority' and substitute 'The Cause' as in Figure B then a rather different picture emerges. Here we can recognize interpretations of violence that flow from acceptance of political beliefs or goals that are not (entirely) in line with those of the prevailing authority and may be opposed to that authority (Defining in terms of 'The Cause' merely dramatizes the same issue which underlines varying degrees of acceptance of authority). Box 1 now refers to actions by the forces of law and order! Box 2 can include the brigades out on the streets, the freedom fighters and paramilitary organizations. Box 3 refers to more or less the same people – the cynical and instrumental – who are not involved in the political battle. Box 4 similarly includes the sick people – often the same people, drug-takers, alcoholics, derelicts. What is important is that in any society the standpoint represented by Figure A may exist *at the same time* as the standpoint represented in Figure B; that is, the same act of violence may by some people in society be perceived according to Figure A but by other people according to Figure B. In a sense the numbers who adopt Figure B instead of Figure A give some indication of the stability of the particular authority structure in a community.

Although in simple form these schema do not merely highlight competing definitions of violence, they also illustrate how particular acts of violence may, at successive stages, be modified or defined differently even if the basic perspective is unchanged. For example terrorist bombings may be immediately described by the police or the media as senseless violence – the acts of psychopaths (Fig. A, Box 4). Should the bombers be apprehended and convicted how-ever, they may be treated differently; regarded and explained as 'Enemies' (Fig. A, Box 1) their political motivation is clearly recog-nised – they become 'special category' prisoners. The reality of many violent acts may be successively negotiated or redefined. On occasions even when told the reasons for some violent acts we may refuse to accept them as plausible or rational; an extreme example might be the 'explanations' offered by Charles Manson and his followers for ritual murders – explanations which were universally rejected and seen as ridiculous – 'Manson is sick'.

Of course my concern here is not to argue for the correctness of any particular interpretation of any act of violence, but simply to draw attention to the importance of social definitions and, in particular, of the decisions of onlookers as to whether the violent act is legitimate or not. Walter[12] elaborates other aspects of the same point: 'when a violent protest is socially prescribed as a legitimate means of *control* or *punishment,* according to practises familiar to us, the destructive aim is measured and the limits made clear. Social definition . . . often *extracts* it from the category of violence – at least from the standpoint of society . . . Violence is generally understood as unmeasured or exaggerated harm to individuals, either not socially prescribed at all or else beyond established limits. It is often socially defined to include the processes that *originate* as authorised, measured force, but that go beyond the prescribed conditions and limits'. Thus, indicates Walter, it is important to our understanding of certain forms of violence to remember the interaction which occurs between the forces of authority and opponents, insurgents or protesters. The interaction (directly through confrontation or more indirectly through propaganda and policy changes may set off violence. Equally it may result in a re-definition of force as violence. Although perhaps obvious this is often forgotten and blame is frequently rather cavalierly attached to one side or another by the supporters of one side or another. In the United States, Skolnick's report on protest movements to the National Commission on the Causes and Prevention of Violence had to explain this and emphasis it. Despite media reports to the contrary, the report says violence has not been usual in protests and, insofar as it has occurred, it is at least debatable whether the responsibility has not been as much that of the official forces as of the protesters. Violence may be initiated by protesters in some instances and by official forces in others. But it is crucial to remember that the violence may emerge from the interaction or confrontation between protesters and official forces[9, 14].

It is perhaps worth adding, since the discussion has touched on clashes between protesters and official forces, that at a more general level violence ought to be located within prevailing authority structures. As Emmanuel Marx says, we know from anthropological studies of societies where individual or interpersonal violence has (within prescribed limits) been accepted as usual and in some cases even desirable. It is really only with the development of the modern nation state and the centralisation of political authority that we find rulers claiming a monopoly of force and proscribing interpersonal violence and even threats of violence[15]. This claim to monopolise the rights to use violence and the claim to receive allegiance from citizens has become usual in modern states. Yet we should also remember[11] that the political map of the world and the Sovereignty of nation states is arbitrary and the result of accidents of history; we are not entitled to assume that there will not be further shifts in sovereignty and continual realignment. In other words while the state's insistence on its right to monopolise force and receive allegiance may be usual so too is the refusal to recognise such claims.

Some commentators who argue along these lines seem to take it that all protest and violence is of a 'political' nature. This seems unnecessary, and, in any event, misguided. It is probably better simply to understand that much protest and violence is purposeful and may be sensible or rational. Two different studies may illustrate this viewpoint.

According to Tilley a common historical view of industrialization is the 'cyclical interpretation'. It is, he says, a popular notion that the process of industrialization was initially met with a haphazard and chaotic response, this was succeeded by some group and collective violence but thereafter integration was achieved, acceptance gained and a coherent and peaceful society re-established and maintained. Such a view argues Tilley is simplistic and distorts the facts. There is little evidence that violence has vanished from society or even died down; what *has* happened through the various processes of industrialization is that the *forms* of violence have altered. Violence has continued but its manifestation has changed; Tilley suggests three major types of collective violence – primitive, reactionary and modern.

Primitive violence includes some of the examples mentioned above. The feud, the brawl, the tribal conflict, the small local intense battle and feuding between religious groups. What characterizes this type of violence is that it is small, it is based on community groups possessed of a strong sense of identity which are pitted against other community groups. Typically over many centuries it gradually blurred into a different type of collective violence – reactionary violence. By this Tilley means the reaction of people to the break-up of feudalism; a reaction against the impositions of new taxes, the running down of the cottage industries, the reliance on large machines, the import and export manipulation with its consequent effect on food prices and thus on people's lifestyles. Ordinary men, women and children reacted against changes in the way of things and specifically to the fact that some rights they had previously enjoyed were being eroded from. The reaction may be conceptualized as a reaction against the formation of the Nation State. And surely Tilley is correct in saying that we do not understand these people or their cause if we simply call them mindless rioters or mobs. Finally there is modern collective violence different from the previous two types insofar as it is based on or stimulated by specialist associations. Rather than particular local communities, or haphazard groups of ordinary people, specialized associations with relatively well-defined (sometimes political) objectives are now prevalent. Organizations for women's suffrage, and trade unions organizing strikes may serve as examples. Tilley argues that in European countries – liberal, democratic or socialist – it is clear that the Nation State has gained victory over local powers but that this has engendered a proliferation of special purpose associations.

In Tilley's argument there is no evidence that the amount of violence (if such can be quantified) has significantly changed but its manifestations have. The types or modes of collective violence have altered as the social structure itself has been transformed. Reactionary violence was prompted by antagonism to the centralization and existence of the National State; modern violence is not – it assumes the National State though it may not accept the present management. To understand such changes in violence we must look to the social and political processes of the day. If we do this and locate the violence in terms of the prevailing social structure then we may make sense of the violence without saying it is all sensible, we may comprehend it without endorsing it. Similarly, again, the National Commission in America came to understand that the racial riots in the sixties grew from the deeply held grievances of the blacks.

Analogously, but in an entirely different context, Taylor and Walton[16] suggest ways of understanding acts commonly defined as mindless, stupid or irrelevant. Industrial sabotage is frequently so regarded but Taylor and Walton advise caution in imputing irrationality simply on the basis of superficial impressions. Behaviour that may seem meaningless to observers may be explicable to the actor, his friends or workmates. And we are reminded, of course, that actions judged strange or even lunatic in one historical period may later come to be regarded as sensible or even praiseworthy.

Industrial sabotage may be prompted by frustration. Workers under pressure or tension who feel themselves powerless to change their situation or improve it, may smash something or lash out. Essentially spontaneous this action does not challenge authority but it can be a safety valve or it can be for fun. To understand it requires us to have regard for the work situation and the pressures or constraints on the individuals involved. Other acts of sabotage may not be similarly impulsive, may be deliberate and calculated. But frequently the conscious aim is simply to ease the work situation or increase productivity, albeit the procedures adopted may

37

cause damage or appear as strange to outsiders. Finally acts of sabotage may be prompted by a desire to gain power, may be politically motivated. Taylor and Walton suggest that this type of sabotage was more prevalent before than it is today because of the institutionalization of conflict through 'trade union' activity.

Just as it is unnecessary to accept uncritically the historical examples previously given, so it is irrelevant to my argument that Taylor and Walton have not adequately explained all types of industrial sabotage. It may be misleading to understand all acts of sabotage as coherent and unambiguous statements such as 'we matter', 'we want to be considered', 'we want the rules changed', 'we want power'. But Taylor and Walton are entirely right in their endeavour to reduce the number of acts of sabotage, or violence, that are regarded as meaningless. It is of little help to talk of bad people or human nature; that is rather unconstructive. To look to the perpetrator of the act and attempt, even when he cannot articulate the reasons for his actions himself, to understand him and his situation may help us to comprehend his actions. And Taylor and Walton quite properly invite us to consider whether their findings and the proferred explanations may not have relevance in the wider society outside the work situation (an invitation accepted by Pearson see Chap. X).

My arguments have touched on various aspects of different forms of violence and the discussion is bound to be superficial in places. No particular synthesis or understanding of 'violence' is offered but some mistakes commonly made in talking of violent acts and violent men have been indicated. If we come to accept the usualness and the normality of violence we may begin to view it in other than purely emotional terms. If we stop assuming all violence is either immoral or bad we may also, partly as a result, stop perceiving it as irrational. If we put violence in perspective and in its particular context we may understand it the better. Some of the perspectives suggested above contain different and often contradictory ideas, concepts and explanations; but it is better to attempt to evaluate and define these rather than merely thinking and talking as though violence is bad. Then we might move from condemnation to comprehension.

References
  (1) BIENEN H. (1968). *Violence and Social Change,* Chicago University Press, Chicago.
  (2) SOROKIN P. (1937). Social and Cultural Dynamics, Vol. III: *Fluctuation of Social Relationships, War, and Revolution,* Allen & Unwin, London.

(3) CALVERT P. (1970). *A Study of Revolution,* Clarendon Press, Oxford.

(4) FEIERABEND I. K. and R. L. (1966). 'Aggressive behaviours within Politics, 1948–1962: A cross national study', Vol. 10, *Journal of Conflict Resolution,* p. 249.

(5) GRAHAM H. D. and GURR T. R. (1969). *The History of Violence in America* – A Report to the National Commission on the Causes and Prevention of Violence, Bantam, New York.

(6) JONES G. S. (1972). 'History: The Poverty of Empiricism', in Blackburn: *Ideology in Social Science,* Fontana, London.

(7) TILLY C. (1969). 'Collective Violence in European Perspective', in Graham and Gurr: *The History of Violence in America,* p. 4.

(8) ROBERTS B. C. (1969). 'On the Origins and Resolution of English Working Class Protest', in Graham and Gurr: *The History of Violence in America,* p. 245.

(9) *National Commission on the Causes and Prevention of Violence:* Task Force Reports, Vols. 1–13 (1969), New York.

(10) SKOLNICK J. H. (1969). *The Politics of Protest,* Clarion, New York.

(11) MACFARLANE L. S. (1974). *Violence and The State,* Nelson, London.

(12) WALTER E. V. (1969). Terror and Resistance: *A Study of Political Violence,* Oxford University Press, Oxford.

(13) GUSFIELD J. R. (1967). 'Moral Passage', The symbolic process in public designations of deviance, Vol. 15, *Social Problems,* p. 175.

(14) BALBUS I. D. (1973). *The Dialectics of Legal Repression,* Russell Sage, New York.

(15) MARX E. (1972). 'Some Social Contexts of Personal Violence', in Gluckmen: *The Allocation of Responsibility,* Manchester University Press, Manchester.

(16) TAYLOR L. and WALTON P. (1971). 'Industrial Sabotage: Motives and Meanings', in Cohen: *Images of Deviance,* Penguin, London.

Chapter III **A history of violence**
John Robottom

By contrast with many other nations the contemporary English have a very poor sense of their own history. The Celtic peoples of the United Kingdom are better served but even they not as well as the citizens of the newly independent countries of the third world, or most of those in West and East Europe, where writing history is a major cultural activity and learning it fills a large part of the school-child's timetable. The fault for this state of affairs lies equally with the scholarly historian whose specialised techniques and intra-professional disputations have made his craft incomprehensible to the common man[1] and with teachers who provide from one school to the next a bewildering range of unco-ordinated patches from the past. The reason is not far to seek: that sense of pride in achievement in military, constitutional and social matters which gave us the history so gleefully satirised in '1066 And All That'[2] seems both factually and morally inappropriate. The consequences may be serious if we follow Arthur Marwick in believing:

'it is only through knowledge of its history that a society can have knowledge of itself. As a man without memory and self-knowledge is a man adrift so a society without memory . . . and self-knowledge is a society adrift[3].'

The people of such a society may lack the will and knowledge to challenge statements about contemporary issues which are given apparent authority and indisputability by being cast in what purport to be a 'true' historical framework. The challenger may even be exposed to the charge that, by arguing against a self-evident truth, he is insensitive to a grave social issue. This risk faces anyone who asks what truth there is in the frequent assertions of the view that violence is on the increase in our contemporary domestic society, especially when they are supported by supposedly definitive evidence in the form of statistics or by being related to some other putative historical trend such as a decline in parental authority, an increase in personal income, a waning of religious and moral sanctions and so on. A simple answer would be that, despite the existence of figures, we do not know enough of the facts to make a quantitative investigation of the amount or intensity of violence in English history. More often, however, apparently historical assessments are invalidated by the demonstration that not only the form of violence but the ways contemporaries had of identifying the problem have changed from one age to the next.

In one sense, the further back one goes the more the use of

violence is inseparable from other features of social activity and political organisation. England in the age of the Vikings and the early medieval period was a land plagued by marauders, territorial warfare, violence committed in the name of religion and ethnic oppression. There was more justice than law, exaction of the blood price for violent crime and murder was for a long time more important than the punishment of the offender as such. The task of the monarchy was to contain domestic warfare (and to channel the impulse to fight into service against national enemies) while establishing throughout the land respect for the king's peace under-pinned by a growing body of customary and statute law. Their ultimate success was aided by, if it did not rest upon, changes in the economic and social priorities of society which led to the development of the towns and cities of early modern times. It is this new urban culture which is the starting point for a proper perspective on violence in English history.

Town dwellers, high or low, are historically not warriors. Until as recently as World War I the great majority of England's soldiers were drawn from the countryside; it was the unemployed labourer from East Anglia or the dispossessed Scottish crofter who built the British empire. The urban activities of commerce and manu-facture flourish best in conditions of civic peace and for four or five hundred years the greatest part of the effort to contain violence has been directed at the preservation of order and the promotion of seemly behaviour in our towns. These rather different goals have often converged in the thinking of the two types of agency at work: those concerned with law enforcement, constables, Bow street runners, watch committees and the modern police and those seeking to civilise behaviour, charity movements, the early Methodist Church, voluntary societies and the social work services of today. Most of the violence with which they have been concerned has been muted in its physical outcome. Actual bodily harm is not normally part of the intention of street demonstrators, brawlers, robbers or even political rioters; it patently is when a man mounts his horse or takes up pike and goes to war. Thus there are always difficulties about defining the point at which different forms of turbulent behaviour deserve the label of 'violent'.

Yet the difficulty should not deter us from drawing the contrast between the frequency with which mobs or mobiles of earlier times broke into behaviour of a primitivite, destructive and aggres-sive kind and the tiny number of such incidents in the past hundred years. Andreas Franciscius, visiting England in 1497, gave its capital city this feeling testimonial:

'Londoners have such fierce tempers and violent dispositions

41

that they not only despise the way in which Italians live but actually pursue them with uncontrollable hatred . . . they sometimes drive us off with fists and blows of the truncheon[4].'

This was tame stuff, however, compared with the terrifying tergiversations of the mob as it swung its destructive way into the smarter squares of eighteenth century London to the cries of 'No Popery', 'Give us back our eleven days', 'Wilkes and Liberty'. These events lie at the beginning of a hundred years, from the mid-eighteenth to the mid-nineteenth century, which constitute a sort of golden age of challenge to law and order. Provincial towns suffered food riots (one historian has catalogued 22 for 1866) and the violent destruction of turnpike gates. Gangs of labouring men marched to break machinery in the Plug and Luddite riots and, joined by craftsmen and lesser tradespeople, to demonstrate for parliamentary reform or the People's Charter.

A couple of generations of historians have quarried for evidence to support one pet theory or another. The many rocks they have thrown at each other need not concern us but some of their conclusions are germane to a general discussion. The more exacting the research the less is it possible to reach the conclusion that behind the disturbances lay a generalised predisposition to violence either in individuals or groups. There may have been fewer who minded a bloody nose in an age when early death, terrible mutilation after accidents were commonplace and when the prize-fighter and the cockpit were the popstars and football arenas of the day; but this is a long way from proving keen anticipation in the prospect of violence. If this were so we should find the same people participating in different riots but this is rarely true[5]; even in movements which have a general political objective it is nearly always the case that those participating are the victims of some cruel turn in economic fortune – an increase in food prices or a downward turn in the market – or have been moved by some local grievance – a harsh decision in the magistrates court or frustrated hopes of a political gain.

There might be relevance to the present day in studies of the response of the authorities to potential trouble. Where these were inept, short-sighted or limited by the absence of appropriate means of enforcing order the result could be disastrous. For many incidents it is possible to trace how protest turned into violence or an attack on property became a bloody battle as a consequence of the lack of a readily available policing force. Bad enough is the picture in the early part of the period of army or militia units cutting down returning rioters and seizing ring leaders for a later public hanging. A solution adopted from 1796 when Volunteer

Yeomanry could be recruited from among the relatively well-to-do was disastrous. It was the local Yeomanry who turned the Manchester reform meeting in St Peter's fields at which all the leaders had called for a respectable and peaceful occasion into the bloody incident of 'Peterloo'.[6, 7]

Senior cabinet ministers learned faster than local authorities. A tension which has repeated itself in recent years is evident in correspondence in which Robert Peel or Lord John Russell, Home Secretaries in the 1820s and 1830s, urged restraint on magistrates and lords lieutenant pressurised by the local propertied classes into calling for military help against trouble makers. The evidence for the need was often the flimsiest of rumours that drilling had taken place on a nearby common or a pike discovered in a weaver's cottage. Increasingly the government shunned the use of barely-leashed local Yeomanry and relied instead on the restraining hand of men such as General Napier who commanded the northern forces at the time of Chartism and commented with satisfaction that 'Half the land has been openly in arms and not a drop of blood spilt on the scaffold'. But even this was a transitional stage; in the forties and fifties the historians' typical clue to government measures is a report in *The Times* that a hundred metropolitan policemen were entrained in London and bound for a disaffected area.

The creation of a nation-wide police force in the years between the Metropolitan Police Act, 1829, and the County and Borough Police Act of 1856 has been signalled as the major step in the conquest of violence in industrial Britain.[8] There are, of course, other factors which have led to an undeniable reduction in mass unrest since mid-Victorian times: the development of a more open political community fed on compulsory schooling, a new popular press (from the 1890s), a steadily widening franchise (which nevertheless left a quarter of all males without the vote until 1918 as well as all women), bidding by political leaders for workingmen's support. Yet, valuable as it is to remind ourselves that our contemporary Red Lion and Grosvenor Squares are small beer compared with the years of Chartism such generalisations can distract attention from questions of fundamental constitutional importance. Speaking in the market place in Nottingham in 1839, Richard Oastler, MP told his audience:

'I recommend a man to arm in his own cottage, to be able to stand on his own threshold in the habitments and equipment of a free man, and then be able to talk with the enemy in his gate . . . Englishmen, patriots, Christians, arm, arm, arm and preserve the rights which your forefathers died to purchase.[9]

This is maybe the language of incitement to violence but what lay behind it, and what was in the minds of his audience, was an assertion of the right to political equality. Oastler was appealing to the Bill of Rights of 1689 – itself the outcome of a military and political coup in 1688 – which gave every freeborn Englishman the right to bear arms in self-defence. Seventy-four years later George Lansbury was making a similar point to a suffragette rally in Caxton Hall:

'Let us teach this make-believe Liberal government that this is a holy war, and it is a war for women's and men's rights the world over . . . and that it is a war in which we will do our best to preserve human life, but it is a war that will have no regard for property of any kind whatever . . .'[10]

The ludicrousness of the picture of either this pacifist Socialist or Tory MP striking a physical blow in support of his aims shows how great are the limitations of language. Metaphors of warfare and physical struggle may come readily from the lips of men determined to alter what they – but not those in authority – see as a total injustice – especially in a society which uses as a commonplace phrases such as 'the rights for which our forefathers fought and died'. If those who make the rhetoric of violence have difficulties so have those who must define its meaning in terms of possible action. This is an obligation which has fallen heavily on the police and Home Office in the twentieth century and which has often exposed them to criticism. But the obligation stems from identifying a responsibility different from that of the early years of the force when the police were seen primarily as a means, more flexible and less lethally armed than the military, of limiting protest. There were thirty years of conflict over the right to hold public meetings in Trafalgar Square and Hyde Park before it was established that a central principle of English public life lies not only in freedom of speech, and indeed protest, but in the provision of occasions to exercise it unmolested.

In 1855 the Home Secretary banned, with doubtful legality, a meeting to protest against a Bill prohibiting Sunday trading. The ban was ignored and the police used truncheons on the crowd turning the occasion into a violent struggle in which 49 police were injured. In 1866 Hyde Park gates were locked, again by order of the Home Secretary, against a demonstration in favour of the Second Reform Act. A battle again broke out as rioters broke down the iron railings and in some cases used them as weapons. Public and parliamentary criticism of the Home Secretary was widespread and in 1872 an Act of Parliament gave the present freedom to use the Park to express dissent. It took two serious clashes in Trafalgar Square and nearby streets before the present arrangements allowing meetings on weekends and bank holidays became the stated practice in 1892. Both resulted in injuries, and the second a death, from injuries inflicted by the police. On both occasions the Home Secretary and police were justly accorded a large share of the blame for mishandling the control of the demonstrations. It was H. H. Asquith who defended the two Lib-Lab MPs who were arrested after the second demonstration, and, a few years later, it was he, as Home Secretary who announced the present arrangements.[11]

The broad apparent principle since then has been that the prevention of disorder should be the chief criterion for prohibiting meetings in a public place. This involves the considerable disadvantage that a subjective or discretionary judgement has to be made. This is obviously the case when a Home Secretary decides whether or not to allow a meeting (under powers granted in the Metropolitan Police Act) or local police exercise their rights to ban or limit processions under the Public Order Act of 1936 (which followed widespread concern at the failure to prevent violence at Fascist rallies and marches)[11]. Discretion is often at work when a magistrate's order is made binding accused persons over. George Lansbury went to prison after refusing such an order after his Caxton Hall speech as did Bertrand Russell in 1961 and followers of Ian Paisley in 1966. Such cases almost invariably lead to some disaffection as does the failure of the police completely to control events at meetings which do take place. These occasions have led to judicial[12] and police enquiries, which may well be necessary if the present tenuous balance between order and liberty is to be upheld. One disadvantage may be that they add weight to the practice of much of the reporting media of both highlighting the occasional disorder and also of anticipating it. This has probably been a major factor in encouraging the view that violence is on the increase and runs the risk of creating a condition of moral panic which may develop into calls for illiberal measures. An N.O.P. survey in 1968, taken just *before* the October 27th Grosvenor Square demonstration showed a majority, although small, in favour of banning political demonstrations altogether and a larger group in favour of controlling them by the use of tear gas and water cannons. The latter suggestion received the support of Sir Oswald Moseley while 67 MPs voted in favour of an unsuccessful bid to introduce legislation deporting non-British subjects taking part in demonstrations.[13] The vindication of the Home Secretary's refusal to ban the demonstration lies in accounts in *The Times* of astonished commentary in continental and US papers about the absence of weapons in the hands of either police or demonstrators: a stark contrast with the vicious struggles that took place in Paris and Chicago in the same year. Karl Meyer of *The Washington Post* made the point explicit under the heading; 'Tolerance: Britain's Lesson to the World.'[14]

Newspaper reporting in October 1968 draws attention to the high degrees of sensitivity to the possibility of violence which has become a feature of our post-war society. Characteristically there were more headlines and more reports before the event than after, both in the popular and 'serious' papers. Once again the historian must run the risk of appearing insensitive to an important issue – for there were after all 42 arrests, 4 police injured and about 50 demonstrators 'hurt' according to *The Times* – when he uses an incident such as this in support of a contention that actual violence has decreased even in the relatively short period of this century. But the assertion can be supported. Take the reports in *The Times,* given the rank of third most important headline, for the Liverpool riots of August 4th 1919 when about half of the local police force were on strike. We read, not only that 420 rioters were charged the following day and that one died of injuries, but that in the London Road:

'CID did not hesitate to belabour the marauders with their heavy batons . . . bayonet charges were the order of the night . . . and a volley of rifle fire was tried as an expedient'

while in the Scotland Road:

'after they had fired a volley in the air they turned some of their shots lower. One man was hit and was taken to the hospital with a wound in the neck.'

Shortening our perspective to fifty years ago we find that the General Strike, sometimes represented as a week of good-humoured sporting fixtures between police and strikers led to 3,149 prosecutions for incitement to sedition and for violence in England and Wales[15]. Another myth may be that 'tribal' activities such as those of mods and rockers or football hooligans are a new and unwelcome feature of post-war affluent society. They probably represent more exactly the coming forward of different groups and generations at risk rather than an aggregate increase in disorder. In 1893 an observer at a football match in Shrewsbury noted: 'The shouting and horseplay on the highways were a terror to peaceful residents passing homewards'[16] and it was at the first Cup Final in 1923 that the crowd totally occupied the pitch before the game. It is both intriguing and salutary to remember that perhaps the most harrowing task of many local police forces in the 1880's was to control the, often deliberately provocative, marches of Salvation Army units and keep them apart from their opponents, the macabrely named 'Skeleton Army'. These incidents – which like much hooliganism in our day were worst in south coast resorts, and notably in Worthing, resulted in imprisonment for 600 Salvationists in 1884 and a claim that in 1882 669 were knocked down or brutally assaulted.[17]

It seems clear that increased awareness of violence and anxiety about its consequences have distorted the reading of the history of public order. This has also happened, although the high level of public sensitivity seems to carrry fewer regrettable consequences, in the field of person against person violence, assaults on children, by one member of a family on another, or those committed in fights and brawls.

Home Office figures show fairly constant rates of increase from the early years of the century, and an apparently alarming acceleration in the post-war years. A serious criminologist would immediately point out that it is in this area, in contradistinction to, say, the theft of motor cars, that there is the greatest 'dark area' – i.e. the space between the number of actual crimes and recorded crimes. So tiny is the proportion of all forms of person against person violence known to the police – in sexual offences it may be only 10 per cent – that it is perfectly consistent with the figures to argue as strongly for a decrease as for an increase in actual crime.[18] To this must be added the difficulty of assessing the significance of the statistical lurch upwards which takes place when any form of behaviour becomes a crime as a result of legislation and the increase in awareness which follows from adding to the numbers of workers concerned with an aspect of community welfare.

A useful case study is that of violence against children, where the first truly effective legislation was the Children's Act of 1908, but for a quarter of a century beforehand there had been vigorous campaigning to bring the various forms of child assault to the statute book. It was in this period that many of the great agencies for the care of children were founded – Dr Barnardo's Homes, the Church of England Children's Society and the NSPCC in 1884. The reports of the National Society's officers show how difficult it was to work in communities where neighbours would not co-operate, where police preferred to leave investigation and prosecution to the NSPCC and where there was a general insensitivity to the problem. In the 'Classic Slum', Robert Roberts recalls Salford before the First World War:

'No-one who spent his childhood in the slums during those years will easily forget the regular and often brutal assaults on some children . . . Among fathers administering such punishments were men who had received forty-eight strokes of the birch – at the local prison for small misdemeanours. Whenever my mother (a shop-keeper) heard of a heinous case, as with the woman who boasted in the shop, " My master allus flogs 'em until the blood runs down their backs" she quietly put the "cruelty man" on. In its city windows the NSPCC displayed photographs of beaten children and rows of confiscated belts and canes. Gallantly as it worked, the Society hardly touched the fringe of the problem.'[19]

No wonder that legislation, which would make crime out of all too commonplace behaviour, was an objective of the Society. A small example of this lies in the The Dark Stain, a shilling booklet printed in 1907, in which the author builds up a profile of the many hazards to which children were exposed.

He analyses the 39,000 cases of cruelty recorded by the NSPCC in the year ending March 1907 to find that they involved 115,002 children and that of these 31,518 were insured for a total of £164,887. In another analysis he takes the Registrar-General's figures for the five to six hundred infants who died annually as a result of over-laying and distributes the cases among the days of the week to show that by far the greatest incidence was on Saturday night and Sunday morning from which he infers that drunkenness by parents or baby-minders was the chief cause. There are harrowing descriptions from a street which housed many women beggars:

'A woman in the street found that a neighbour with a blind child was doing well by begging with it. The woman deliberately put poison in the eyes of her own daughter, a pretty little girl of six, in order to blind her and make her more valuable for begging purposes.'[20]

These incidents of violence to children all became crimes the next year when child insurance, the use of children for begging (and prostitution were made illegal and suffocation as a consequence of drunkenness became a culpable offence. Equally satisfactory to the author of 'The Dark Stain', who noted that in 1906 the NSPCC could only prosecute in 5.5 per cent of cases known to it and that inspectors often covered populations of a quarter to a third of a million, would have been the duty laid by the Act on the police to enforce laws against cruelty, and the fact that most offences could from that time be handled in the summary courts. Thus a group of Edwardian reformers achieved one of their goals – an immediate and dramatic increase in the crime figures. A similar statistical increase in recorded offences is presumably one goal of

48

those concerned today with the protection of battered wives and babies.

They, however, work in a climate of public sensitivity and anxiety which is almost incomparable with that of seventy years ago. The controversy over the Maria Colwell case and discussion of legislation which might diminish the 'natural rights' of parents both illustrate the extent of the shift of opinion and sentiment; not just as far as the view that violence to children concerns us all but on to the feeling that 'the state' or 'the authorities' have failed when a single child is ill-treated.

A rather different sense of failure, but accompanied by a similar readiness to blame those in authority, is evident in the commonly expressed view that the development of a welfare society has coincided with an increase in violence in the streets. Discussing one aspect of this, Stuart Hall has shown how public concern about an apparent up-surge of muggings in 1973 was fed by the media's selection of news and by authoritative statements from police spokesmen and others. Thus, an inferential structure was built up which directed attention to one offence among many and, indeed, by ascribing particular characteristics to certain assaults, created a new category of recorded crime.[21] Stuart Hall's main concern was with the formation of attitudes among the lay public, but changes in inferential structure have occurred among more professional enquirers. Consider the following case study, of Mr T.

'. . . has been ten months out of work. He lives with his mother and explains that the cause of his distress was a quarrel with three friends in a train while leaving the races. They were all drunk, began to quarrel, and then he found himself on the line and an engine went over his hand . . . his last offence was breaking his mother-in-law's leg and assaulting his wife for which he received six months.'

Interesting material for a present-day seminar on the control of violent hooliganism, maybe – but in fact the case was in 1896 – and the author, Mrs Bosanquet of the Charity Organisation Society, precedes it with this clue to her inferential structures:

'To those who regard betting as one of the legitimate pleasures of the working class we recommend the study of the following case.'[22]

It requires only the quickest of skimmings through the novels of Dickens, the reporting of Charles Booth or Henry Mayhew or a modern account such as Kellow Chesney's 'The Victorian Underworld'[23] to recognise that violence was a predominant characteristic of life in the lower of the two nations of the time. Yet it is, quite startlingly, impossible to find any attempt to describe it as

49

a distinct phenomenon or to ponder the causes and nature of violent behaviour as such. It is always wrapped up in one or another social construction. To Mrs Bosanquet it was a natural and expected concomitant of gambling, for others drink was the evil and yet other writers thought it simply a matter of recognising criminal breeding. Terry Coleman quotes the following reporter's description of a man, sentenced to fifteen years transportation for drunken brawling, who

'May be considered a type of the class to which he belongs. His stature is rather below the common height, but his broad frame gives evidence of immense strength. His countenance is forbidding in the extreme. Every feature indicates habitual crime.
"For evil passions, cherished long,
Have ploughed them with expression strong"
while his rough matted hair completed the aspect of a finished ruffian.'[24]

Seebohm, Rowntree and Charles Booth produced great urban studies which were free of this sort of reach-me-down categorisation, but still neither provide satisfactory evidence for a study of violence. There is plenty recorded in Booth's 'Life and Labour'. If a stranger went near number 10 Parker Street for instance:

'he is sure to be asked for money which, if given, would as surely go to the public houses. Perhaps a quarrel will begin and in two minutes one woman has hauled another down, while a third will seize the apparent victim by the hair and with the other hand fetch heavy blows on her face, others join the fray and the whole are swearing and fighting . . .'[25]

Yet the purpose of the house by house investigation of Parker Street was to demonstrate not the incidence of violence but the more generalised pattern of a life debased by lack of regular employment, ignorance and squalor which was the common lot of those in 'class A' of the poor. For these Charles Booth proposed state action to eliminate what Rowntree termed 'below the line' poverty but even when this early welfarism was placed on the political agenda after the Liberal victory of 1906 it was expressed in terms which did not necessarily advocate a gentler society. For a theme running through many of the polemics of the time, and very forcefully in 'The Heart of the Empire' by C. F. G. Masterman, the first minister to supervise national insurance, was that the city had a debilitating effect on the natural virility of British citizens.[26] Alarming support came from the finding that four out of every ten who volunteered for service in the Boer War were unfit.

The heart of the empire theme did much for the cause of social reform; but for that of women's suffrage it was a cause of the frustration which helped to divert the movement into paths of violence. Thus, a liberal MP could say in 1909:

'. . . so long as this country is constituted as the directing power of a huge empire . . . it is of vast importance that our policy should be directed in the same masculine, virile way – it may be a brutal and bad way – but it must be directed in the same way and towards the same end as the policy of competing nations';[26]

and a *Times* leader, commenting on the suffrage question in 1908 could proclaim:

'. . . the underlying assumption in the national franchise is that the voter, who has to decide on the well-being and even the existence of his country, can argue out views for his country's own good on equal terms with his fellow, and in the last resort can knock him down if he chance to be the better man. No such assumption could be possible were women to have the vote.'[26]

A corollary of these attitudes exists in the extent to which heavy-handed physical punishment featured as an agent of discipline until comparatively recent times. Geoffrey Gorer remarked on its prevalence in 1955[27] and some of the interviews in Jeremy Seabrook's 'City Close-up'[28] confirm the existence of a nostalgia for the practices on which Robert Roberts casts a different light:

'Caned in school for any fault, these children were often severely beaten again at home for having been punished at all. A certain joy died early in them. Broken in spirit, scurryingly obedient, bleak in personality, they would be the slaves now of anyone who cared to command them.'[19]

It is clear indeed that the study of violence only gains meaning when it concerns itself with the wider context of contemporary values and social forms. There may even be merit in attempting to gain the most wide and general perspective on the subject, such as might arise from reminding ourselves that the past hundred years or so have seen the development of a society with an openness in both physical and social configuration which makes it incomparable with that of mid-Victorian England. Describing the city of that time, Geoffrey Best tells us:

'the amenities and institutions of the propertied, their homes and business premises, their parks and promenades, their religion and their politics . . . reticulated like an arterial system . . . through a turbulent land of often desperate need, customary roughness and endemic violence – a land teeming with tramps and vagrants, gypsies, nomadic and seasonal labourers, beggars and spongers, housebreakers, sneak-thieves, pickpockets, horse-thieves and loafers.'[29]

It is hard for us, especially if we have been reared with the picture of the friendly bobby on the beat maintaining social order by his presence and an occasional cuff on a juvenile ear, to realise how impenetrable some of the dark areas were to the police who entered into the brick warrens only in forays, often physically rough, to pluck out a few malefactors. The beat policeman, reinforced by innumerable gatekeepers and watchmen, confined himself to the territories of the propertied and respectable. His 'move along there', applied to urchins and even working men who strayed out of their territory; it was a tiny expression of this social order, and a quite natural consequence of the fact that there were two classes of shops. The city centres catered for the carriage trade; but for the great majority the front-parlour and corner shop sold all the necessities of life. In pre-1914 Crewe there were streets where as many as one in every four houses was a shop and where there is only rarely even an altered doorway or window to remind us of the fact.

There were just as much two classes of life style. For the respectable there were activities which were essentially improving: church services, concert music, plays, museums and libraries. For the rest, drinking, low music hall and the rough and tumble, punctuated by sporadic viciousness of a life in the mean, filthy streets, innocent often of elementary water and sewerage services. For the comfortably placed this life lay utterly beyond their experience, although they were fed vicarious glimpses when they paid into the funds of the local ragged boys' home, whose officers would venture into the abyss to pluck out some waif, or by reading accounts of novelists and journalists who had penetrated this strange and fascinating world.

The half century before World War I saw the first stage in the mighty confluence of political, social and physical development which has given modern Britain an openness of feature in almost complete contrast to the land described by Geoffrey Best. But this first stage was sometimes a very unsympathetic penetration of the values and standards of one section of Britain into those of the great majority. Haussmann drove boulevards through Paris to facilitate riot control; Britain's Corporation Streets and Victoria Roads established bridgeheads for the infiltration of gentler life styles. From them spread out the elementary Board schools which would educate the ironically described 'new masters' of the land, the public bath-houses and – a little later – the Carnegie libraries and the churches with their hectoring way-side pulpits. Sometimes quite specifically bourgeois notions gained sway. Margaret Hewitt has described how the concept that a woman's place was in her home and with her children was first applied to the working classes rather than demanded by them.[30]

If developments since 1919 have been more neutral in their cultural impact it is partly because so many of them are public. Many a council estate suburb bears witness to public expenditure not only on house, and sometimes shops and the occasional pub, but on a vast range of social provisions which manifests itself in schools, employment exchanges, ante-natal clinics and health centres, youth clubs and so on. Today's public provision also makes the assumption of mobility, expressed in the public transport and road systems which link suburb, work and city centre. A third factor reducing the assertion of the more classically bourgeois standards, although often tending to increase property ownership is the broad 'consumer revolution'. Town centre stores, holiday camp proprietors, the limited companies which own football clubs all fret at restrictions on trading hours, traffic flow and any other factor which keeps their customers away.

This massive rechiselling of Britain's social architecture has created a framework which must be considered in any discussion of violence in contemporary society. At times it seems to create new opportunities for unruly behaviour. It was the Duke of Wellington who was opposed to cheap railway fares on the grounds that they would enable the 'lower orders to move about'. Some incidents on football specials might seem to confirm his gloomy forecast until we remember that we – unlike the Duke's contemporaries – see nearly all the violence that does take place and can realise how trivial in quantity it is compared with that in the dark places of his own day. It may be the case that open access to city centres is an occasional spur to hooliganism especially when those there are faced with intolerant stares and uneasily suspicious attitudes and a situation develops in which bystanders, police and those in 'the crowd' fall back on an essentially Victorian concept about who has a right to be there. I can remember a few years back an occasion when a couple of thousand adolescents (including some of my pupils) crowded into the central square of a midland city to find themselmes stalked by wary (although very circumspect) police and gaped at by theatre and cinema goers who were rewarded by nothing worse than the thrill of hearing a couple of bottles drop and shatter on the pavement. Next morning a grim headmaster warned in assembly against 'going into places where you don't belong'. In 'Working Class Community' Brian Jackson describes a similar affair and points out how the situation created a vague resentment against the authorities whose territory the crowds had invaded. He also points out how the press seeking a reach-me-down explanation tried to fix the, totally inaccurate, 'race riot' label.[31]

This process of social interpenetration of high and low, the inter-marrying of cultures so that a cup-tie and the Alf Garnett Show engage the attention of men and women on both sides of the cultural tracks, the paradox that we all have so much more that is public as well as owning so much more privately, has been itself the major force in eliminating violence as an endemic condition in British life. The medical analogy is maybe apt. Only after preventive medicine has wiped out an endemic disease can resources be concentrated on the few remaining acutely ill. The central thesis of this essay is that both public and specialist awareness of violence – itself a term which has only recently gained its connotations of capricious and deviant behaviour – has increased as the major threat has declined. The remaining incidences of violence are just as much a cause for concern and treatment as an outbreak of typhoid or small-pox, but in both situations exaggeration and panic are surely unhelpful.

References
(1) BARRACLOUGH G. (1967). *History and the Common Man*, Historical Association, London.
(2) SELLARS W. and YEATMAN R. (1930). *1066 and all that*, Methuen, London.
(3) MARWICK A. (1970). *The Nature of History*, Macmillan, London.
(4) FRANCISCIUS A. (1953). *Itinerarium Brittaniæ: A Journey to England in 1497*, C. V. McFault, Barcelona.
(5) RUDÉ G. (1959). *The Crowd in the French Revolution*, Oxford University Press, Oxford.
(6) READ D. (1958). *Peterloo: the Massacre and its Background*, Manchester University Press, Manchester.
(7) MARLOW J. (1969). *The Peterloo Messacre*, Rapp and Whiting, London.
(8) CRITCHLEY T. A. (1970). *The Conquest of Violence*, Constable, London.
(9) NOTTINGHAM JOURNAL, 29 March 1839 (see: ROBOTTOM J. and others (1965), *Working Class Unrest in early Nineteenth Century Nottingham*, University of Nottingham Archive Teaching Unit No. 2).
(10) WILLIAMS D. (1967). *Keeping the Peace*, Hutchinson, London.
(11) BROWNLIE I. (1968). *The Law Relating to Public Order*, Butterworth, London.
(12) CMND 5919. *The Red Lion Square Disorders of 15 June 1974: Report of Lord Justice Scarman, February 1975*, HMSO London.
(13) THE TIMES, 23 October 1968.

(14) THE TIMES, 28 October 1968.
(15) MOWAT C. L. (1955). *Britain between the Wars,* Methuen, London.
(16) WALVIN J. (1975). *The People's Game,* Allen Lane, London.
(17) BISHOP E. (1964). *Blood and Fire,* Longmans, London.
(18) MORRIS A. (ed.) (1974). *The Law-breakers,* BBC, London.
(19) ROBERTS R. (1971). *The Classic Slum,* Manchester University Press, Manchester.
(20) SIMS G. R. (1907). *The Dark Stain,* Jarrold and Sons, London.
(21) HALL S. (1975). *Mugging: a case study in the media, The Listener,* 1 May 1975.
(22) BOSANQUET H. (1914). *Social Work in London 1868–1914,* J. Murray, London.
(23) CHESNEY K. (1970). *The Victorian Underworld,* Maurice Temple Smith, London.
(24) COLEMAN T. (1968). *The Railway Navvies,* Penguin, London.
(25) FRIED and ELMAN R. (1971). *Charles Booth's London,* Penguin, London.
(26) GILBERT B. B. (1973). *The Heart of the Empire,* Harvester Press, London.
(27) GORER G. (1955). *Exploring the English Character,* Cresset, London.
(28) SEABROOK J. (1971). *City Close-up,* Allen Lane, London.
(29) BEST G. (1971). *Mid-Victorian Britain 1851–75,* Weidenfeld and Nicolson, London.
(30) HEWITT M. (1958). *Wives and Mothers in Victorian Industry,* Rockliff, London.
(31) JACKSON B. (1968). *Working Class Community,* Penguin, London.

Chapter IV The biological value of aggression
H. Swanson

Agonistic behaviour, of which aggression is a component, is seen in every living vertebrate species. This implies that in evolutionary terms, aggression must have a strong positive survival value. In this chapter I would like to suggest various functions for aggression, which may apply to humans, by using illustrations from the animal kingdom.

Agonistic behaviour is defined as any behaviour associated with conflict, including both attacks and reactions to being attacked, which may be fighting back or fleeing. It includes bloody battles as well as more subtle manifestations such as threats and submissive gestures.

This behaviour is confined to conflict between members of the same species i.e. intra-specific aggression. There may of course be aggression between different species, particularly in those which bear a predator-prey relationship to each other. Thus a lion will use his claws and teeth to stalk and attack a zebra but his motivation is quite different from when he is defending his territory against another lion. When he is jumping on his victim he does not flatten his ears or show any other signs of anger; he is merely satisfying his need for food.[1] Although an animal may use the same weapons such as claws and teeth for predation as for fighting, it has been shown that different brain centres are involved. Thus while stimulation of one area of the brain of a cat through implanted electrodes will cause it to attack a mouse liberated in the room, stimulation of another area will cause it to ignore the mouse and instead attack another cat, the experimenter or even a brush.[2, 3]

The first reaction of most prey animals to attack is flight. However, if this becomes impossible because escape is cut off, an animal will fight to defend itself. In fighting for its life, or that of its young, it will use its most lethal weapons. Since survival of the species is ultimately at stake on both sides of the predator-prey relationship, it is advantageous for both species if the adversary is killed or injured, and therefore no-holds-barred fighting has been selected for during evolution.

Table 1 Functions of aggression

BETWEEN SPECIES	WITHIN SPECIES
Predation	Dispersal of population
Defence against predators	Maintenance of social stability

Inter-specific aggression may also occur if two species are competing for the same food or nesting sites. However, under natural conditions this is unlikely as species sharing a common habitat usually occupy separate ecological niches and thus do not compete with one another. This is demonstrated dramatically in coral fish, where many species feed on the abundant food supply, but each species has adapted for a certain type of prey. Many different kinds of fish can therefore co-exist peacefully, but no more than one member of the same species, (identified by its characteristic brilliant colouring) can be tolerated in a given area.[1]

When potential enemies have to share common resources, such as a watering hole, they adjust their habits so that they use it at different times of day.[4] Only when conditions become unnaturally difficult, as for instance, when food becomes very scarce during a drought, will formerly compatible species be forced to literally 'fight' for survival.

What can be the value of aggression between members of the same species? The fact that aggression between individuals should lead to the preservation of the species appears as a paradox at first sight. The observation that only a single representative of each type of fish inhabits a defined area demonstrates one function of agonistic behaviour, that of spacing of the population. If too many members of a species inhabit the same area they may soon exhaust their food supply. Thus territorial behaviour has evolved as a mechanism for population dispersal over the available habitat.

One theory of population control is that animals breed to their maximum capacity and that their numbers are kept in check by predators, exposure, disease and shortage of food.[5] Although these factors are certainly important, observations have shown that most members of a given population are healthy and well-fed and that the food supply shows no sign of becoming exhausted. It must be emphasised that this applies to natural conditions, where animals are living in ecological balance with their environment. An alternative theory was therefore proposed by Wynne Edwards[6, 7], who suggested that animals limit their numbers before there is over-exploitation of the food supply. Territorial behaviour would seem to be an ideal adaptation of this requirement. This can take many forms, but the most usual is for a single male and his family to defend a certain area of land which contains sufficient resources for survival of the breeding unit. In some species e.g. lions, the territorial unit may comprise several males and females.[8] The size of the territory can be adapted to the food supply, so that in good years the territories are small while in poor years they can be enlarged. A well-known study on grouse in Scotland[9] has shown that this indeed happens. Since only those pairs of birds which own a territory will breed, less birds will produce young in lean years but each family will have enough food to survive comfortably. Excess non-breeding birds are driven to the edge of the moor where, living conditions being less desirable, they will probably succumb to predators. Because it is difficult to make accurate counts, the evidence for territory formation being the principal means of population control in many species is still speculative.

It is doubtlessly an advantage for breeding units to own a territory where they can feed freely and bring up their young unmolested. Territorial behaviour has been most widely studied in fish and birds: the bright colours of tropical fish and many birds act as signals to others to keep their distance. It is usually the males which are brightly coloured as it is their job to defend the territory while the more drab coloured (and therefore better camouflaged) females look after the young.

In seasonal breeders, the testes regress during the non-breeding season and during this time the males may not show any territorial behaviour. As the breeding season approaches, the testes start to secrete the male hormone, testosterone, which induces the desire to seek a mate and stake out a territory. Furthermore, the sex-typical characteristics, such as brightly coloured plumage in birds or antlers in deer, also appear at this time. It is an interesting sidelight on the economy of nature that the same visual displays which act as deterrents in other males may also serve to make the territory owner more attractive to females.[1, 10]

How does an individual acquire a territory? If he is engaged in a serious battle with an evenly matched competitor, both he and his adversary could be seriously wounded or even killed. Obviously it would not be to the advantage of the species if the best specimens were to be mutilated at the beginning of the breeding season. Animals with potentially dangerous weapons have therefore evolved elaborate rules and rituals to govern their fights for dominance.[1, 11, 12] Rattlesnakes could easily kill each other with their poisonous fangs, but instead of biting they intertwine their bodies and when one has put the other down he emerges as the victor, while his opponent retreats. Similarly, giraffes intertwine their necks rather than use their lethally sharp hooves. The familiar sight of red deer with their antlers locked or the sound of rams butting their heads together are evidence of ritual dominance contests. The rules are well understood by the combatants and the loser will indicate that he concedes defeat by appropriate submissive gestures. Thus, although wolves and dogs use their teeth for both fighting and predation, as soon as the loser presents his neck to the winner, the latter is inhibited by this submissive gesture from following up his advantage, and killing his adversary.

Table 2 Attributes of conventional competition

Symbolic rewards: territory and/or status
Ritualization of fights
Acceptance of status after resolution of conflict

It now becomes apparent that animals seldom fight directly for food or even for a mate, but that their conflicts take the form of conventional competition for symbolic rewards.[7] Having won a contest for dominance, the victorious male is now in the position of acquiring and holding a territory. Ownership of territory will qualify him as a potential mate for one or more females, and when the young are born, he and his family will have exclusive rights over the food supply.

Upon acquiring a territory, the owner will keep intruders at a distance by the previously mentioned visual displays, or by auditory displays such as the singing of birds and the whistling of prairie dogs. Most mammals have a highly developed sense of smell and they mark their territories, particularly the boundaries, with deposits of urine and faeces or with specially developed scent glands.[13] A male which has acquired a territory defends it against intruders. He will feel most confident at the centre of his territory, and will defeat a much larger adversary. Familiarity with his environment gives him a strategic as well as a psychological advantage. His confidence decreases near the borders which may be adjacent to the territory of another male. Thus conflicts between territory-owners usually occur only at the boundaries where the oscillating desire to fight or flee causes them to interact in a series of chase-flight sequences. Since one of the functions of aggression is to select the fittest animals for breeding (by allowing them to acquire and defend territories) it is not surprising that the same hormones which control sexual behaviour also control aggression.

Table 3 Types of social organisation

TERRITORIAL	HIERARCHICAL
Small group	Large group
Relative dominance	Absolute dominance
(chase-flight at boundary)	(attached to individual)
Few interactions	Many interactions
(chase-flight at boundary)	(dominance/submission rituals)
Defence of territory	Defence of group

Incidentally, some females join in the defence of the territory (especially the nest) and there is evidence that in these species female hormones may also increase the tendency towards aggression.[14]

Not all animals are territorial. Large herbivores have to wander from place to place in search of suitable grazing land. Such animals usually join together in large herds as a protection against predators. The herds of wildebeest, zebra and gazelles which frequent the plains of East Africa may appear to the casual tourist as an amorphous group but the trained observer will detect a well-defined social structure. A large herd is composed of a number of sub-groups, the members of which all know one another. Leadership in a herd is also established by means of conventional competition. Whereas in a territorial situation, dominance is relative, insofar as the dominance of an individual varies with the distance from the centre of the territory, in non-territorial animals, dominance is absolute.[15] The leader retains his position no matter where he is and is recognised by threats and other ritual displays. He is often, but not necessarily, the oldest and largest male and his sleek and well-kept appearance suggests that he seldom engages in fights.[16] Once others stop making the appropriate submissive gestures in response to his threats, his authority is challenged and this is a sign that he will soon lose his position. Although farmers are able to recognise the leaders in their herds of cattle[17] and flocks of sheep (and may take advantage of this when moving the animals from place to place), threat displays recognisable to humans are most conspicuous in monkeys and apes. As these animals are very active, frequent encounters between members of the troop require instant awareness of relative status. Fights may break out between the lower-ranking animals, but these stop immediately when the leader appears.

Some kind of hierarchy exists within any group of animals which live together, no matter what the size of the group and whether or not they are territorial.[15] The simplest is the family structure where the order of dominance descends from the male to one or more females and then to juveniles. As soon as the juveniles start to threaten the status of the head of the family, they are driven away. The females usually stay with the family group longer than the males, who may form gangs with other youngsters of the same age, until they are old enough to start a breeding unit of their own. It may take several years after reaching sexual maturity before a young male has acquired sufficient self-confidence to challenge an older male for a territory or for a place in the hierarchy which will give him access to a receptive female. This applies to such widely differing species as elephants, horses, wolves and monkeys.

In some groups, as for instance in domestic chickens, the hierarchy is linear and this is where the classical 'pecking order' was first observed: A pecks B, B pecks C etc without reciprocation. Usually the structure is much more complex, involving shifting relationships between dominants, sub-dominants and inferiors. Females may form part of the hierarchy, or have a separate one, such as in hyenas, where females are bigger and dominant over males.[18] It has been noted that in chimpanzees and some species of monkeys, the offspring of dominant females are more likely to become dominant in their peer play-groups and will often become leaders when adult.[19, 20]

Hierarchy may also play a part in population control. Wolves and wild dogs live in packs whose size is critical for efficient hunting. They can usually only support one new litter per season, as food has to be brought back for the young and mother. In this situation, only the dominant male and female are allowed to mate. The others are inhibited from mating, through social pressure rather than active interference by the leaders. If the inhibitions break down and a second litter is born, it is usually destroyed by the dominant animals; this is in the best interests of the pack.[18, 21] Inhibition of mating by anyone except a dominant pair (which may be behavioural or due to regression of the sex organs) has also been observed in laboratory colonies of gerbils.[22]

It should be emphasized that although a certain amount of aggression occurs in the establishment of a hierarchy, once this has happened, relations between members of the group are peaceful. Not all displays are threats – there is much so-called 'bonding behaviour' whose function is to induce cohesion between individuals.[23] Everyone is familiar with the social grooming of monkeys and apes and boisterous play among juveniles. There is much contact seeking, with animals sitting close to one another and sleeping together. The bond between parents and their offspring may last for years in chimpanzees, elephants, horses and other slowly maturing mammals. In other species the pair-bond between mates may last a life-time.

In contrast to their behaviour towards the members of the 'in group', most animals will be very aggressive towards strangers, whether they be neighbouring troops or individuals who try to intrude into the group, even though several troops may have overlapping home ranges. In earlier days, zoo-keepers who were not aware of this put unfamiliar animals together without chance of escape often found that bloody battles broke out in which individuals were sometimes killed.[24] Now great care is taken to introduce animals to each other on neutral ground before putting them in a cage together. This is also advisable with smaller animals kept as pets or in the laboratory, such as mice, hamsters and gerbils.

It should now be realised that in addition to dispersal of population, a second function of aggression is maintenance of social stability. There is some fighting when a hierarchy is established, or altered through some change in social structure such as the death of the leader by predation or other causes, the emergence of a challenger amongst the juveniles or the intrusion of a stranger. The more stable the established hierarchy, the more peaceful living conditions will be, occasional threat gestures being sufficient to keep order. Such a situation is most conducive to successful breeding and rearing of an ideal number of young. It is interesting to note that there may be great differences in social organisation not only between species, but between animals of the same species living in different habitats. Specific behaviour patterns have been selected over many generations to provide the best fit with the special requirements of the environment.[7]

Having established that under appropriate conditions, aggressive behaviour may serve a useful function, let us now look at the internal and external factors which will cause aggression actually to occur. The notion that aggression is a drive which gradually builds up and has to be 'released' at periodic intervals – the so-called 'hydraulic theory' – is now largely discounted.[16] Unlike hunger, a true drive whose increase is accompanied by a progressive drop in blood sugar until it is satisfied, there are no physiological changes which take place if aggression has not been 'discharged' for some reason. However the neural mechanisms underlying the capacity for aggressive behaviour are present in all individuals. The threshold for excitation is controlled mainly by internal factors while the releasing stimuli are provided by environmental cues.

Is there a hereditary basis for aggression? Some breeds of dogs are reputed to be more aggressive than others, as are some individuals in a litter.[25] Mice have been inbred for generations so as to produce many strains, each of which is genetically almost homogenous. It is possible to grade the various strains according to the amount of aggression shown in standardized tests.[26, 27, 28] In species with a relatively short life span, it is possible to breed for more or less aggression by selecting animals who show the appropriate behavioural trait. Compared to the wild stock from which they originated, laboratory rats are remarkably peaceful because aggressive individuals were either killed in fights or removed by experimenters. In animals where artificial selective breeding has not taken place, and in humans, it is likely that individuals will have varying thresholds for aggression, depending on their genetic constitution.

The hereditary make-up provides a framework for the behaviour patterns which make up the 'personality' of both humans and animals and which evolve by a continuous interaction between heredity and environment. The old argument about nature versus nurture is rather irrelevant, since it is now recognised that neither factor can operate independently. When the question arises as to whether there is an aggressive 'instinct' it should be realized that even in lower animals there are very few true instincts, defined as innate patterns of behaviour which are invariably elicited by specific stimuli. Thus the tendency to grab something when falling is probably instinctive but even the species-characteristic song of birds can be modified by learning.[29, 30] Usually the environment is sufficiently constant for behaviour patterns appropriate to the species to emerge in succeeding generations, but a change in environment, particularly if it occurs early in life, may produce abnormal behaviour. Thus monkeys reared without contact with other young monkeys may be incapable of showing normal sexual or maternal behaviour.[31] There has been evidence in recent work that the anatomical connections between nerve cells in the brain can be modified by varying experience during development.[32]

One of the mechanisms by which genes express their influence on behaviour is through the action of hormones, particularly sex hormones, during the period of pre-natal differentiation. The mammalian testis is active during foetal life in secreting the male hormone – testosterone, which causes the differentiation of the genital tract along male lines. At the same time, testosterone 'programmes' the still plastic brain so as to make it more responsive to male hormones in adult life and to facilitate the expression of masculine behaviour patterns.[33] Because mice and rats are born in a very immature condition, it is possible to alter these behaviour patterns by hormone treatment shortly after birth. Thus female mice injected with a single dose of testosterone at birth will show male-type copulation when mature.[34] Other types of sexually dimorphic behaviour may also be affected. Normally only male mice are aggressive; when they are castrated their threshold for aggression decreases, but is restored to normal by testosterone treatment. Female mice, on the other hand, do not show aggression even when ovariectomized and treated with testosterone. However, female mice which had been 'masculinized' in infancy will respond to testosterone as adults in the same way as males i.e. by increased aggression.[35, 36]

The role of sex hormones in facilitating aggression during the breeding season has been mentioned previously in connection with the establishment of territories and hierarchies. Castration is a long-established practice in animal husbandry for reducing aggression. It should be emphasised that hormones allow behaviour to occur but do not cause it. They produce a change in internal state which lowers the threshold towards external stimulation. Other changes in body chemistry, such as a lowering of blood sugar associated with hunger or an increase in adrenal secretion during stress, may also affect the threshold for aggression.[37]

We can thus summarize the internal factors which predispose an individual to be more or less aggressive: heredity, organizational and activational hormones, and changes in body chemistry. To what extent can these tendencies be modified by experience? What is the role of learning and social conditioning? It has been shown that mice born to mothers from an aggressive strain will show less aggression when adult if they are suckled by non-aggressive foster mothers than litter mates reared by their own or another aggressive mother.[39] Furthermore mice are more likely to fight if, while immature, they regularly see other mice fighting in nearby cages.[38] Monkeys born to mothers who hold a dominant rank in the hierarchy are 'trained' to dominance and are more likely to be dominant when adult than those reared by a submissive mother.[20] It has often been suggested that the play-fighting shown by most young animals is training for real fighting, but the evidence of controlled experiments suggests that there is no correlation between these two classes of behaviour.[40, 41] On the other hand, victory in a real fight or even conventional competition for dominance will have positively reinforcing qualities. Thus an animal which has won a fight is more likely to start another fight and moreover, is more likely to win. Conversely, once a pattern of defeat has been established, this also is self-perpetuating.[42] Presumably this is how permanent hierarchies are established in a natural population, where defeated individuals avoid confrontations by showing the appropriate submission gestures or else emigrating. Bluff, due to confidence after a victory, is an important factor in maintaining a position of dominance. It seems that animals can be 'trained' to use varying degrees of violence to resolve conflicts. If a number of strange dogs are confined in an enclosure where they would be likely to fight but are prevented from biting by being muzzled, they are less likely to engage in fighting once the muzzles are removed.[38] However, behaviour patterns which have evolved over many generations through natural selection will show a certain resistance to alteration through training.

The social structure of a group can influence the amount of aggression shown by individuals. In colonies of gerbils there is very little fighting in a stable society with a well-established hierarchy. However if this is disturbed by the death of the leader or some other individual, the attainment of sexual maturity by a new generation, or the introduction of strangers, there is liable to be an outbreak of fighting.[22]

The physical characteristics of the space in which animals are kept can also influence their social structure and consequent behaviour. Thus if four or more adult male mice are placed together in a large enclosure, they will fight until one emerges as dominant, and they will keep this relationship for a long time. On the other hand, if the enclosure is divided in two by a partition and four mice are placed on either side, then a dominant will emerge in each half. When the partition is removed each of the two dominants will defend his half of the enclosure as his territory. It might be mentioned that only males are attacked, females and juveniles being free to go where they like; sex is recognised by olfactory cues. Which animals become dominant is determined by the interaction of the genetic constitution and previous experience, which makes up their personality. Failure to recognize the importance of the individual in social interactions can lead to misinterpretation of findings. Thus it has been observed that a mouse living in a cage by himself becomes very aggressive when matched against another mouse under standard conditions. With 2 mice living together, fighting will occur in 50 per cent of cases, with 3 mice in 30 per cent and when more than 10 mice live together, fighting hardly ever occurs.[43] A statistical interpretation may lead to the fallacious conclusion that crowding decreases aggression in all the animals. An alternative explanation might be that a single mouse will invariably be a territory-holder without experiencing defeat, while in grouped mice, the one who becomes dominant will probably be the only one to show aggressive tendencies.

It should now be apparent that a predisposition to aggressive behaviour is caused by multiple factors operating on different levels of organization, from genetic to social. We now have to consider the specific precipitating or 'releasing' factors which provoke an individual to express overt aggression. A theory proposed by Archer[44] suggests that fear and aggression are variants of a single response. Which one is expressed in a certain situation depends on interaction between the internal state and the relative intensity of the stimulus. The interplay between the conflicting urges to attack or flee is seen most dramatically at territorial boundaries. Incidentally, the same hormone, adrenalin, causes physiological changes which prepare the body for either fight or flight, such as increased respiration and redistribution of the blood to muscles.

The common factor which evokes fear or attack is a discrepancy between the actual world and what is expected (Fig. 1). At the simplest level, an intrusion into the body surface producing pain, particularly if unexpected, will usually result in an expression of anger and attack against the agent causing the pain. If the agent is inaccessible or threatening, the aggression may be directed to some other object or a fear reaction will occur.

Most animals will only tolerate another to come within a certain distance of their body.[45] There is an invisible aura around each individual called the 'personal space'. Thus birds spaced out on a telephone wire are just out of reach of each other's beak. The size of this envelope depends on the species and the circumstances. Many so-called 'contact' animals like to sleep in a pile (e.g. hamsters and gerbils) although at other times they can be quite intolerant of close neighbours. Instrusion into this personal space, particularly around the face, will usually provoke aggression. In territorial animals, the territory might be seen as an extension of this personal space and again intrusion will precipitate attack. Conversely, removing an animal from his familiar surroundings into a strange environment will usually evoke fear.

Finally, frustration caused by some barrier or obstacle preventing an animal from reaching a desired goal, might be interpreted as a discrepancy between what is expected i.e. the reward and what is obtained (no reward). Many workers consider frustration as the most important cause of aggressive behaviour.

Whether fear or aggression, or either, is evoked as a response to a specific situation depends on several factors. The internal condition such as the hormonal state and the degree of arousal as well as the strength of motivation are important in setting the threshold for response. The degree of discrepancy will determine whether the reaction is fear or anger (Fig. 2). Mild discrepancy will provoke aggression but more intense simulation will produce fear. Thus mild pain on initiation of an attack may provoke counter-aggression but if more severe wounds are inflicted, anger will be replaced by fear which will be expressed by submission or flight. The arrival of a stranger represents only a slight disturbance of familiar surroundings and thus evokes attack, but removal into a strange place means a complete loss of known landmarks and will

Fig. 1

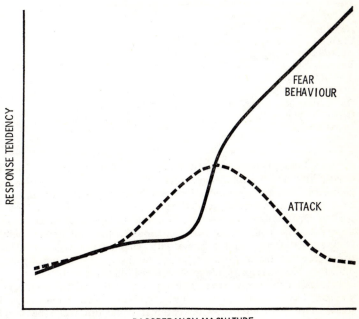

RESPONSE TENDENCY

FEAR BEHAVIOUR

ATTACK

DISCREPANCY MAGNITUDE

67

provoke intense fear. Fear is less if other familiar animals are present. Thus while a single chick might be terrified at the first appearance of a large object like a red balloon, a group of chicks will soon overcome their fright and attack the threatening object. Also if an animal is being chased and his escape route is blocked, he will turn and attack his pursuer in a most vicious manner. Such examples suggest that there is indeed a close link between fear and aggression.

Table 4 Factors influencing threshold for aggression

PHYSIOLOGICAL	EXPERIENTIAL
Heredity	Early socialization
Organizational hormones	Previous victory or defeat
Activational hormones	
Body chemistry	
ENVIRONMENTAL	SITUATIONAL
Distribution of living space	Degree of discrepancy
Density of population	Strength of motivation
Social disorganization	Appropriateness of target
	Blocking of escape

Can ethology, the systematic study of animal behaviour, teach us anything about human behaviour? It is easy, almost a parlour-game, to draw glib analogies between selected patterns of animal behaviour and certain aspects of human behaviour. Thus the concept of territoriality can be seen in humans in their attachment to their favourite chair, their bedroom, their home and finally their country. Decorating of the home with personal possessions and a name-plate on the office door, might be interpreted as a form of marking. The concept of hierarchies is well-illustrated in such rigid structures as the army, royalty, the government and the civil service and more subtly in the status symbols which delineate one social class from another. Conventional competition can be seen as the drive for power and/or money and assertions of dominance and submission are seen in the more or less formal greeting rituals and courtesy gestures. The greater tendency to aggression in males, the conflict between father and son, the formation of gangs of juvenile males, all have parallels in one or more animal species.

A number of popular books have appeared over the last few years[1, 46, 47, 48, 49], in which human behaviour is explained in terms of such analogies. These books have been severely criticised[50] by scientists who feel that they present potentially misleading over-simplifications. In particular, they feel that in a social climate

Fig. 2

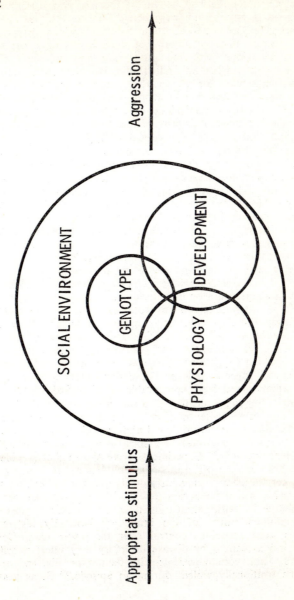

where violence is held to be on the increase, the contention that aggression is innate may engender a fatalistic attitude in which violence is condoned and efforts to reduce it are considered useless. It is apparent that the authors of these books have not studied human behaviour with the same care and rigorous scientific methods with which they studied animals, and consequently some of the suggestions for attenuating human aggression may seem naive. However, they have performed a useful service by making the public aware of the findings of ethologists and suggesting that a biological approach may provide new insight on human behaviour.

Recently, ethologists have started to apply carefully controlled methods of observation to human behaviour. By the use of slow motion or speeded-up film, one-way screens etc, they are discovering many previously unsuspected cross-cultural similarities in facial expressions and gestures, some of which can already be detected in tiny babies.[23] We are beginning to appreciate the complicated interplay between heredity and experience in the moulding of personality, the social factors which predispose to conflict, the changes in body chemistry which vary the threshold for aggression and the external factors which may precipitate over-action.

The various methods and devices which have been advocated to prevent violence are unrealistic if they assume that aggression is due to a single cause or that it can be eliminated through education. Even if it were possible, it would seem undesirable to suppress completely the aggressive drive in human society. It would be more useful to analyse and eliminate these factors which may change normal competition and assertiveness to unnatural violence. In spite of the complexity of human behaviour, the basic emotions of fear and anger are elicited by similar factors to those affecting other animals and have comparable physiological manifestations.

Scott[38] has suggested that disturbances at any level of organization may cause violence (Fig. 3). At the genetic level, there is evidence that some chromosomal abnormalities (e.g. males with an extra Y chromosome) may be associated with abnormal tendencies to violent action.[51, 52] Experiments have shown that specific parts of the brain initiate whilst others inhibit aggression. Thus by stimulating certain areas, a previously docile monkey will exhibit sudden rage and attack the experimenter, while a bull may be stopped in mid-charge by radio stimulation of a small receiver implanted in the inhibitory centre of the brain.[53, 54] Normally higher brain centres exert conscious control over the lower ones. However, brain lesions caused by disease or injury may interfere with this control. Thus, certain patients with temporal lobe epilepsy may become irrationally violent during an episode.[37] Some years ago

Fig. 3

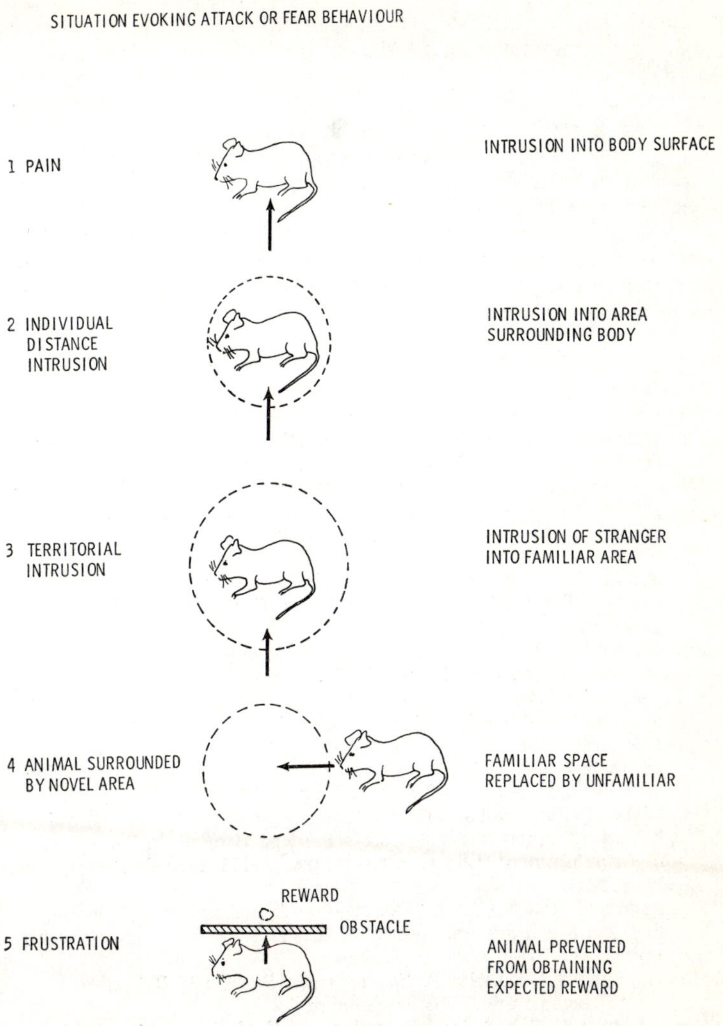

SITUATION EVOKING ATTACK OR FEAR BEHAVIOUR

1 PAIN		INTRUSION INTO BODY SURFACE
2 INDIVIDUAL DISTANCE INTRUSION		INTRUSION INTO AREA SURROUNDING BODY
3 TERRITORIAL INTRUSION		INTRUSION OF STRANGER INTO FAMILIAR AREA
4 ANIMAL SURROUNDED BY NOVEL AREA		FAMILIAR SPACE REPLACED BY UNFAMILIAR
5 FRUSTRATION	REWARD OBSTACLE	ANIMAL PREVENTED FROM OBTAINING EXPECTED REWARD

71

a student who climbed a tower and indiscriminately shot passers-by was later found to have a brain tumour.[55] If properly diagnosed, such people may be helped by surgery or drugs.

Most outbreaks of violence are not, however, caused by brain tumours, but by the interaction of heredity, previous experience and specific precipitating factors in the social environment. Psychologists and sociologists have proposed many conflicting theories as to the causes of abnormal aggression. Although they seem plausible, it remains to be proven by well-controlled scientific investigations whether personality disturbance due to childhood deprivation, constant exposure to violence, and excessive frustration, result in inappropriate aggressive responses. The application of ethological methods to the study of human behaviour might lead to a fuller understanding of the biological base of aggression, as a step towards the analysis and subsequent elimination of some of the causes of violence.

References
(1) LORENZ K. (1963). *On Aggression*, Methuen, London.
(2) WASSMAN M. and FLYNN J. P. (1962). 'Directed attack elicited from the hypothalamus', *Arch. Neurol.* vol. 6, pp. 208–219.
(3) LEVINSON P. K. and FLYNN J. P. (1965). 'The objects attacked by cats during stimulation of the hypothalamus', *Anim. Behav.* vol. 13, pp. 217–220.
(4) LORENZ K. and LEYHAUSEN P. (1973). *Motivation of Human and Animal Behavior*, van Nostrand Reinhold, New York.
(5) LACK D. (1954). *The Natural Regulation of Animal Numbers*, Clarendon Press, Oxford.
(6) WYNNE-EDWARDS V. C. (1964). 'Population control in animals', *Scientific Amer.* vol. 211, pp. 68–75.
(7) WYNNE-EDWARDS V. C. (1971). 'Space use and the social community in animals and men', in *Behavior and Environment* (Ed.) A. H. ESSER, pp. 267–280, Plenum Press, New York.
(8) BERTRAM B. (1975). 'The influence of social factors on reproduction in wild lions', *Anim. Behav.* vol. 23, p. 237.
(9) WATSON A. and MOSS R. (1971). 'Spacing as affected by territorial behavior, habitat and nutrition in the Red Grouse', in *Behavior and Environment* (Ed.) A. H. ESSER, pp. 92–111, Plenum Press, New York.
(10) ROTHBALLER A. B. (1967). 'Aggression, defence and neurohumors', in *Brain Function*, vol. 5 (Eds.) C. D. CLEMENTE and D. B. LINDSLEY, pp. 135–170, UCLA Press, Berkeley.
(11) EIBL-EIBESFELDT I. (1970). *Ethology: the Biology of Behaviour*, Holt, Rinehart and Winston, London.
(12) ALCOCK J. (1975). *Animal Behavior – an Evolutionary Approach*, Sinauer Assoc, Mass.

(13) RALIS K. (1971). 'Mammalian scent marking', *Science,* vol. 171, pp. 443–449.

(14) PAYNE A. P. and SWANSON H. H. (1971). 'Hormonal control of aggressive dominance in the female hamster', *Physiol. Behav.* vol. 6, pp. 355–357.

(15) LEYHAUSEN P. (1971). 'Dominance and territoriality as complemented in mammalian social structure', in *Behavior and Environment* (Ed.) A. H. ESSER, pp. 22–33, Plenum Press, New York.

(16) DIMOND S. J. (1970). *The Social Behaviour of animals,* B. T. Batsford, London.

(17) BOISSOU M. F. (1975). 'Effects on social experience on dominance relationships in domestic cattle', *Anim. Behav.* vol. 23, p. 237.

(18) VAN LAWICK-GOODALL H. and J. (1970). *The Innocent Killers,* Collins, London.

(19) CROOK J. H. (1970). 'The socio-ecology of primates', in *Social Behaviour in Birds and Mammals* (Ed.) J. H. CROOK, pp. 103–166, Academic Press, London.

(20) KAWAMURA S. (1967). 'Aggression as studied in troops of Japanese monkeys', in *Brain Function,* vol. 5 (Eds.) C. D. CLEMENTE and D. B. LINDSLEY, pp. 195–224, UCLA Press, Berkeley.

(21) ZIMEN E. (1975). 'Pack size regulation in wolves', *Anim. Behav.* vol. 23, p. 237.

(22) SWANSON H. (1975). Population control in confined colonies of hamsters and gerbils', *Anim. Behav.* vol. 23, p. 237.

(23) EIBL-EIBESFELDT I. (1971). *Love and Hate,* Methuen, London.

(24) SOUTHWICK C. H. (1969). 'Aggressive behavior in Rhesus monkeys in natural and captive groups', in *Aggressive behavior* (Eds.) S. GARATTINI and E. B. SIGG, pp. 32–43, Excerpta Medica Foundation, Amsterdam.

(25) SCOTT J. P. (1962). 'Genetics and the development of social behavior in mammals', *Amer. J. Orthopsychiatry,* vol. 32, pp. 878–893.

(26) GINSBERG B. and ALLEE W. C. (1942). 'Some effects of conditioning on social dominance and subordination in inbred strains of mice', *Physiol. Zool.* vol. 15, pp. 485–506.

(27) SOUTHWICK C. H. and CLARK L. H. (1966). 'Aggressive behavior and exploratory activity in fourteen mouse strains', *Amed. Zool.* vol. 6, p. 559.

(28) VALE J. R., RAY D. and VALE, C. A. (1972). 'The interaction of genotype and exogenous neonatal androgen: agonistic behavior in female mice', *Behav. Biol.* vol. 7, pp. 321–334.

(29) THORPE W. H. (1958). 'The learning of song patterns by birds, with special reference to the song of the chaffinch', *Ibis,* vol. 100, pp. 535–570.

(30) HINDE R. A. (1969) (Ed.). *Bird Vocalization,* Cambridge University Press, New York.

(31) HARLOW H. F. and HARLOW M. K. (1962). 'Social deprivation in monkeys', *Scientific Amer.* vol. 207, pp. 136–146.

(32) GREENOUGH W. T. (1975). 'Experiential modification of the developing brain', *Amer. Scientists,* vol. 63, pp. 37–46.

(33) BARRACLOUGH C. A. (1972). 'Modifications in reproductive function after exposure to hormones during the prenatal and early post-natal period', in *Neuroendocrinology,* vol. 2 (Eds.) L. MARTINI and W. GANOG, pp. 62–100, Academic Press, New York.

(34) MANNING A. and MCGILL T. E. (1974). 'Neonatal androgen and sexual behavior in female house mice', *Horm. Behav.* vol. 5, pp. 19–31.

(35) BRONSON F. H. and DESJARDINS C. (1970). 'Neonatal androgen administration and adult aggressiveness in female mice', *Gen. Comp. Endocrinol.* vol. 15, pp. 320–325.

(36) EDWARDS D. A. (1970). 'Post-neonatal androgenization and adult behaviour in female mice', *Physiol. Behav.* vol. 5, pp. 465–467

(37) MOYER K. E. (1971). 'The physiology of aggression and the implications for aggression control', in *The Control of Aggression and Violence: Cognitive and Physiological Factors* (Ed.) J. L. SINGER, pp. 61–92, Academic Press, New York.

(38) SCOTT J. P. (1973). 'Biology and the control of violence', *Int. J. Group Tensions,* vol. 3, pp. 4–19.

(39) SOUTHWICK C. H. (1968). 'Effect of maternal environment on aggressive behavior in inbred mice', *Communi. Behav. Biol.,* vol. 1, pp. 129–132.

(40) BEKOFF M. 'The development of social interaction, play and metacommunication in mammals; and ethological perspective', *Quart. Rev. Biol.* vol. 47, pp. 412–434.

(41) GOLDMAN L. and SWANSON K. K. (1975). 'Developmental changes in pre-adult behavior in confined colonies of golden hamsters', *Dev. Psychobiol.* vol. 8, pp. 137–150.

(42) BRONSON F. H. and ELEFTHERIOU B. E. (1965). 'Adrenal response to fighting in mice: separation of physical and psychological causes', *Science,* vol. 147, pp. 627–628.

(43) VALZELLI L. (1969). 'Aggressive behaviour induced by isolation', in *Aggressive Behaviour* (Eds.) S. GARATTINI and E. B. SIGG, pp. 70–76, Excerpta Medica Foundation, Amsterdam.

(44) ARCHER J. (in press). 'The organization of aggression and fear in vertebrates', in *Perspectives in Ethology,* vol. 2 (Eds.) P. P. G. BATESON and P. KLOPFER, Plenum Press, New York.

(45) MCBRIDE G. (1971). 'Theories of animal spacing: the role of flight, fight and social distance', in *Behavior and Environment* (Ed.) A. H. ESSER, pp. 53–68, Plenum Press, New York.

(46) ARDREY R. (1967). *The Territorial Imperative,* Collins, London.

(47) ARDREY R. (1970). *The Social Contract,* Collins, London.

(48) MORRIS D. (1967). *The Naked Ape,* Jonathan Cape, London.

(49) MORRIS D. (1969). *The Human Zoo,* Jonathan Cape, London.

(50) MONTAGU M. F. A. (1968) (Ed.). *Man and Aggression,* Oxford University Press, New York.

(51) HOOK E. B. (1973). 'Behavioral implications of the human genotype', *Science,* vol. 179, pp. 139–150.

(52) MEYER-BAHLBURG H. F. L. (1974). 'Aggression, androgens and the XYY syndrome', in *Sex Differences in Behavior* (Eds.)

(53) R. C. FRIEDMAN, R. M. RICHART and R. L. VANDE WIELE, pp. 433-453, John Wiley, New York.

(54) DELGADO J. E. (1967a). 'Aggression and defense under cerebral radio control', in *Brain Function*, vol. 5 (Eds.) C. D. CLEMENTE and D. B. LINDSLEY, pp. 171-193, UCLA Press, Berkeley.

(55) DELGADO J. E. (1967b). 'Discussion of paper by I. Eibl-Eibesfeldt', in *Brain Function*, vol. 5 (Eds.) C. D. CLEMENTE and D. B. LINDSLEY, pp. 88-90, UCLA Press, Berkeley.

(56) ROBINSON B. W. (1971). 'Aggression: summary and overview', *The Physiology of Aggression and Defeat* (Eds.) B. E. ELEFTHERIOU and J. P. SCOTT, pp. 291-304, Plenum Press, New York.

The author would like to thank John Archer in particular for giving permission to use Figs. 1, 2, 3. They are taken from:
ARCHER J. (in press). 'The organization of aggression and fear in vertebrates', in *Perspectives in Ethology*, vol. 2 (Eds.) P. G. BATESON and P. KLOPFER, Plenum Press, New York.

Chapter V Violence—nature or nurture?
Vladimir Kahan

The seeds of violence seem well implanted in our society. From earliest days the young are confronted, pressed to the edge of their biological patterns. As age increases these pressures are maintained, often ahead of the capacity of the child to cope. Disapproval is readily available, and non-acceptance is commonplace. Policies of reassurances are not only uncommon but are regarded as 'spoiling, letting them get away with it, give them an inch . . .' and similar refusals to acceptance. Not surprisingly the prophesy comes true; 'too little, too late' is a well known state of affairs, and hard wrung concessions are not the best basis on which to build mutual confidence.

It is common experience that much social control in early life is attempted by forms of implicit or explicit confrontation. Disapproval, rejection, sanction, aggression, violence, come together in smacking, and corporal punishment, by parent or teacher, often against a background of uncontrolled threatening, and attacking, outside home or school rooms.

Following other concepts, some social control is attempted through relationships, affection, tolerance, example, helping the young from an early age to live with the stresses of non-requital of wishes and the witholding of acceptance for disapproved acts. Both approaches are complicated because they are usually inconsistently employed, aggression and affection inter-weaving in both the formative and formed periods. Social, cultural and educational influence come into play at different levels colouring both. They, in their turn, are affected from the victim's point of view, by a mixture of unpredictable alerting and reassuring situations.

Capacity to cope with people, places or changes in settings can be taught by modifying learning situations to the point of provoking innate excitation to arousal, followed by reassurative procedures leading to a return through dispersed arousal and alert, to the previous state of relaxation. Alerting is ordinarily brought about by changes in the environment, up to the point of their presenting a difference noticed by the individual (nearly all new patterns alert or alarm). Reassurance is gained by support, or the extinguishing of alert by familiarising the new situation through other means. Arousal, with acted out sharp responses is a fact in itself, and when it happens the condition, and the experience of it, are permanently laid down neurophysiologically, even though it may be modifiable emotionally and meaningfully by later experience.

There is little evidence of innate, on going, aggression as part of the 'nature' of living creatures. It is noticeable that as zoology moved from cataloguing to morphology and later to observing creatures in their habitats the belief in aggression as a 'basic quality' gradually diminished. Animals believed to be innately aggressive became fewer, species by species, as it was observed that to produce transient attitudes of aggression, alarm, defence of the young, or hunger, were required. Buffon in his Zoological Dictionary described the cow as a vicious animal, 'when attacked, it defends itself'. For very many years there have been anecdotes of encounter between man, and 'wild' animals in which the joyful surprise of the reporter at not being attacked as expected, is vividly described. They were useful early side lights on animal behaviour in the wild, showing that when not alarmed, protecting their young, or hunting, animals do not exhibit spontaneous aggression. The human animal demonstrates responses appropriate to his species and the methods of domestication of Western man may well account for the belief that man is wilful, and innately sinful inasmuch as the connection of real or imagined sinfulness rather than the acceptance of 'innocence' is implicit in much popular and special early child management.

This contribution views human behaviour, violent behaviour especially, as a balance between the behaver and the setting, and believes that the study of the behaver is a first requirement. This needs to start at the beginning; not only is the child father to the man, but the child follows the unborn babe with his multifacetted natural equipment and later experiences. This study of behaviour, with its special reference to violent behaviour, and its development, looks at modes of species behaviour, and the social attitudes and environments that almost seem to be planned to bring about violent reactions, as well as later social training that engenders and facilitates violent reaction in the behaver. They require consideration, as do possibly beneficial aspects of violent acting out, whether controlled and socially acceptable or otherwise. As a positive rather than a passive element some societies, to some effect, attempt to minimise personal and social aggression, and thus provide opportunities to look at the advantages and disadvantages of personal, group or collective non-violent behaviour.

In relationship to man and the variety of human societies there is a wide range of accepted explanations for violence or aggression, Anger, aggression, violence, arising from whatever situation have had religious or philosophical interpretations over the centuries, continued and personalised by psychologists taking up individual lines of interpretation especially for the last fifty or so years.

Behaviourists and later animal behaviour investigators such as Lorenz[1] saw aggression phylogenetically, and as being associated with bonding between individual creatures. Frank saw some human violence as expressive acts of passion, which, other circumstances being allowed for, seemed to occur more in the presence of male chromosome preponderance. Speigel of Brandeis University[2] saw social violence in humans as having three foci; the intrapsychic state, the group situation, and cultural value orientations. It has been suggested that violence is associated with cultures which concentrate on pursuing the development of interpersonal relationships. This tends to lead to a high level of cultural striving and achievement with an accompanying high intensity of intra-psychic conflict providing tensions associated with violent acting out, against a reactive controlling violence by the community. Intrapsychic stress is seen broadly as a cause not only of violence but of mental unease and illness, and both are strongly associated with social attitudes which admire achievement gained as the result of a high level intensity of goal seeking. The changing balance of views of the causation of violence, from speculative individual psychodynamic explanations to wider neurophysiological, culturally based, and learned responses, provides some wider grounds on which to consider prevention, management and measures for rehabilitation. Graduated learning situations, reaching alert, but stopping before full arousal, except when this is deliberately part of a plan of progressions, is the way in which the young develop patterns of conflict responses to inner needs such as hunger, people, places or changes in settings. Arousal produces physiological changes leading to 'fight or flight' and fight is violence. This is not elective, although it may be learned. It is the physiological result of an inner situation in which reassurative elements were lacking, and the alerting was not dispersed. The excitatory explosion is the psychophysiological reaction to arousal rather than a chosen specific response, and develops from mechanisms laid down as basic experiences. In the light of neuro-physiological knowledge conscious directive elements play only a small part, if any, in this reaction.

It is the belief of the writer that the devlopment of the basically simple biological reaction sketched in the above paragraphs is the foundation on which personal and social adjustments are made.

It is the purpose of this chapter to attempt to discuss a few aspects of violence and its genesis, only as far as it may be useful in considering the wide field that the concept of violence covers. By dictionary definition violence is 'the quality of being violent, to outrage, to injure'. Aggression is defined as 'beginning a quarrel'. These activities, similar and inter-relating at first sight, are very different even though for purposes of social management they inter-weave, and seem to displace, and replace, each other both in the assessment of what they are, and what society does about them.

To consider violence first. There is the excitatory acting out which is the principle theme of this chapter. In addition there are imaginative forms of violence, verbal and physical, but without the fact of physical contact. Of these forms of violence words, tone of voice, gestures and movement all play a part and aim to outrage, but do not develop into direct physical contact. On the other hand there are forms of violence of a direct nature intended to injure in cold blood such as boxing, and prize fighting, and other activities in which contact is a major part. There are fringe implications of injury in games such as football and, even from time to time in cricket, when differentiation between the wicket and the batsman is blurred by social competitiveness. In delin-quency a need to outrage or injure, quite apart from acquisitive gain, is known to be an important element. It is a major motive for offences such as vandalism, arson and even self injury and can be seen to lead by degrees to individual non-conformity, or organ-ized forms of violence and aggression against groups, the Estab-lishment or its defenders.

There are other circumstances in which violence is not of the excitatory sort implicit in the sources of violence of a phylogenetic type, but is a 'cool' use of manipulated outrage as part of socially approved conflict situations, even though basic excitatory acting out often appears in them at one point or another. The meaning of the term violence, both by definition and experience becomes even more difficult to understand when social violence is expressed by governments in terms of war, or acts of aggression. Violence, sometimes originating in anger, sometimes on a more calculated basis, is passed along socially accepted human channels who some-times feel outraged, sometimes not. The situation may be one in which an executant impersonally, and without feelings of aggres-sion, outrage or violence, may be creating outrage and injury of which he is only remotely aware. These anomalies, common to many societies, seem to be appropriate and rational sequels to the preparation received by individuals in the society in which they occur. There is a pattern in personal and social life in which induc-ing violence and reinforcing its appearance and development ap-pear to be an intentional part. It starts in the earliest days of infancy. Beginning with the baby and parental control exercised through rationalised ignorance of infants' emotional needs, it leads readily to systems of inconsistent giving and witholding of appro-val, or non-provision of support. To the attitudes which do not differentiate between the child and his offending are added confrontations beyond the capacity of the child to understand. Reinforcements such as tapping, 'chastisement', deprivation of liberty or 'time out' in isolation, are preparations for later difficulties such as emotional blunting, over dependence, or social indifference. As the social responsiveness of the child expands, increased mental and physical strength, lead to wider investigating, and neighbourhood and educational pressures come into play. In the former setting adult tolerance and acceptance depend on the child not offending the feelings, preconceived ideas, or property sense of the neighbours. At school, perhaps as part of a preparation for the facts of life, organised rejection of the individual child in favour of the needs of the group, subject, school organisation or teacher, and the development of 'special virtues' continue the earlier process.

Side by side with the encouragement to violence and aggression implicit in such experiences, there is a strong resentment on the part of society at the success attending its attempts to transfer its own aggression to the young. This learned violence induced in the young is often regarded as offensive, outrageous, and self generated. It is customarily met by reprobation and retribution administered through relationships – damaging procedures such as rejection and personal punishment without providing opportunities for self improvement through restitution, or other openings which might develop a sense of worth and useful social fortification.

It is often doubtful where violence starts and the ordinary process of excitation of activity and drive and the rest of human energy and extroversion end. As already noted definitions of violence suggest that when activity injures or outrages it is violence, but interpretation is difficult. Is violence an environmentally determined concept? There is justification in considering human needs and their relationship to violence in terms of growth and development. Needs, early in life, are physical as well as emotional and psychological. For example, one early basic physical human need is for warmth; young babies being highly susceptible to cold. They also have a great need to be protected from intestinal and respiratory infections. The less tangible areas of human need are a more recent study, but a body of knowledge has accumulated that makes possible an understanding of much of the interaction between human beings and their environments, physical, personal, and social, from the earliest days. Underlying the activity of all living beings, especially mammals, is responsiveness to stimulation. This quality of excitability develops into recognisable patterns of psychic motor reactivity, and this is thought of as behaviour. The manner in which this reactivity is managed plays a great part in the way that succeeding stimulation is dealt with. Human needs tend to move rapidly from urgent physical ones to a need for a stable setting of personal human relationships in which emotional and mental needs also are met. Human contact starts with a simple immediate object relationship which if sufficiently well based and properly carried out is able to lead on to the development of additional and more complex emotional attitudes and inter-dependencies. They in turn open up the way to observing, and accepting, increasing and widening environmental demands. Successful emotional learning makes possible the expansion of personal interdependence in relation to the widening and changing demands which are made on the developing child. However, human beings, particularly in their early stages also have a great need for non-change, i.e. continuity of setting, especially in its human relationship element. This sensitivity is primary and deeply rooted. Should changes happen too often, or too quickly, confidence-damaging effects come about, and when this happens very young human beings fail to register favourable impressions, and do not lay down reactions which enable them to cope with this situation and later ones, without damaging loss of emotional and physical control.

It is in relation to this mechanism that imprinting has its importance, so that individuals react in certain recognisable and expected ways in particular situations. The study of severely emotionally handicapped children within a controlled milieu supports the findings of general behaviourist studies in the animal field. The behaviour of children, especially severely disturbed ones, demonstrates various models of reaction which clarify the responses to situational pressures of normal children and adults, and thus enable them to be studied more clearly. Very disturbed children are often more directly reactive, and demonstrate long retained elements which participate in all action decisions, but are usually deeply embedded and concealed in social behaviour.

They are particularly reactive in relation to changes in material settings; in some cases the rearrangements of toys in a different way from the previous arrangement produces uneasiness. Smelling objects, mouthing them, touching surfaces, opening doors to look into cavities are variations on the theme of fear of change, and unforeseen possibilities, that need reassurance through recognition. Older, more experienced, children who are verbal, explain how their feelings of security have been lessened because familiar bricks and mortar have been altered from what they were before. They can be seen to pay attention to facial expressions, keenly observing them,

81

differentiating between smile and grin and are made especially uneasy by unsmiling faces. Investigation of teeth as dangerous objects, learned from their own biting and chewing, can be observed, and panic reactions when restrained against their wills. The confrontation of eye to eye gaze is often avoided, and instead observations are made by rapid side long glances. Cutting off contact by eye shutting, and fingers in ears when tension becomes great enough occurs and continues into late childhood, as does withdrawal from verbal communication. Over a wide range of situations there are previous histories which contain highly unfulfilling early situations in terms of intimate personal relationships, and it would be reasonable to suppose that many of these children, often specially vulnerable, have reacted to arousal by flight or freezing which has gone beyond social utility and reversal.

There is physiological evidence, experimental at present, as well as psychological and psychiatric findings, to suggest that no prior experience is completely lost. The creation and modification of mind by brain activity, arising out of electrochemical activity originating in sensory nerve receptors, provides a mechanistic link between mind and the outside world. New experiences change, modify, and enrich earlier ones, but the earlier ones physically persist and are not lost. Such a concept goes a long way in accounting for behaviour, and can have much to do with the genesis of violence and aggressive reactions. It can also be used to play a part in its avoidance.

In addition to the facts of environmental experiences, it is likely that inborn variations of excitatory responsiveness to requital and non-requital of physical and emotional needs play an important part. Excessive reaction by withdrawal, or acting out, instead of a response followed by a ready return to the prestimulated state may be governed by constitutional factors as may the degree of excitation produced by the stimulus.

Physical and emotional maturation, associated with growing older, produces anatomical and physiological activity leading to alterations in goal reactivity, but still partly dependent on earlier imprinting. This in its turn, affects the degree to which later stimuli alert, arouse, or are extinguished. At any given point of time when the excitatory system is stimulated into activity the reaction, physical or emotional, depends on a conscious or unconscious selection of action depending on previous experiences, good or bad, and the new stimulus and the reaction to it becomes part of the 'memory bank'. If the threat to the 'defences' is strong, arousal, with hostility or withdrawal, takes place. Where earlier experiences have enabled the subject to protect his vulnerability, excitation does not so readily lead to acted out arousal. This concept is basic to understanding human violence and its prevention and management. The process arises out of innate responsiveness due to organic excitability which brings about reactions which lead to the production of environmental responses.

It is an on-going process with continuous building and modification of personality, and reactivity both to the inner and outer environments. At the same time, physical development opens up new modes of abilities in the growing child. Attention seeking, neuromuscular testing out with locomotion and manual deftness, recognition of the environment at a further distance, all are aspects of innate development and play their part in the way responses to outside stimulation are received, incorporated and acted upon then, and later. Over the recent past, schools of individual psychology, James, McDougal, Watson, Freud, Jung, Adler, and others, have drawn attention to behavioural and emotional phenomena. They have interpreted them in the light of the dynamic theories they developed. All provided explanations for violence and aggression, and these were based on psycho-emotional experiences, understandable to themselves in terms of past experience, ambient culture and the acceptance of the special nature of man.

The study of species reactions, rather than exclusively human reactions and their development from primary experiences with imprinting of new patterns in response to special experiences and the effect this had on goal selection, has demanded some revaluation in relation to the source areas of violence and aggression. The concept of violence and aggression based on inner drives of aggression, or on frustration of specific areas of physical and emotional reactivity, needs reviewing in the light of the mobility of object attachment that has been demonstrated by human and animal behaviourists. The demonstration of ways in which attachments can be engineered, during sensitive periods and in sensitive areas, implies that individual reactivity to the environment can be greatly modified. Violence, with aggression, may be a more modifiable expression of innate excitability, depending largely on inappropriate goal seeking and needs, than has been thought to be the case. Confusion between excitement, violence, and aggression, may well have originated in the earlier acceptance that aggression and violence were primary modes of feeling and action rather than expressions of excitation which are malleable and modifiable in both qualities and goals. The border between them and undirected neurophysiological acting out, as in some types of epilepsy is still unclear, but is suggestive. Experiences, stimulations, are engrammed and are lost only with difficulty as a result of damage to, or deterioration of, the brain. These 'engrams' are physical, and produced by reverberating semi-permanent activity in the brain where they relate to the very many circuits that are already in action. It is in pursuit of presenting the child with reassurative engrams, rather than arousal ones, in as many contexts as possible, that supportive management is especially desirable. It is while the earliest stages of development are being passed through, that the terms of reference to which later experiences will relate are being laid down. Human young show adverse excitation as anxiety, tears or anger in the face of threat or frustration, and many reassurative repetitions are needed to bring about a desired end, or to extinguish an undesirable one. Much of the basic structure of personality is the product of intellectual/emotional reactions which have occurred in the very early years of life; of hundreds, if not thousands, of repeated experiences, and in itself, is a measure of the massive contradictory elements that go into socialised behaviour. It is along this continuing experience/engramming process that human reactivity may be directed towards better controlled mental and physical activity, or towards acted out excitation resulting in aggression or violence.

Personality is affected by genetic endowment from conception as well as by environmental factors. The difficulties of identifying genetic endowment as an element in the development of personality and social reactivity are so well known as to have lead to its neglect as a valid consideration except in circumstances where it is gross to the point of clinical recognition in terms of physical, emotional, or intellectual abnormalities.

Nevertheless it seems reasonable to suppose that inherited tendencies are not only to do with external physical family similarities, or limited to recognised hereditary illnesses. Various strengths of neurophysiological and neuro-anatomical responses, affecting the quantity or quality, of response to the environment, its recording and absorption, may well have a part to play. This possibility, not to say likelihood, needs to be especially recognised as an element in the situation when provision for identifying causes, developing measures of prevention, modes of management, and rehabilitation of the violent are under consideration. It is a problem affecting individuals; chromosome studies, much expanded in recent years, may have an important contribution to make in the future especially in the field of protecting the genetically vulnerable. In fact, measures designed to deal with violence on a large public scale need to take into account innate vulnerability as well as the environmental factor. Environmental elements include pre-birth influences, and the special baby/mother relationship as well as interspersed relationships during the first days, weeks, months, and years. Baby rearing in the home occurs in a wide variety of settings with a wide variety of maternal and family attitudes. Family, neighbourhood and educational management are further environmental experiences which accumulate and add to the body of knowledge with which the child will be equipping himself for facing life, be they the pressures on his ability to control his excitability and physical activity within himself and his home, or the neighbourhood and school. The degree to which early experiences have been enabling rather than disabling will affect the capacity of the child to seek skills at school, and to enjoy demonstrating ability and maturity, thus helping him to find a worthwhile image of himself as a preparation for adolescence and adult life.

The highly sensitive biological equipment that has to cope with the many pressures implied by this short presentation of an aspect of child development, is a mechanism readily vulnerable to many psychological and material stresses even though it mediates what usually appears as balanced and knowledgeable behaviour. Man is essentially a nervous, fearful creature, and the child is even more reactive and less stable. A certain amount of inhibition can be, and is, developed by direct fear of external forces. Rejection, disapproval, and physical threats have, and can still be seen to produce socialised behaviour. Rejection and disapproval when kept within 'arousal' level may have immediate effect in limiting acting out and containing the victim, but they may make long term negative reactions a greater possibility when pressure cannot be continued. Physical violence, or the threat of it, as a mode of control is a lesson to outrage, to injure, and is a green light to the young for violent acting out of their own tensions especially when retribution is not likely to follow.

In this chapter juvenile violence is being considered chiefly as a behavioural situation leading to aggressive social difficulties between the behaver and his setting. This may be at interpersonal or impersonal levels, in the home, neighbourhood, or school, whether day, residential, ordinary, or special. The behaver, as has already been suggested has received ideas of what he can expect from his environment. They are often confused, inconsequential, and usually lacking in expected satisfactions. It is often a fair reflection of an environment which has, and still is, managing him with a general lack of harmonious, consistent attitudes, and in which there is a low priority in the direction of personal concern for the behaver's emotional needs as an individual. In addition, the various elements, parenting, family life, school, street experience, are kaleidoscopic in terms of peer and group relationships, let alone the rapidly changing feeling tones in any or all these settings.

These undependable environments continue as a series of successive situations starting from home, and going on to play or nursery groups, to infant school; later to primary, and then to secondary school. Education at each level is a group orientated activity and makes group demands a priority rather than concerning itself with individual needs, personal, emotional, or educational.

Many children by personal good fortune, emotional toughness, or being cherished at especially vulnerable periods of their development, adapt to the threatening unknown which has an implicit arousing quality if defences have not been developed by accumulation of supportive experiences. These experiences start at a primitive and basic interpersonal level, and are later expanded both by skill learning, and the development of a self image by the incorporation of attitudes of trusted adults.

Most violence occurs in ordinary situations, at home, in the street, or at school; some occurs in special situations, in institutions, in which the violent young are placed to receive care and management through the stimulation of their arousal systems. These individual arousal systems contain the collected learning of the years during which confrontations have taken place characterized by anxiety, failure, helplessness, or sheer physical inadequacy to take on the adult controlled world. The young in these circumstances have learned to expect attack, or frustration, to act out violently, or to freeze; their reactions become predictable responses. It is likely to be unproductive to confront them with methods of management which they can recognise as similar to those they have had to try to cope with for most of their conscious lives. Different settings, be they interpersonal or institutional, can be reassurative, supportive, or threatening. It is possible, not even very difficult, to organise and establish reassurative supportive systems which use what has been learned about human relationships and human needs as a basis for providing opportunities for the violent person to re-adapt his attitudes as the first step towards re-assessing life as it confronts him.

Some approaches to management on these lines have been made both in residential and day settings. The primary condition is to bring about relaxation of tension. Natural suspicion associated with years of distrust, failure and social bankruptcy needs to be dissipated. The experiences themselves, juvenile offences, truancy, living rough, unemployability and offences with violence, confirm the hopelessness of moralising as a method of help in many cases.

Evasion of situations in which approval depends on achievement is to be expected. To attempt to overcome this by intensifying measures of exhortation or threat which have failed in the past is unrealistic. An approach which includes interest and concern for the person presents an opening that may start to make an impact. The front on which such efforts need to be made must be socially and tolerantly wide, and of sufficient depth in time and resources for progress and regression. There is a need to avoid confrontations, eye to eye, with *quid pro quo* reward and punishment until the point is reached when the inadequate and worthless feeling youth or girl feels he or she has something with which to match the situation. Much non-residential work with the violent is on too narrow a base, with insufficient back up resources. In addition, too easy return to the milieu in which the undesirable behaviour is acceptable, leads to the victim having additional personal/moral conflicts to cope with during treatment.

The personal acceptability of the violently reacting child or young person has to be made manifest even when his behaviour is not, both at an interpersonal level, and also in the personal social demands made environmentally. Whether through day attendance, or in a residential setting. Avoidance of confrontation by assertion or threat is of prime importance, and even the simplest organisational limitations need to be explained from first principles, and discussed for as long as it takes to reach an agreement.

Violent behaviour, on the other hand, may or may not be accepted, depending not only on what that behaviour is, but also what it means to its perpetrator. The use of violence may be conscious, in cold blood, or hot headed and impulsive but in both cases may be seen by the individual as part of himself. There are many violent people who claim 'It's not me, it's my temper', disassociating themselves, at various levels, from their conduct.

To attempt to help the violent before their problem has been ventilated, shared, confidence gained, and a personal link established, is rarely successful. The underlying states of arousal in the violent with established patterns of aggressive defence do not ordinarily allow the penetration of much that is not relevant to the justification of their resentments. As Churchill said many years ago, 'Jaw, jaw, jaw, is better than war, war, war'. This is as true in interpersonal relations as it is in political situations. Time for the cooling of feelings, familiarisation of people and ideas allows the development of other solutions to problems and has an important role to play. Time needs to be seen as a major factor in the establishment of an atmosphere in which the violent can reorientate some of their expectations of threat, increase their limited self confidence, and bring into effect alternative ways of coping with personal situations.

Much has been said and written of physical containment for the socially aggressive violent delinquent. The difficulties of providing treatment or care unless the individual is present is the justification. Less is heard of the counter productive aspects of closed doors, moral judgements, punishment hierarchies and the perpetuation of the failed measures of 'before'.

The re-establishment of self respect, with its learning processes based on the requital of human needs for emotional support, and acceptance, does not pre-suppose a 'no demand' permissive atmosphere. Such a setting may have been necessary at an earlier period of development, during infancy and earlier childhood. At more advanced ages, from 12–13 years on, many new important, even though secondary, factors have entered personality make-up. The psychophysiological changes of puberty, adolescence, or adult development, combined with years of living often need modifying to assist the working out of identity problems in terms of inner feelings, against the background of the real life situations.

Few people can resist interested concern especially when it is presented in a manner that accepts the recipient as an equal in the human dilemma. It should be unpatronising, and manifestly aimed at helpfulness rather than personal or social criticism and dominance. Verbal, personal contact at this level needs to take place in a setting where acted out undesirable behaviour can be absorbed without the expected resentment being shown. The testing out of the helper, or therapist, by the aggressive young is part of the reason for the aggression, and is often the aggressor's major yard stick for acceptability. Acceptance by the adult, or authority situation, of the aggressor is one of the major touchstones used before trust, confidence, or liking starts to make a bridge between the behaver and his setting. Without this process, any place of control is a challenge to get away from. Recognition of the distinction between the behaver and his behaviour as a basis for modifying responses, is of primary importance.

To extinguish the arousal of social aggression, overt or covert, against persons, ideas or institutions becomes a practical proposition in setting designed to be unthreatening, especially when the topics discussed can be similar to those which previously led to disapproval by criticism or passive unacceptance. The behaver, responding to his inner life of experiences, associated with expected frustration, needs an unusually accepting, but structured setting in which to live before his natural, excited acting out is no longer necessary because later experiences have modified earlier learned aggressive defences.

Unacceptable systems of approval and disapproval, rewards and punishments, are natural provocations and bring the need for containment by locked doors, barred windows, or 'time-out' in solitude, in their wake.

The 'bad behaver' can be kept in an open setting in which adults present him with physical presence, relationships through shared experiences and feelings, comradeship, interested concern over a wide range of situations and activities. Such a policy of manifest concern for the youth or girl, in which privacy is as planned as contacts, and is used as part of 'ego building' is more likely to be helpful than provocatively making institutions absconding proof with bars, locks, and walls.

References
(1) LORENZ K. (1963). *On Aggression*, Methuen, London.
(2) SPIEGEL J. P. (1972). 'The dynamics of violent confrontation', *International Journal of Psychiatry*, 1093, 10b, September.

Chapter VI Day-to-day aggression between parent and child
John and Elizabeth Newson

This paper appears in slightly longer form as a chapter in Newson, J. and E.: *Seven Years Old in the Home Environment*, Allen and Unwin, London, (1976).

In this chapter we propose to concern ourselves with the normality rather than the pathology of violence: to consider how far violence (or the threat of violence) plays an everyday part in ordinary family life. In order to make our discussion usefully specific, we will narrow our focus to one age-group: the seven year old child in conflict with his parents. The data which is presented here is abstracted from a much larger longitudinal study of 700 children growing up in Nottingham during the 60's and 70's; the greater part of the research material consists of long interviews in depth with the children's mothers, recorded in their own homes at regular intervals through the child's life.[1,2,3]

In simple terms, conflict occurs between parent and child (and particularly between mother and child), at seven as at earlier ages, as a result of the mother's attempts to socialise the child and the child's resistance to her efforts. The extent of seven-year-old resistance can be gauged by mothers' replies to one of the questions we asked about the child's general personality: 'Is he the sort of child who usually agrees with what you want him to do, or does he tend to object to things quite a lot?' Only 37 per cent were said to be generally agreeable to parental requests; 37 per cent were variable, and 26 per cent of all children objected to things 'quite a lot'. Sex and class differences are insignificant but professional and managerial class boys tend to be less 'agreeable'. Obviously these findings are of interest in terms of general personality dimensions; here we would merely make the point that conflict is by no means a dead issue at seven.

Publican's wife:

'She objects. Objects very strongly. She's got a will, you know. She thinks that she won't listen to you, she has to do it *her* way. You have to clamp down on her to make her do it.'

Coal driver's wife:

'He'll agree, but his face'll disagree and he'll sulk about it – but he won't come out openly and say.'

Before discussing the issues involved in open conflict, we must also remember that there is an area of sub-conflict, as it were, that bears on this: the mutual friction generated by parent and child. We asked, as we had at four years old, 'What about disagreements? What sort of things make you get on each other's nerves now, you and N?' Oppositional or 'disobedient' behaviour was in fact often cited in this context; but there was also a miscellany of annoyances which did not relate to amenability, but had more to do with the rough edges of irritation that can appear in the relationship of any two people living at close quarters. To the extent that general friction, whatever the source, can fuel open conflict, this seems relevant to the issue. The wording of the question also allowed the mother to volunteer examples of the ways in which she thought she got on the child's nerves; and the overall impression at seven, as at four, is of a two-sided impact. Obviously parents were sometimes using their authority to 'go on' at their children in an effort to curb behaviour that they found annoying rather than actually judged as 'naughty'; almost equally, however, children seemed to be going on at their parents. Nagging, in short, appears to be normal on both sides.

Builder's labourer's wife:

'She's really awkward at times, and she'll say "Can I have so-and-so dress on?" – well, it's probably dirty, ready for washing, and I'll say "No, you can't" – "Well, can I have me shorts on?" And I tell her, you know, that it's not suitable weather for them, and then she'll start showing off a little bit. Of course, she'll get a slap, then I feel easier then; and many a time she'll say to me, "I'm leaving, I am!" And I'll say, "Go on, then, the bag's upstairs". She'll say, "I am, I'm leaving!" and I'll say "Well, all right then". But nothing ever comes of it, I think she just does it to aggravate me.'

Cook's wife:

'Well, she must have her *say*; and you tell her to "shut up and don't answer me back". But she must say what . . . "I'm *not* being cheeky, Mummy", and I can't seem to get through that it *is* cheekiness. I just can't make her see – she thinks that she's got something to say, and so she's going to say it. Even if she's going to get smacked, she'll still say it! (So she's really putting her point of view, as far as she can see?) That's right, yes, and in her little mind I don't think she realises how cheeky she's been – whether I'm wrong or not there, I don't know, but whatever the consequence is going to be for her afterwards, she must have her say and explain herself. (And it comes out to you as cheekiness?) Well, especially when you say, "Now shut up, I don't want to hear another word" – "But . . . I'm only . . .", and she'll carry on, you know, you just can't get it through. "Now I don't want to hear anything else about it, and that's it!" But *no*, she will *not*, and you *will* hear it, it doesn't matter what you're going to do to her, you'll hear it; and it annoys me at times.'

A typical way for a child to frustrate his mother's wishes at seven is by almost infinite procrastination. On a number of counts it is an effective strategy on his part. It gives him an opportunity to make verbal objections if he wishes, yet does not quite commit him to the risky course of outright refusal. It leaves his options open so that if his mother becomes dangerously impatient he can hastily comply, while there is a good chance that she will abandon the struggle and do the job herself, help him to do it, or even produce a bribe. And if he does misjudge his mother's tolerance and she 'clips him one to buck his ideas up a bit', he will at least have the satisfaction of protesting righteously that he was 'just going to do it'. 11 per cent of mothers smack for 'being slow' and these results show no class or sex differences.

Although procrastination can come very close to a tacit refusal, both child and mother are aware that the situation is still open-ended, and that a showdown is not yet necessary. An explicit refusal by the child is quite another matter, as is immediately reflected in the proportion of mothers who say they would smack him in response to this: 56 per cent overall, compared with the 11 per cent who smack for slowness. Only a small minority of 8 per cent, without class or sex differences, would neither reprimand nor punish in the face of the child's refusal: for instance, 'I've had that many kiddies, I don't bother now, I do it myself', said an unemployed labourer's wife. Obviously also a rebuke can sometimes be implied in the *way* a mother may say 'Don't bother, I'll do it myself'; the child may receive the message that he is at best unhelpful and at worst immature. We can reasonably assume, then, that almost always the child's refusal is met by disapproval, which in more than half of these cases is expressed in physical punishment.

It seems relevant to emphasise that, at the moment in the interview when 56 per cent of the mothers volunteered that they would smack their child in the situation specified, *neither punishment in general nor physical punishment in particular had yet been explicitly raised by the interviewer*. The questions at this stage were deliberately framed rather neutrally: in fact, looking again at the four questions which bring us to this point, it is feasible to imagine them all being asked the other way round, in terms of how the child might react if faced by a refusal. The mother's *disciplinary* function, as opposed to her social relationship with the child, is not predicated by questions 156–9; and it is not until Q.160, when she has already had the chance to commit herself spontaneously to smacking, that this topic is introduced by the interviewer.

156 What about disagreements? What sort of things make you get on each other's nerves now, you and N?

157 Do you find that N takes a long time over doing as you ask him?
158 What do you do if he's being very slow over this sort of thing?
159 What happens if he simply refuses to do something you want him to do?
160 How do you feel about smacking children of this age?

Implications of the punishing act

These questions and parents' reactions to them highlight the basic issues which emerge when we come to consider differences in disciplinary styles. Some conflict between parent and child is almost inevitable: it arises because parents require children to do things, or to refrain from doing things, and this interferes with the child's autonomy as a person with wishes and feelings of his own. In disciplinary conflicts, by definition, we have a situation where certain individuals exercise their rights as people of superior status (in age, power and presumed wisdom) to determine what younger and less experienced people, of inferior status, may or may not do. If the child complies willingly, of course (even if his willingness has been engineered by offering him the illusion of choice), his self-esteem can be kept intact; but whenever he is forced into an unwilling compliance by the threat of sanctions, whether these be pain inflicted or approval withdrawn, he will inevitably suffer in some degree feelings of powerlessness and humiliation.

Punishment is the word we use when sanctions are enforced by one person on another in an effort to secure compliance despite resistance: or sometimes in order to re-emphasise the power relationship when it appears to be threatened by sustained resistance or refusal. In the latter case, it is the hope of the punisher that *next time* his power to compel will be restored.

Punishment can take many different forms, ranging from beatings of greater or lesser severity, through the token slap, deprivation of normal rights or privileges and deprivation of property, to social ostracism. If this discussion is to mean anything, it seems important to define as punishment situations only those which involve a deliberate act in which a socially more powerful person demonstrates that he can subject a less powerful person to his will. In the context of human relationships, it can obscure the issue to label *any* aversive stimulus as punishment. The burnt child fears the flame, but it is stretching a point to say that a flame can *punish* a child; equally, if a wife says to her husband, 'Do you think I did right?' and he replies 'Not really', this may be aversive but cannot under normal circumstances be usefully discussed as punishment.

The definitive boundaries are of course blurred; but at least we can say that subjection is always implicit (and often explicit) in punishment. Thus its effect is mainly to hurt the child's pride, whether or not it is physically painful. Punishments are directed at the child's sense of self-esteem, and are intended to deflate his ego, and this is so whether they consist in the mother deliberately turning her back on him or beating him with a broom-handle.

The other side of this coin is that punishment in some sense absolves the child from responsibility for his action. For the present it bears the message 'I am making sure you pay for what you've done'; and for the future it adds 'if you do it again, you'll pay for it again', with the corollary ' – so you mightn't think it worth it'. Whether now or in the future, the punishing parent thus accepts responsibility for settling the account, and thus *the child's conscience is bypassed*. To this extent punishment can even be a refuge and a comfort to the child.

When these children were four, we tried to come closer to what was happening when a mother smacked her child by describing it in the following terms, which still seem to hold good at seven:

'. . . smacking happens as one element in a *pattern of understanding* between the mother and the child. The mother has a fairly consistent set of principles, roughly corresponding to her authoritarian or democratic attitude, which she hopes in time to communicate to the child by her words and actions, and through which she expects to socialise him into the sort of person she values; and, within this framework of principle, she not only smacks but tries to evaluate for the child the meaning of her smack. It is probably true to say that the precise form of an aggressive act is less important than the fact that it has occurred; and it is certainly true that the objective force of a smack is less significant to the child than the spirit in which it is delivered.[3]

In other words, we have argued that issues as to how often and how hard children are smacked may be less important in the child's socialisation experience than the impact upon him of the mother's general outlook upon the whole disciplinary situation; leaving aside children who are physically cowed by brutal treatment (which the great majority are clearly not), smacking in ordinary families can be more usefully considered as a kind of punctuation within the context of a continuing dialogue than as a simple aversive stimulus. *As* punctuation, however, it clearly has significance in altering the feel of the situation: just as the disciplinary confrontation in itself crystallises issues of power and status, so the use of physical punishment underlines a relationship of 'I'm bigger than you' as opposed to 'I'm wiser than you'.

Counting the blows

However, the significance of frequency of smacking is rather greater in older children because of the age characteristics involved. At four, although the possibilities of verbal control are very much greater than at one year, they are still imperfect enough for some mothers to discount them altogether. This is reflected in the fact that 75 per cent of all mothers were smacking once a week or more when the child was four. By seven, the verbal alternatives to smacking are more obviously available, and this proportion drops at seven – to 41 per cent. However, because they are now a minority group, if a large one, these mothers can be assumed to be more committed to a 'smacking philosophy' than the majority group, taken as a whole, who smacked thus often at four.

Again frequency is likely to tell us something about the mother's philosophy because it distinguishes between those who smack as a day-to-day measure – as part of their normal vocabulary, as it were – and those who use it as a last resort because everything else has failed, or because the situation itself is exceptional, or simply because they've had a specially bad day. The mother who says 'I suppose at weekends he gets more, because he's at home more then' clearly has a different *approach* from the one who, asked when she last smacked James, says 'I seem to remember an argy-bargy in the bathroom . . . it *might* have been this year . . .'.

The frequency of smacking also has significance for the child in terms of how he evaluates any individual incident: to return to the punctuation metaphor, an exclamation mark will have more impact if used once in an article than if it is sprinkled ten to the page. The mother who wishes to use smacking for dramatic effect will obviously have to set this against a *general* policy of non-smacking, and the smack itself can be relatively light: while the woman who smacks as 'just part of the daily routine' not only finds that 'children forget about it so quickly', but is likely to resort to harder and harder smacking when occasionally she does want to make a more dramatic statement.

The categories given in Table 1 are exclusive, in the sense that no child appears in more than one. 8 per cent overall are smacked once a day or more often; a third are smacked at least once a week but not as often as once a day; 28 per cent are smacked at least once a month but less than once a week; and almost a third are smacked less than once a month or not at all. Sex and class differences can be most clearly seen in the 'once a week' and 'less

Table 1 Actual smacking frequency reported by mothers

96

	Social class					Summary		Overall population
	I&II %	IIIwc.* %	IIIman** %	IV %	V %	I&II+IIIwc. %	IIIman,IV,V %	%
Once a day or more								
boys	4	7	12	14	11	6	12	11
girls	2	8	6	5	5	5	6	6
both	3	7	9	9	8	5	9	8

Significance: trend ↗ p=0.06; m.class/w.class n.s.; between sexes p<.05

	Social class					Summary		Overall population
Once a week or more excluding those above								
boys	35	40	41	38	53	37	42	41
girls	17	18	27	22	44	18	28	25
both	26	29	34	30	48	28	35	33

Significance: trend ↗ p<.01; m.class/w.class p=0.08; between sexes p<.001

Combining above two sections, to show children who are smacked *at least once a week* trend reaches significance at p<.001 level

Once a month or more,
excluding those above

boys	26	31	22	22	17	28	23	25
girls	29	31	33	35	23	29	32	29
both	27	31	28	29	20	29	27	28

Significance: trend inconsistent, n.s.; m.class/w.class n.s.; between sexes n.s.

Less than once a month

boys	35	22	23	26	19	29	23	25
girls	52	43	34	38	28	48	34	38
both	44	33	29	32	24	38	29	31

Significance: trend ↗ $p < .01$; m.class/w.class $p < .02$; between sexes $p < .001$

* wc = white collar
** man = manual

than once a month' categories: it is very obvious that boys in general tend to be smacked a good deal more often than girls, and that smacking decreases considerably for both sexes as one moves up the class scale.

Feelings and beliefs

Before asking mothers how often the child in fact was smacked, we had already asked a series of questions exploring mothers' subjective feelings about smacking as a principle. The first four of these questions asked them to consider smacking in general; the next, to gauge their emotional feelings upon smacking their own child. In addition, we later asked two further questions which are worth looking at briefly at this point, since they also ask the mother to examine her feelings about discipline.

160 How do you feel about smacking children of this age?

161 Do you think parents should try to do without smacking altogether, or do you think smacking is a good way of training children?

162 In general, do you think smacking has good results with children of this age?

163 Any bad results?

165 What effect does (smacking) have on you? – do you feel relieved or upset in any way (or is it just a part of the routine)? (*Last clause omitted only if mother clearly does not smack routinely*)

196 Do you find that how strict you are depends a great deal on your own mood at the time?

197 When do you most approve of yourself – when you're being strict with N, or when you're being easy-going?

We have no space here to give detailed results; very briefly, the salient finding was that mothers are somewhat mixed up between their beliefs and their feelings. The class and sex differences which emerge from the frequency tables are not in any simple way reflected in attitude patterns. Thus, for instance, there are numbers of middle-class women who, while more or less accepting the principle of smacking, do not in fact make use of it very much in practice; while there is also a group of working-class women who smack quite often while disapproving of it in principle. Considering how relatively commonplace smacking still is at seven, it is interesting to see that *almost three-quarters of all mothers are emotionally upset by it* – 'feeling churned-up inside' is a typical description; multiplied by the number of children she may have of smacking age, this adds up to considerable and repeated emotional expenditure for the individual woman. Some described an initial feeling of relief that was quickly superseded by disturbing emotions: 'I feel terribly upset – it may relieve a certain amount of pent-up tension in me, but it makes me feel dreadful'.

The rather poor fit between principle and practice is borne out by more detailed referral to the transcripts. There is a strong feeling of parents being pushed by the demands of the moment, by the personality of the child, by their own personal inadequacies where they would have preferred 'not to let it come to a smack', and by their worries about the future. This last is of course (as we also saw at four) very basic to the socialisation process: parents would often prefer to 'let things ride for the sake of peace and quiet' if it were not that they are haunted by the thought 'What will he be like later if I let him get away with things now?' Although it is true that middle-class styles of discipline, because more verbally based, place more responsibility on the child for *long-term* good behaviour, it is by no means the corollary of this that working-class mothers have no eye to the future: their discipline may be short-term effective, but it is certainly long-term intended. Mothers generally in fact have in common *the aim that the sanctions they impose should result in a socialised child,* and each tries to follow what she sees as the means to this end. So central is this aim that we make no apology for quoting at length in illustration of the theme.

Gardener's wife:

'If I didn't stop them, they'd be the gaffers of me all the while; so I've got to put my foot down one way, and shouting I don't always do it. So you might as well give them a good hiding and done with it . . .
Well, I think if they never have a good hiding they think they get away with a lot, now they do, when they get older. We had good hidings, yet we never did them things what's going off today, did we?'

Foreman's wife:

'They need a little bit – whatever they say about smacking, you can't give them all their own way, I mean you've got to have them a *little* bit frightened of you, haven't you? *I* think you have, anyway.'

Business executive's wife:

'I can't see where (smacking) has any effect, quite honestly. (You don't think this a good way of training them?) No, I don't.
I think it's much better to try and reason with them, even if it takes much longer; because after all, when they've been smacked the smack is gone, and they are more likely to forget what it's

even for; whereas things you say are likely to come back in their minds a little bit.

Stoker's wife:

'He believes in smacking, my husband; but he don't really have to do it, because they take notice, like, you know, of him. (He's stricter than you?) Ooh – yes! In fact my husband never falls out with me only over that. He says "I'm trying to bring them up right and you're too soft-hearted" – that sort of business. But I can't be hard enough, I've tried but I can't. Some people's very firm, aren't they? And that's what we really fall out about – I ought to be firmer. He keeps them in their place, everyone round here says so; while I'm making them rogues like they are – in a way by being kind to them, you know.'

Designer's wife:

'I *am* fairly strict with him, yes – only because I like to see a well-disciplined child, and I do feel that unless you're strict with them from the beginning all the way through, you can't expect them to behave in a reasonable way later on. I suppose, er . . . I don't take a *pride* in being strict, but it's the results I'm after. I'm trying to think it's going to be better for him in the long run.'

Machine operator's wife:

'I don't try to smack 'em an awful lot. In a way it's a difficult age, seven – if you hit 'em too much you can turn them the wrong way, but if you don't hit 'em you can turn them the wrong way as well, you see – you've got to try in between. I have to try and use my intelligence, if I've got any, and try and work it out myself.'

The formalization of aggression

Another way of finding out how important smacking is to a mother is to ask what she does in specific *situations* of conflict. To a certain degree, asking the mother 'What do you do in such-and-such a case?' formalizes the behaviour she reports, in the sense that she thereby identifies it as her normal, more-or-less *chosen* response, even if she is not altogether happy with it. To this extent, behaviour reported in this way probably has more significance to her style of child-rearing (as perceived by herself) than sampled behaviour would, which might be more subject to the pressure of circumstance.

In the same way, the aggressive act itself can be gauged in terms of formality. Almost any mother may hit out in a fury when tried beyond her tolerance; differences here may be basically a matter of individual tolerance level. Slowing up the act of smacking, however, immediately invests it with purposiveness and underlines for the child her intention to discipline him. In the pre-school years, to say 'Wait till I get you home', and to smack the child once they got home, had a similar effect of formalization; at 7, to take down a boy's trousers or turn up a girl's skirt in preparation for smacking, to fetch an implement, or even to own an implement as such, all signify the mother's *acceptance of smacking as punishment* as opposed to her use of it as an expression of anger. To the extent that some mothers would never dream of formalizing it in these ways, however hard pressed, this divergence represents a real difference in attitude rather than just degree – though, obviously, smacking is likely to hurt more on poorly protected skin or where an implement is employed.

Overall, 17 per cent of mothers sometimes take a boy's trousers down (or turn a girl's skirt up) in order to smack. This behaviour happens slightly more towards girls than towards boys (significant at .05 level), which probably reflects only the fact that the mother can turn up a skirt herself, whereas taking down trousers needs some degree of co-operation from the victim. Class differences are not significant except in one respect: 28 per cent of Class III white collar mothers of boys, as against 13 per cent in all other classes, are prepared to take down their sons' trousers for smacking (class difference significant at .02 level). Mothers of girls in this social class do not behave differently from other classes.

Administrative assistant's wife:

'Oh yes, I make a job of it. Because it's the drama more than anything else that seems to have the effect on him. He's screaming and shouting long before I've even got his pants down.

HP collector's wife:

'Er, no, I haven't done. I think his Dad has, you know, because er – it hurts him more, you know. But um . . . I don't think he likes you to do it, you know – take his trousers down and smack him – because even when he's getting dressed, he don't like anybody to look at him . . . you know . . . things like that . . .' (mother a little embarrassed).

Of course, the baring or partial baring of the child's buttocks is intended to make the punishment degrading as well as physically uncomfortable; and it may be that, as in the last quotation, working-class parents in particular (whose sense of sexual modesty is more acute) may feel this is going too far – they wish the child to be shamed, but not quite to that degree. Inhibitions of this kind

Table 2 Smacking: mothers who use, or threaten to use, an implement[1]

	Social class					Summary		Overall population
	I&II %	IIIwc* %	IIIman** %	IV %	V %	I&II+IIIwc %	IIIman,IV,V %	%
Implement already used								
boys	29	26	27	20	25	27	25	26
girls	22	18	19	17	10	20	18	18
both	25	22	23	18	17	24	21	22

Significance: trend not sig.; mid.class/w.class n.s.; between sexes p < .05

	I&II %	IIIwc* %	IIIman** %	IV %	V %	I&II+IIIwc %	IIIman,IV,V %	%
Implement threatened only								
boys	51	71	68	60	67	60	66	65
girls	29	37	38	56	59	33	44	41
both	40	54	53	58	63	47	55	53

Significance: trend ↗ p < .001; mid.class/w.class p < .06; between sexes p. < .001

Implement: threat or use

boys	80	97	**95**	80	92	87	91	91
girls	51	55	**57**	73	69	53	62	59
both	65	76	76	76	80	71	76	75

Significance: trend ↗ $p < .01$; m.class/w.class n.s.; between sexes $p < .001$

* **wc.** = white collar

** **man.** = manual

[1] Actual implements used are not here distinguished. In both use and threat, order of preference is: first, strap or belt; second, cane or stick; third, slipper; fourth, miscellaneous objects.

do not apply to the use of implements as such, however. We asked this group of questions as follows:

166 How often does N in fact get smacked?

167 Is it just with your hand, or do you use a slipper or a cane or anything like that? (If hand only) Do you ever *threaten* to use something more?

We thought it important to ask about threats of this nature because once the threat had been made (or once the implement was known to have been used on older siblings, or to exist at all), it seemed to us that the issue of physical punishment had already moved into a new dimension: in a word, the dimension of beating, not smacking.

22 per cent of all seven-year-old children have received corporal punishment via some implement; a further 53 per cent have been threatened with this, making the remarkably high total of three-quarters of this population for whom being struck in this way is at least within the bounds of conscious possibility. This overall percentage is consistently high in all social classes, except that Class I and Class II mothers are less likely to *threaten* with an implement; they are, however, just as likely as other groups actually to use one. There is a perceptible sex difference in actual punishment with implements, and a much bigger sex difference when it comes to threats of their use: combining both tables, 91 per cent of boys are either threatened or actually hit, compared with 59 per cent of girls. A breakdown of the type of implement used suggests that cane and stick are rather more favoured by middle-class parents, and strap or belt by working-class parents. Slippers and other more *ad hoc* implements such as yardsticks, wooden spoons and the dog's lead appear in too small numbers to analyse their social class distribution.

The threat of cane or strap may not necessarily have prognostic significance as to actual use. Nevertheless we reiterate that, at the very least, the mother's appeal to its existence does in fact subtly alter the feel of potential conflict situations between her and her child: just as the cane in the corner of the junior school headmaster's office colours the collective perceptions of his schoolchildren even if it has not actually been used within the memory of any child.

Unemployed labourer's wife:
'He'll sit and sob (when he doesn't want to go to school).
I've often had to run him out wi' a stick, many a day – and he'd stand there and he *wouldn't* go.'

Sales representative's wife:
'Well, usually I think I use my hand; but if I have a stick I can

wave it about and it has a great effect, but I don't like smacking with a stick. (Do you sometimes?) Yes, I have smacked them with it sometimes on the bottom.'

Table 3 An index of mothers' reliance on corporal punishment

Item	Based on question	Mother's response	Score
1	158. What do you do if he's being very slow . . . ?	Physical punishment	1
		Verbal rebuke or ignores	0
2	159. What happens if he simply refuses to do something . . . ?	Physical punishment	1
		Verbal rebuke or ignores	0
3	166. How often does N in fact get smacked?	1+per day	3
		1+per week (< 1 per day)	2
		1+per month (< 1 per week)	1
		Less	0
4	184. What do you do when he is rude to you?	Smack	1
		Other punishment/ reprove/ignore	0
5	185. Has he ever picked up any bad language? . . . What do you think you should do . . . ?	Smack	1
		Other punishment/ reprove/ignore	0
6	167. (If any smacking) Is it just with your hand, or do you use a slipper or a cane or anything like that? (If hand only) Do you ever *threaten* to use something more?	Implement used	2
		Implement threatened only	1
		No threat or use of implement	0
7	168. Do you ever take his trousers down/ turn up her skirt to smack him/her?	Yes	1
		No	0
	Score range: 0–10		

Table 4 High and low scorers on corporal punishment index

	Social class					Summary		Overall population
	I&II %	IIIwc* %	IIIman** %	IV %	V %	I&II+IIIwc %	IIImanIV,V, %	%
High scorers 5+ (top 31%)								
boys	29	33	44	41	44	31	43	40
girls	12	20	24	21	36	16	25	23
both	21	27	34	31	40	24	34	31

Significance: trend ↗p < .01; mid.class/w.class p < .01; between sexes p < .001

Low scorers 0, 1, 2 (bottom 38%)								
boys	41	29	29	27	21	35	27	30
girls	57	51	45	47	33	54	44	47
both	49	40	37	37	27	45	36	38

Significance: trend ↘p < .02; mid.class/w.class p < .05

* wc. = white collar
** man. = manual

Presser's wife:
  'Oh, I threaten many a time. I threaten my yardstick. I've got a yardstick in that corner, you know. I threaten that, many a time. (Have you ever used it?) No, never. (Do you ever intend to use it?) No, I don't, I might break it.'
Lorry driver's wife:
  'I've got a stick there, but that's a warning – a be-gooder-or-else!'

Reliance on corporal punishment: an index

Although we have distinguished between the incidence of physical punishment and the formality with which it is administered, and have pointed out that threats of an implement do not necessarily lead to its use, we thought it meaningful to combine these various aspects into one comprehensive index which would measure the degree to which corporal punishment featured in the lives of individual children: whether this was because it was frequently resorted to, invoked in many different situations, formally ritualised or merely threatened. Internal comparison of scores on these various points did in fact produce a significant degree of consistency $(p < .001)$: the measures of incidence (items 1–5 in Table 3) were found to correlate at approximately 0.3 with the measures of formality (items 6–7). Table 3 shows how the index of corporal punishment is made up: and Table 4 analyses this population in terms of high and low scorers on this index, and their distribution by social class and the child's sex.

The most obvious conclusion from Table 4 is that physical punishment is invoked considerably more for boys than for girls at this age. Though slightly less marked, there is also a distinct and significant tendency for physical punishment to feature more strongly as we descend the social class scale. In particular, physical methods of controlling behaviour are much more likely to be stressed among families in the unskilled manual group, and their girls enjoy a lesser degree of comparative favour than do girls in other social classes. A further analysis of the index scores, to ascertain whether the salience of Class V might be mainly a function of family size, shows no such relationship.

It is our impression that the main burden of the maintenance of discipline at this age rests firmly on the mother. This is partly because she is more often around when such issues arise, but also because it is much less acceptable nowadays for mothers to appeal to fathers as the ultimate sanction. Fathers themselves, in line with their greater participation in nurturing functions, seem unwilling to be cast in the traditional role of avenging judge with mother as prosecuting counsel; and, on the whole, mothers too reject the 'wait till your father comes home' technique as unfair and inappropriate to the modern view of fatherhood. Our questions on which parent smacked most yielded a decisive 79 per cent for the mother, with only 10 per cent of fathers taking this role; only in the unskilled manual class did fathers increase their percentage, to 16 per cent, and there were no other class or sex differences reaching significance. It is clear that the contemporary father's increased participation in child rearing falls short of the disciplinary role.

That mothers generally do accept this division of roles is shown by their answers to a further question. Where one parent did tend to smack more than the other, we asked: 'Is that because you (husband and wife) disagree about smacking, or is it just that you are (he is) more often there when it's needed?' Only 14 per cent of these respondents disagreed with their husbands about the principle of smacking, and there were no class or sex differences. The circumstances of disagreement are indicative, however: the couple were four times as likely to be in disagreement when the husband was the major smacker as when the wife was.

Encapsulating the power structure

Most of this chapter has been concerned with confrontations between mother and child in which the mother's superior strength as opposed to her greater moral wisdom has in the end been invoked – whether by an act of violence on her part or by drawing the child's attention to the possibility of such an act. Either way, her physical mastery has been made explicit.

Many mothers would say that this has therefore been a story of defeat, and not on the child's side either: 'I have failed if she has to be smacked', says a clergyman's wife. Although, as we have seen, most mothers smack at least occasionally and most also imply some approval of the principle by at times threatening the use of an implement of punishment, it must be understood that the role of smacking remains a means to a more important end than the immediate conflict: it serves the need which parents feel to maintain their credibility as power figures who must undoubtedly win in any significant battle of wills. The inevitable occasional clash of interests between parents and child may become testing-times, when parents suspect that their long-term ability to influence their child's behaviour (a basic notion to the parental role) could be irretrievably diminished if they are seen to lose.

Controlling the child's behaviour thus often becomes a kind of game in which parents try to choose strategies appropriate to what they see to be at stake: and for most parents what is at stake is, to a greater or lesser extent, the myth of their own invincibility.

In other words, few parents really want to maintain their authority wholly by brute force, because this would in fact tend to undermine their additional credibility as benign charismatic powers who do not need to punish their children in order to gain their co-operation and respect. Parents would like to be obeyed because of their superior wisdom and experience, because the child acknowledges that they have his long-term interests at heart, because they love him despite his faults, and because they choose *not* to exercise all the power they have to compel his submission.

It is when the child challenges them on these grounds that they need to demonstrate their invincibility; and this they may do in ways which are partly dictated by expediency. How they feel about resorting to a show of physical strength at this point will depend upon whether their child-rearing attitudes are deeply based in the democratic principle, when they may well fear that they are betraying their ideals ('I have failed if she has to be smacked'; 'I should feel I'd lost all face with Mark'); or upon whether they believe strongly in an authoritarian stance, in which case they have little reason to have moral worries about the necessary showdown which 'makes him understand who's boss'.

Once again we have to reiterate that smacking happens, not in a vacuum, but as a part of a continuing dialogue of words and behaviour in which the mother's intent is conveyed in many and various ways. Hugs and kisses are one kind of message; smacks carry another; words are the vehicles for others again. Disciplinary behaviour as a whole has to be seen (as it is by both child and mother in the context of all these kinds of messages, which *taken together* convey to the child an image of what he is, what he might be and how these personae match his parents' hopes and apprehensions. And because smacking itself almost always takes place in the midst of a barrage of words, this account has been, even at a behavioural level, only half the story.

References
(1) NEWSON J. and E. (1976). *Seven Years Old in the Home Environment*, Allen & Unwin, London.
(2) NEWSON J. and E. (1963). *Infant Care in an Urban Community*, Allen & Unwin, London.
(3) NEWSON J. and E. (1968). *Four Years Old in an Urban Community*, Allen & Unwin, London.

'Everyone is agreed that the present management of families in which children are abused is far from satisfactory. There are too many deaths and too many children suffer harm which damages them for the rest of their lives. To the extent that one factor is the mishandling of the parents during their own childhood, the condition is self perpetuating and the management of the children of one generation must affect the children of the next. Rehabilitation of the family may, therefore, be more important to society than punishment.'

(Dr Alfred White Franklin)[1]

In the last three or four years hardly a month has passed without reference in the daily press, or the media, to a battered child. Despite the tragic Maria Colwell case with its attendant public enquiry and findings, children in this country continue to die or suffer permanent brain damage as the result of injuries inflicted by their parents or guardians. Even as I write, a child is dead and another enquiry about to commence.[2]

In this chapter, with the aid of case material, I would like to share some of the things we have learned during the course of our research, to look objectively at difficulties that arise, and ways in which we might offer a more effective and meaningful service to the families involved.

Historically, much of the earlier research carried out has been medically orientated and in this sphere Professor C. H. Kempe of the University of Colorado Medical Centre, Denver, has become one of the world's leading authorities. He recently redefined the battered child as 'any child who received non-accidental physical injury (or injuries) as a result of acts (or omissions) on the part of his parents or guardians'.[3] While there have been many other definitions, this seems to be the most widely accepted. Following his work, a number of significant contributions were made in this country, largely in the area of medical recognition and diagnosis but little was done to examine this as a social problem requiring a multi-disciplinary approach within the community.

In 1967 Arthur Hughes of the NSPCC wrote an article drawing attention to this fact.[4] Later that year, following discussions in the United States between the Revd Arthur Morton, Director of the Society, and Professor Henry Kempe, it was decided that, in keeping with its long tradition of service to abused children and their families, the NSPCC would pioneer a research project to look into this problem in depth and add to the body of knowledge on the subject.

The project began in October 1968 and early the following year the Battered Child Research Department was established. It retained that title until October 1974 when the new National Advisory Centre on the Battered Child was opened and superseded the original department.

The Centre provides a twenty-four hour on-call treatment service and a therapeutic nursery. In addition, consultative and educative facilities are available on a national scale.

Since the department's inception a number of studies have been completed and two major research reports published.[5, 6] Currently, assisted by a grant from the DHSS, two new research projects are being undertaken.

The first is concerned with the analysis of video recordings of mother-infant interaction; its purpose being to discover and demonstrate to workers in the field essential behavioural differences between parents who physically injure their infants and those who do not.

A second project is aimed at devising a method of investigating subsequent health and educational development in children who have suffered non-accidental injury.

Let us now look at some aspects of the problems as they present today.

The incidence of non-accidental injury

There has been growing concern of late about the various figures quoted on the incidence of child abuse, particularly with regard to children who die. While we know that children are continuing to suffer in this way, we do not have accurate figures available for the country as a whole. It would seem that we may well need some form of national notification before this is possible. In a recent government circular on the subject, it was suggested that all local authorities set up registries for their own areas.[7] These will be of value in highlighting trends and perhaps regional variations.

Some research has already been carried out and gives a more enlightened estimate than has been possible before. The Centre, for example, has been responsible for a National registry of NSPCC cases in which children under the age of four have received inflicted injury. We know that when we presented our last report three times as many referrals were being received by the Society as at the time the project began.[8] Additionally, pilot schemes under the auspices of the NSPCC have been set up in

111

seven large metropolitan areas. Of these a register for the metropolitan area of Greater Manchester has been in operation two years while another in the Leeds Metropolitan District has been open for a year.

Available statistics show that 'The rate of reporting (in Leeds), is 1.1 cases per thousand children under four. The first year of the register in Manchester indicated a similar figure of 1.07 cases per thousand children under four. The second year of the Manchester register, 1974, showed a slightly higher reporting rate of 1.2 per thousand children under four.[9, 10, 11]

Other recent estimates are 1.4 per thousand children under four, on the basis of figures produced by Dr Malcolm Hall in Preston[12], and 1.0 per thousand children under four (severe abuse only) in NE Wiltshire.[13]

If the register figures, which were obtained by the use of standard and regularised registration procedures, are indicative of the position in other areas, they would suggest an incidence of between 3,000 and 3,500 children under the age of four sustaining non-accidental injury in England and Wales each year. It should be stressed, however, that until we have more information from other sources, these figures can only be seen as indications. With regard to the number of death involved, the latest study carried out by a Home Office research unit based on a sample of 334 children from 297 families, found that between a quarter and a third of the total sample died as the result of inflicted injury and a further 7.5 per cent were permanently maimed.[14]

There are also indications that, due to the variability in the way in which post-mortem examinations are carried out and the manner in which deaths are certified by the coroners' courts, some caused by non-accidental injury may be recorded as death from natural causes.

A classic example of recording is the following extract from a coroner's report.

Age:	7 months.
Marks of Violence:	Bruises on right jaw, shoulder and arm; left knee and mid back. Scars on left loin, left shoulder and right jaw.
Are all other organs healthy:	Healing fractures of right 9th rib: healed fracture of left humerus: subcutaneous haemorrhage over both thighs: haemorrhage into lower intercostal muscles.

THE CAUSE OF DEATH AS SHOWN BY THE EXAMINATION APPEARS TO BE:
BRONCHOPNEUMONIA

Any further remarks: There is widespread evidence
of injury, but this did not lead
to death directly.

Coroner's Verdict: Natural Causes.
2nd May, 1975.

There appears to be a need to lay down guidelines for coroners to ensure that all cases that reach the court are given a full examination. This should include a full skeletal survey. It is also suggested coroners might obtain a social report on the family of a dead child to aid them in their consideration of the case. In this way more accurate information would become available.

Next, we come to some of the salient points that have emerged from the research, starting with the children.

The children
Both NSPCC studies showed that the greatest number of children fell into the five months or under category and that the younger the child the more likely it is to be injured and the more serious the injury is likely to be. This knowledge should not detract from the fact that children of any age can and do suffer non-accidental injury, but such children are not so vulnerable or as helpless as the younger ones.

Some of the records studied indicated that use of the juvenile court, which could offer protection to both the child and the parents, was sometimes delayed, occasionally with tragic results. An example of such a failure in protection is the case of a child referred at the age of four months, with scorched buttocks and minor bruises.

'There was evidence of a fractured femur at six weeks. From the age of four months to seven months, slight bruising to the forehead was noticed on four occasions. At the age of seven and a half months the child was found dead and a postmortem revealed eight old fractured ribs and previous brain damage.'

Trauma to the soft tissues of the face and mouth appeared in 43.5 per cent of the cases.

Examples of plausible explanations offered for this type of injury were the following:

'He caught his dummy on the cot' (laceration of inside of mouth);
'He was struck in the face by his elastic rattle' (bruises to the jaw).

The more violent attacks on the face are given more realistic explanations:

'I lost my temper and bit him' (bite on cheek).

This child had previously been hospitalised for facial bruising. 'He was lifted by cheeks and flung down by father' (bruises to cheeks).

This child had suffered previous injuries.

It becomes clear that bruises and injuries which appear to be of a minor nature may signify the beginnings of increasingly violent forms of injury. The high incidence of trauma to the face may, like bruising, be an aid to early diagnosis of a nurturing problem which, if modified, might avert serious injury to a child.

The high risk to a subsequent child, in families where a first born has been injured, is a finding of particular importance to all those who take the responsibility of weighing the risks of supervised home care for the non-accidentally injured child against an alternative protective course of action. Records showed that in families where the first child was injured there was a 13 to 1 chance a subsequent child would be injured.

Two out of every five children admitted to hospital because of injury had previously been injured to an extent sufficient to warrant medical attention and three out of every five who were discharged home after hospital treatment had to be readmitted on account of subsequent injury.

Finally we come to the correlation between low birth weight and non-accidental injury. In both samples (13 per cent in the first study and 14.50 per cent in the second) the incidence of low birth weight was approximately twice the national average. The most recent NSPCC study carried out in the Manchester Metropolitan District, found that 37.8 per cent. of children notified to the register who had sustained non-accidental injury, had birth weights of less than 2,500 gms compared with 7.2 per cent of children from families of similar social class.[15] The proportion of non-accidentally injured children with a birth weight of less than 2,000 gms, is almost ten times that in the comparable population.

The parents

A number of suppositions are prevalent concerning the parents involved. Some suggest that the majority are of psychopathic personality and cannot be helped. Others say they are individuals of low intelligence. Psychological studies carried out at the National Advisory Centre, with the co-operation of parents, do not support these propositions.

Tests (Wechsler Adult Intelligence Scale) of a group of battering parents matched with a control group for parental and child age, ordinal position of the child, social class, educational level, type of living accommodation and nationality showed that the mean IQ's of *both* groups on verbal and performance scales fell within the normal range. The majority are neither mentally subnormal nor frankly psychotic, although personality problems of long standing are commoner among battering parents than the general population.[16]

Close contact with families in which children have received non-accidental injury reveals that in many cases the parents themselves were from early childhood, consistently subjected to an experience of disapproval and rejection. Whatever they did was never enough to gratify their own parents and they have grown up feeling denigrated and worthless.

Dr Steel, the eminent American psychiatrist says, 'throughout life they have pathetically yearned for good mothering, returning again and again to their mother, seeking for it but not finding it and ending up with disappointment, lowered self-esteem and anger.'[17]

As a result of their emotional deprivation, the mothers tend to be immature and lacking in self control. Depression and anxiety are common, although hostility may mask the symptoms. Fathers often present as introverted individuals hard to get to know and lacking in parental warmth. The families are frequently living in social isolation with no real friends.

While we know that non-accidental injury occurs to children from all strata of society, we are seeing the greatest number from the lower socioeconomic groups. This is not surprising, when one considers that families in these groups are generally under much greater social stress and have fewer avenues of relief. Unwanted and unplanned pregnancies are consistent factors in their ongoing problems, as are marital difficulties.

Distorted perception is a common occurrence, with demands being made that the young child cannot possibly meet. In many instances parents expect the child to provide all the love and warmth that has been missing from their own lives and when the child is unable to meet their expectations, they express feelings of great rejection.

Illustrative quotes from parents
'I felt no love for the child when it arrived and on getting home from the hospital, felt very distressed by a feeling of fear and inadequacy. This was accentuated when the baby cried to the point of almost uncontrollable rage and revulsion. The need to stop the noise was as overwhelming as that of a drowning person to clutch as something solid.'
'My mother never had any time for me. I could never do anything that would please her and I can never ever remember her putting her arms around me. If I tried to get close she

115

would just push me away and say don't be silly.'

'I didn't want to have a baby in the first place! I tried to get rid of it twice! I've never liked them, although I don't know why, they're such poor little mites.'

'I know he hates me. When I try to feed him he just turns his head away, he knows what that does to me! Once a short time ago, I was so angry, I took the teat off the bottle and tried to ram the bottle right down his throat!'

Another factor involved and described by Joan Court[18] concerns the collusion that occurs between parents. Clinical experience with these families supports the view that the 'innocent' partner in a battering situation is always consciously or unconsciously aware of what is happening. In many cases the partner is present when the actual episode takes place or sets the scene for the disaster. This leads to a question raised of late concerning the possible correlation between battered children and battered wives. The initial country-wide NSPCC study[19] identified a group classified as being characterized by essentially antisocial behaviour of the predominantly aggressive type. There were indications that these adults were habitually aggressive and that their behaviour tended to be released against any source or irritation.

In a report[20] on the first five years of the Battered Child Research Department's work, nine mothers describe their husbands as having been physically violent towards them at some time. In these families, the main lines of tension, aggression and violence flowed between the parents rather than between parent and child. Children were more likely to be injured by accident rather than design. In three cases the violence was serious, frequent and associated with drink. The three men involved often resorted to violence in other situations. Although there was occasional violence towards the children, the disorder in the family was based primarily in the psychopathology of the father and thus in the marital relationship rather than in the parent–child relationship.

The majority of non-accidentally injured children do not appear to come from families in which the wife is also injured. There is however, some overlap and we will always see a number of parents who are habitually aggressive. These cases make special demands on social workers who, while attempting to protect a defenceless child, are confronted with the possibility of increasing hostility and tension which might further endanger life.

Management, social work intervention and care

In its memorandum of the 22nd April, 1974 on non-accidental injury to children, the Department of Health and Social Security

116

pointed out that 'recent events have left us in no doubt of the need to repeat the professional guidance about the diagnosis, care, prevention and local organisation necessary for the management of cases involving non-accidental injury to children.'[21] It will greatly assist in our understanding if those of us concerned with diagnosis, treatment and ultimately prevention, are able to accept, that in the majority of cases coming to our notice, the parents, due to personality factors already discussed, are to a great degree captives of their own childhood experiences and have no conscious desire to harm their children. In our attempts to offer effective support it may also be helpful to remind ourselves that angry aggressive feelings towards those we love are perfectly normal emotions.

I venture to suggest there are very few people with children who have not at one time or another been pushed to the limit of their endurance and have felt like doing the child an injury, using such expressions as 'If that child doesn't stop I'll kill him,' or 'Take that baby out of my sight before I strangle her.' Many of us will recall instances, when this kind of situation has arisen. How much worse must it be for young parents living with children in social isolation, facing numerous pressures and stresses and unable to cope because of their own limiting experience of nurturing. These are adults who have very low points of tolerance and who do need a considerable amount of reaching out to, in a supportive non-authoritarian manner.

If prevention of injury or re-injury is our aim, our main objective must be this difficult task of demonstrating, within the context of our professional relationship, to parents who are often hostile and highly suspicious, a genuine concern and desire to help. 'It is essentially a matter of making oneself totally available to these needy and hyper-sensitive parents on their own terms. This makes sense if one remembers their previous experience of a parental relationship was basically destructive.'[22]

This must not blind us to the fact that we are going to see some adults who have been so badly damaged in their own childhood that they are never likely to be able to provide the relationship which is so important in a child's development, and where we will have to act, using what legislation is necessary, to secure the on-going welfare and healthy emotional development of the child concerned.

The unheard cry for help
Case Example:
    Mary, a slim attractive 23 year old mother, came to our attention at 1 a.m. on a Monday morning. An hour previous she had

walked into a local children's hospital with her six week old baby unconscious in her arms. Medical examination, including X-rays revealed a severe head injury, (subdural haematoma) three broken ribs and internal injuries to the chest. The child was said to be seriously ill. The Consultant Paediatrician had spoken to the mother who had told him she had dropped the baby earlier that evening when putting him to bed.

He felt the injuries were not consistent with the explanation and was sure that this was a case of non-accidental injury. We were asked to assist.

A social worker from the department arrived at the hospital some fifteen minutes later and found the mother in the children's ward, standing back in the shadows at the head of a cot looking down at her motionless child. There were beads of perspiration standing out on her forehead, her face was deathly white and as she twisted a handkerchief nervously around in her hands, she repeated in a voice that was hardly audible, over and over again, 'My God what have I done? – why didn't they listen to me, oh why didn't they listen?'

Mary's case is typical of many that are seen in our hospitals today. It raises important issues, which if recognised earlier, may have prevented a whole series of events that led up to the child's serious injuries and the mother's anguished question.

A study of Mary's history prior to her arrival at the hospital shows that she had given many early indications of her need for help.

We know that the child was the result of an unwanted pregnancy and Mary had gone to her GP asking for help to obtain a termination, which had been refused. Following this, she had tried to abort herself on two separate occasions by throwing herself downstairs. On each occasion she had been taken to different hospitals and later discharged home without follow up. When the child was born (in hospital) the mother said she didn't want to hold it, look at it or feed it. This went on for four days with the mother turning her back every time the nursing staff came near her.

On the fourth day, after a bitter argument, the mother discharged herself taking the baby with her.

There then followed three visits to different casualty departments and on each occasion Mary complained that there was something wrong with her baby, he would not eat or he would not sleep properly. The child was physically examined each time but X-rays were not taken and nothing was really done to help the mother express her own feelings or anxieties.

A few days after the last incident Mary came to the NSPCC's notice.

There are many other recorded incidents:

The mother who asked her GP to call late at night because her eight week old baby would not stop crying. The doctor visited and suggested the baby needed feeding. Two months later the baby was received into hospital with fractures and bone injuries involving both arms, both legs, six ribs and shoulder.

Another mother went to her local Social Services Department asking that her baby be taken into care for a while because he was difficult to feed and was not eating properly, she felt she just could not cope. On this occasion the mother was told that social services would contact her GP and someone would visit her at home immediately. Two days later the child was received in the children's ward of a local hospital suffering with a subdural haematoma – no-one had called.

It seems that danger signals are still being missed, which, if recognised earlier and acted upon, may well prevent children suffering unnecessarily at a time when the parents might be far more amenable to help than they are at a later stage. Case conferences should be called as soon as possible with a view to the sharing of information so that a proper assessment can be made of the whole family situation. The importance of co-ordination and co-operation between all concerned cannot be over-emphasized.

In the initial stages of contact with these families there is a need for a high degree of skill and sensitivity on the part of the worker involved. As we have pointed out elsewhere[23], a multiplicity of workers can increase family stress and a type of supervision which is limited to an anxious watchfulness without specific treatment goals is not in the child's interest.

In some instances shortage of qualified and experienced personnel has led to trainees being given these cases to handle, and in others, because of frequent staff changes, families have had as many as three different social workers in six months. Quite often the parents involved see this as a re-enactment of their earlier life experiences and feel completely rejected and bitter. This can have very serious repercussions for any future therapy, particularly if when, for the first time in their lives, they are just beginning to respond in a positive manner, a change takes place.

Our work with these families leads us to believe that the first few months of contact and how they are handled is crucial to any positive movement that might be achieved. It is also a period when the parents will test out the relationship in a variety of ways and be at their most demanding. This means a considerable amount of reaching out on the part of the worker and this is time consuming. It is, however, the period when, if the parents are at all amenable to help, they will begin to respond. The long term implications of these difficult cases do not make them suitable for social work candidates under training or for workers who are only likely to be available for a short period of time.

In circumstances where work is progressing with a family and a change of worker has to take place it is of great help to all concerned if the parents can be forewarned and prepared for the change by the outgoing worker, allowing them time to ventilate their feelings, and when possible, introducing the new worker to the family prior to departure. Frequently, the only notice families have received is a short letter saying their social worker is leaving, or has left, and another will visit in due course, occasionally followed by a long delay before anyone is actually able to visit. The build up of tension created for the family by this situation can be a potentially dangerous one for the child. Those of us having administrative responsibilities should also recognise that adequate support and consultation must be readily available for the social workers involved.

To ensure continuity and stability a few social service departments have made specialist appointments. Contributing in this area, the NSPCC has, with the aid of specific grants from DHSS and local authorities, set up a number of special treatment units in metropolitan regions. These units, staffed by qualified and experienced professionals, are linked to the National Advisory Centre for research purposes. They offer specialised treatment and consultative facilities in their locality and have responsibility for handling the experimental registers mentioned earlier.

One other aspect that requires our consideration is the effect these families can have on those of us who are providing a service. Families of this nature have an uncanny knack of highlighting our own inadequacies and continually confront us with situations geared to raising anxiety levels. For the inexperienced this can produce a state of immobility at a time when clear objective thinking is imperative. Richard Galston succinctly grasps the problem when he says 'the anxiety produced by anger which is unassimilated is highly contagious. It lies about like a time bomb waiting to go off and it intimidates others to flee, to put distance between themselves and the source either directly or through the use of one of the many administrative devices available to any clinic or agency.'[24] One of the most important resources called

120

upon from any worker involved in this kind of situation is a capacity to bear the anxiety. Just as we accept there are going to be a small number of families unable to respond to treatment, I think we must also accept and recognise those few instances when the social worker is unable to respond.

Recent therapeutic innovations

With the present decline in the economic situation and a shortage of skilled professionals available, examination of some recent therapeutic innovations that have been tried, might offer some ways in which we can increase the effectiveness of our service and lessen the burden on professional resources to the ultimate benefit of the children and families involved in treatment.

Crisis nurseries and drop-in foster mothers

In setting up provisions for families in which non-accidental injury to children had occurred, we were concerned that we should learn from the experiences of those parents who felt that available services did not meet their particular needs. One of the most pressing of the requirements voiced was for some form of nursery facility where a parent under stress and frightened of injuring their child might leave him for a while, without fear or remonstration. Many parents interviewed had suffered quite traumatic experiences when seeking this kind of help and had consistently met with rebuffs of one kind or another. Some even felt they had been forced into a tragic situation in which they had actually injured their child because they could not get the various authorities to recognise or understand the urgency of the matter or danger involved.

A graphic example of this is the following mother's quote:
'I got to the point where I seemed to have been to everyone!
Things were getting worse and worse, all I needed was a break
but no-one would listen! In the end I nearly killed my baby
and then they said it was *my* fault!'

Taking these points into consideration there are a number of alternatives available.

Nurseries

Essentially any nursery planned to cope with these families has to be extremely flexible, with a staff ready to accept children being brought in for varying periods at any time.

Our own experience has shown that a nursery of this kind has a particular therapeutic value if it incorporates facilities that are available for the use of the parents. They should be helped to feel

121

welcome, with a room of their own in which they can relax without having the children under their feet. One of the positive results from this has been the development, quite spontaneously, of a parents' self help group. With its aid many of the newly referred respond much earlier to treatment.

For the children play therapy is of great value in preparing them for later life and providing some of the outlets they have not been able to enjoy at home. Encouraging results have been observed in those attending the Centre's nursery.[25]

A vital feature is the provision of transport which goes out in the morning to all the homes of the families, bringing the children and any parents who want to come to the nursery, returning them home at night. A member of the staff always accompanies the driver so that, if necessary, she can dress the child and ensure he or she attends if mother is unwell.

The nursery staff are very much a part of the therapeutic team and as such close attention has to be paid to ensure they receive adequate orientation towards their widened role, since they will find themselves as involved with the parents as they are with the children.

Drop-in foster mothers
An alternative, which is of particular value in areas where nursery provisions are poor, is to initiate a system of drop-in foster mothers. These volunteers are paid a small retainer and provide short stay emergency placements for children at times of crisis. In most instances an overnight stay is all that is needed but it is possible to extend this period if necessary.

As with most provisions in this field, the keynote is flexibility and accessibility, with foster mothers having to be prepared to accept children at any time of the day or night. When suitable applicants are selected, emphasis is placed on personality rather than any professional skill. We also try to recruit from as wide a variety of social backgrounds as possible, since we have found that mothers find it easier to relate to someone whom they feel has had the same kind of stresses to contend with. Some of our earliest referred parents who responded to help are now part of this network.

Mothering aides
Since the majority of parents who inflict injuries on their children are not paranoid or psychotic, it is possible to introduce a lay worker into the family at a comparatively early stage, once the initial relationship has been established between the parents and primary therapist.

122

The role of the mothering aide is essentially that of a concerned caring parent figure, either male or female, who is prepared to listen uncritically to the parents' problems, provide practical help and to be available as a life-line during periods of crisis. Henry Kempe[26] suggests the ideal lay therapist or mothering aide is one who is prepared to become meaningfully involved in a major way over a period of eight to twelve months, in the lives of these very deprived parents. This is accomplished through weekly or twice weekly visits, often to the parents' home. At all times the mothering aide is helped to feel that he or she has the full support of the professional staff and there is the closest liaison between the primary professional therapist involved and the volunteer, together with regular weekly group meetings. Training is unobtrusive, being an ongoing process in an informal atmosphere. It is effected largely by using the group meeting as a forum for discussion, with a member of the professional team in attendance.

Family developmental centres

In some enlightened areas medical and social services departments have combined their efforts to set up treatment programmes that will provide residential facilities for the whole family where significant child abuse has occurred. There is for instance, a unit operating at the Park Hospital for Children in Oxford where families are received into a small family unit within the hospital grounds for a period of twenty-eight days and then followed up with supportive services. During this period the whole family experience the rare combination of practical help, medical treatment and applied psychology. As was explained in a recent article[27], the combination of these elements is vital. The idea is that the parents make a completely new start and this they cannot be expected to do, if, when they leave the hospital filled with new approaches to parenthood, the old problems are still there. So far, some 230 families have benefited in this way.

Parents anonymous

The original group came into being in the United States a few years ago and now has branches and chapters in most states. Quite recently groups have been formed in other countries including the United Kingdom. The agency originated as the result of the frustration of an American mother, who like many of those we have spoken to in this country, felt she could not find the kind of help she needed. When asked by a psychiatric social worker what she thought should be done, she suggested the idea of starting her own group composed of mothers with similar problems. From this early beginning the scheme developed to the present day **Parents Anony-mous**. In their literature the organization lays down two major goals (a) to perpetuate an organized programme for parents who fear they might or are actively engaged in any form of physical or emotional abuse towards a child and (b) to help rehabilitate parents who so engage in physical or emotional abuse towards a child.[28]

To be effective it is felt important that a group of this nature should be started by someone who has themselves been in the position of inflicting injury on their own children and that they have a professional person, readily available to the group for consultation.

These are just a few of the methods which have been tried successfully with families where child abuse has occurred.

There are undoubtedly others where, by a combination of enthusiastic volunteers and dedicated professionals, we can further widen our provision.

In this chapter the author is expressing his own views and opinions based on personal experiences. They are not necessarily the official views of the National Society for the Prevention of Cruelty to Children.

References
(1) FRANKLIN A. W. (1975). *Concerning Child Abuse*, Churchill Livingstone.
(2) MEURS S. (1975). Daily Telegraph, 5 July.
(3) KEMPE C. H. and HELFER R. E. (1972). *Helping the Battered Child and his Family*, J. B. Lippincott.
(4) HUGHES A. F. (1967). The battered child syndrome – a multi-disciplinary approach, Case Conference 14, No. 8.
(5) SKINNER A. E. and CASTLE R. L. (1969). *78 battered children: a retrospective study*, NSPCC, London.
(6) CASTLE R. L. and KERR A. M. (1972). *A study of suspected child abuse*, NSPCC, London.
(7) DHSS MEMO 74/44 (1974). *Battered Children, New Government Advice*, 22 April.
(8) CASTLE R. L. and KERR A. M. (1972). Op cit.
(9) NSPCC (1975). *Non-accidental injury to children in Leeds*, unpublished, May.
(10) NSPCC (1975). *Non-accidental injury to children in Manchester*, unpublished, May.
(11) NSPCC (1975). *Non-accidental injury to children in Manchester – The second year*, unpublished, May.
(12) HALL M. H. (1974). *Some aspects of non-accidental injury in children*, Paper presented to Tunbridge Wells Study Group.
(13) OLIVER J. E. *et al.* (1974). 'Severely ill-treated young children in N.E. Wiltshire', Oxford Unit of Clinical Epidemiology Research Report No. 4, August.

(14) STURGES J. and HEAL K. (1975). *Non-accidental injury to children under the age of 17,* Home Office Research Unit Ref. 663/2/25.
(15) NSPCC (1975). Op cit.
(16) HYMAN C. and MITCHELL R. (1974). *A psychological study of child battering,* NSPCC Unpublished Paper.
(17) STEEL BRANT (1970) in *Parenthood* (Anthony & Benedek), Chapter 22, pp. 445, Little Brown & Co.
(18) COURT J. (1970). 'Psycho-social factors in child battering', *J. Med. Wom. Fed.* Vol. 52, pp. 99–105.
(19) SKINNER A. E. and CASTLE R. L. (1969). Op cit.
(20) NSPCC BATTERED CHILD RESEARCH TEAM (1975). *At Risk,* Routledge & Kegan Paul, London. (Expected date publication Nov. 1975).
(21) DHSS (1974). Memo 74/44, April.
(22) COURT J. (1969). 'Battering Parents', *Social Work,* Vol. 26, No. 1.
(23) SKINNER, A. E. and CASTLE, R. L. (1969). Op cit.
(24) GALSTON, R. (1970). *Violence Begins at Home,* Paper presented to American Academy of Child Psychiatry.
(25) NSPCC BATTERED CHILD RESEARCH TEAM (1975). Op cit.
(26) KEMPE, C. H. and HELFER, R. E. (1972). Op cit.
(27) YORKSHIRE POST (1975). 9 July.
(28) PARENTS ANONYMOUS (1974). California, USA.

Chapter VIII On violence in community homes
Spencer Millham, Roger Bullock and Kenneth Hosie

'I was pissed off with his getting at me and I did him over.'
Boy, aged sixteen, in a community home.

'Bill's outburst was quite unexpected for I felt we were developing a good relationship. I have noted that he is often difficult after a weekend at home and this time he would not say anything about it. His aggressive past always makes one careful with him but clearly he needs the skilled psychiatric care we cannot provide here.'
Housemaster's report in boy's file.

'Smith has been here nearly six months, he has absconded on three occasions and each time has incited others to join him. He is frequently surly and aggressive and punishment has had no effect. He has not responded to treatment under open conditions and needs a more structured environment. He is a bully and this serious attack on his young housemaster is his third violent incident in the school.'
Headmaster's letter to the Social Services Department.

Even the most superficial reading of much that is written on violence and the brief glimpse above of an aggressive incident would suggest that violence is not an easy concept to approach. People's perspectives clearly differ. What turns aggression – the creative drive – into violence, the illegitimate use of force, raises all sorts of interesting psychological and sociological questions which we have little time to explore here. Our task is much more modest in its concern with aggressive adolescents in residential situations.

This paper attempts to look at the pattern of violence in a number of community homes, seventeen of which we studied intensively between 1968 and 1972,[1] and four schools which we have visited recently for other reasons.

Academic papers need to contain both discussions of methodology and analysis and these, unfortunately, monopolise the text. Thus, research findings sink in a sea of argument and become unapproachable to a general audience. Hence, this study is divided into two parts; the first section lays out certain general findings about violence in residential settings, while the second comments in more detail on our research methodology and provides statistical evidence.

Introduction
As we come to look at violence, we face the familiar problems

inherent in any investigation of criminal behaviour. We find the same plethora of theory and scarcity of empirical evidence, the same disputes over treatment, containment and deterrence and the same difficulties in delineating how much, in what areas and by what agents violence is said to be increasing. Attempting to provide a general theory for violent behaviour whether biological, psychological or sociological seems just as fruitless as efforts to provide general criminological theories. The nature of violent behaviour, which can range from thumping or being thumped by your teacher to baby battering or planting a bomb, must defy attempts to find background factors which are common to all violent offenders.[2]

Secondly, much criminal behaviour, and this is particularly true of violent behaviour, can only be defined in interaction with others. Robinson Crusoe could not have been a violent psychopath, at least, not until Man Friday showed up. As such, we need to know much more than we do of the meaning that participants give to aggressive actions, the circumstances in which they take place and the immediate history of the incidents. For we know that identical behaviour can have radically different consequences.[3]

Indeed, our definitions of what is violent are largely a response to the consequences of a particular act rather than to its intention. This is particularly important in situations of adolescent violence, because in their defence, boys so frequently remark 'I didn't mean it to turn out like that', 'He took it the wrong way', 'The knife was just to scare people'. Similarly, we know that an enormous amount of violence passes unnoticed, particularly in the family, and we understand very little about the different ways in which violent behaviour comes to the notice of control agencies, be they teachers, social workers or the police.[4] We are similarly rather ignorant of the ways in which these groups deal with the violent situations presented to them.

These confusions, as in most studies of criminal behaviour, mean that anyone embarking on a search for grand theories of violence rapidly runs into difficulties, usually producing generalisations which many cases do not support, or providing theories which explain more violence than we actually get. But still these theoretical debates flourish for, as we shall see, theorising is considerably easier than empirical investigation.

If general theories of violence do not seem to get very far, there has been more success when particular sorts of violence come under consideration. For example, it is possible to construct a coherent and reasonable explanation of violence at pop festivals, soccer matches or on special football trains.[5] None of this is particularly new and explanations usually suggest that the authorities get the sorts of behaviour for which they have prepared.[6] Stan Cohen's book on the seaside violence in the late sixties, *Folk Devils and Moral Panics,* provides a lively account of such riots and conflicts.[7] He emphasises the provocative role of TV, radio and newspapers in creating near-hysteria in resorts like Brighton, Clacton and Hastings, remarking that any scooter-owning lad faced with the prospect of a dreary Bank Holiday would inevitably gravitate to where the action was or, disappointed by Frinton in the fog, rapidly create some. Similarly, much of this would be true of football specials, where police and Alsatian dogs on hostile platforms make the going great on Inter-City, especially as the lads have left Dad behind to watch sport at home on TV.

In contrast, an explanation of armed robbery or violence for gain, would look at other factors involving a calculated estimate of the risks of getting caught and its consequences; whereas, we might seek explanation of sexual assaults, attacks on children and arson as the consequences of psychological disturbance, or view baby-battering as part of a more general cycle of deprivation. Explanations of political violence on the other hand might explore situations in which the democratic process is seen by some as neither democratic nor a process, indeed there is an increasing tendency to blur criminal with ideological violence.[8] However, it is difficult to see that the individuals who engage in such widely varying sorts of violence could display common characteristics, even though terms such as vandal and hooligan are applied to them all.

Violence in community homes

But this paper is concerned with a specific topic: violence among residential institutions, inevitably a minor episode in a wider violent sage. Certainly what one learns about this group should not be loosely transferred to other adolescents in entirely different situations as we know that residential contexts stimulate particular behaviour and responses which are more extreme than in open situations. Institutions engender frustrations which the free know not of.[9] But violence in residential settings is not unimportant. It raises considerable concern among staff, it may diminish their job satisfaction, exacerbate mobility, staff wastage and, particularly important, hinder the residential care of the orthodox majority of children. Violent behaviour in residential schools is also an important criterion by which aggressive boys are transferred, sometimes from open to closed situations, from community homes to secure units or Borstals, and this certainly has a serious prognosis for the child.

However, it should be stressed that this paper in no way represents a survey of violence in schools. It merely contains material gathered incidentally to the main aim of our previous research into community homes, a study which explored the effects of different regimes on children. So our approach to violence has considerable deficiencies which must be emphasised at the outset.

Reliability of evidence

An initial problem stems from the difficulties in using documentary evidence from schools.[11] This is not because considerable material is suppressed or unavailable; on the contrary violent incidents, when they occur, are lengthily reported to case conferences or in boys' records. But such accounts are not written with research in mind, thus the details of any violent incident becomes difficult to unravel. Phrases such as, 'He was aggressive', 'He lunged about', 'He took a swing at', 'He was violent', are common in descriptions of disputes. Who actually gets hit, how often, how hard, and with what results, is usually extremely difficult to elucidate.

Another problem is that the perspectives presented of violent incidents are always staff viewpoints. These rarely correspond with those of the boys. This is not to suggest that staff are unsympathetic or obtuse, but issues of threat, self-defence, anxiety or other child perspectives are rarely explored in subsequent written reports of the incident, even though a child's viewpoint may loom large in post-mortem discussions.

Quite as serious as these problems is the tendency for any ex-post facto account of a situation, particularly in a community home context, to have quite extraneous considerations built into it. The truth is largely filtered. For example, the violent incident may be written up by staff to alert local authorities and the central administration that here is a strong candidate for transfer. Obviously the case has to be made for such a new placement and it would be largely counter-productive to emphasise how this violent lad helps old ladies across zebra crossings, how marvellous he is with staff children or, particularly, to hint that most of the staff felt that Mr Bloggs, the instructor whom the boy hit, has had it coming to him for ages. Similar considerations apply to any report alerting the authorities as to staff vulnerability.

Yet, these problems pale into insignificance when we realise that people perceive the same acts very differently depending on their previous experiences and particularly the regimes or contexts in which they are working. For example, if, before visiting the old approved schools and at the time of the Court Lees scandal we, as research workers, had seen a newspaper headline 'Violence in an Approved School', we would naturally have thought of boys being hit by staff. A year later, however, knowing the schools very much better, we would have thought much more of staff being attacked by boys. Today, if we read of 'Violence in old people's home' we would be less prepared for an article on the depredations of a psychopathic granny and prepare ourselves for an account of exhausted residential staff at the end of their patience. I suspect that we would all entertain similar perspectives about mental hospitals.

This is important because when we set out to measure violence, we largely find the situations we look for.[12] It is interesting that staff anxiety over violent adolescents, which we shall shortly explore, bears little relation to the actual levels of violence in schools. There were several schools in our previous studies of eighteen Approved Schools where staff frequently hit children and where the formal punishment records underestimated the number of violent situations that occurred, but which, nevertheless, were quite happy with their levels of violence. No one seemed particularly anxious in this rumbustious environment except possibly a visitor and in such schools violence was not defined as a problem.

In contrast, in several cosy family group homes for younger children, where staff were particularly sensitive to boys' needs, violent behaviour was often viewed as a major concern. Staff complained that children swore, that they hit each other, that they damaged property or were noisy and defiant. Levels of anxiety did not parallel the number of violent incidents. In contrast, once you begin to explore staff perspectives in more permissive regimes, staff definitions of violence becomes very different. In such contexts, violence is frequently defined as acting-out behaviour and aggressive attacks on staff, even physical attacks, were viewed as valuable crisis moments for exploration and resolution. In such contexts, violence is written about and perceived in a way that is very different from that found in more rigid regimes such as those for boys of senior age. Thus, with all these real problems in the way of any investigation into violence among adolescents in residential homes, it is not surprising that so little empirical research has been undertaken.

Violence defined
Despite these research problems, we have considerable material from seventeen schools, complete case histories of the 1,120 boys in them and have been studying four community homes, two inter-

mediate and two senior, in detail as they made major changes in their regimes. So, notwithstanding all these deficiences in approaching the number and nature of violent incidents in residential homes we made the following explorations.

We have already commented that violence is difficult to define but while we accept that violence may appear in many forms[13] we suggest that most of them are largely irrelevant to our immediate task simply because these sorts of violence have not been defined as illegal or unacceptable. In this respect, such forms of violence are very different from undiscovered crime or middle class delinquency and frequently the parallels drawn between a violent society and widespread criminality are misleading.[14]

We can define violence as 'the use of force in a social situation in a way that those in power define as illegitimate'.[15] In a school situation, it is usually the headmaster and staff, the power holders, that define the sorts of force that are forbidden. In most schools physical attack of boy on boy, of boy on staff or of staff on boy are all areas that are defined as being unacceptable. So, of course, is an attack of staff on staff, but such incidents are comparatively rare. But, as we come to examine these situations, many of the difficulties just indicated are already in operation.

It is very difficult to get a reliable set of figures for attacks of *boy on boy* in schools. For example, there seem to be an awful lot of boys stepping on brooms in some establishments, which is a victim's usual explanation as to how he received a black eye. But serious attacks which precipitate other crises, such as absconding, or which demand medical attention, are fairly reliably entered up in school records. In such cases, while the actual dynamics of the boy-boy incident are difficult to follow, it is clear that violence has occurred. Much more reliable are the figures and descriptions of boys' attacks on staff in residential institutions. Any striking of *staff by a boy*, even if a relatively minor incident, is carefully entered up. In therapeutic communities too, you find this pattern is adhered to, even though the interpretation that is given to such aggression is rather different. Such careful reporting probably springs from the fact that violent behaviour is viewed as having serious and unfortunate prognostic implications for the offender.

However, in one area, where violence is offered by *staff to children*, we suspect that the reporting is deficient. This is not only because it rests with staff themselves to make uncomplimentary reports on their own actions, but also because much of the violence that we as adults offer to children – the vigorous shove, the shaking of a little boy, the grabbing by the scruff of the neck and frequently the clout – are not perceived by us as violence. This is supported by the fact that every report that we found in the schools of assaults of staff on boys all seemed to have come to light as the result of some subsequent action on the part of the child. For example, he has absconded, he has refused to go into the class or workshop, or, of course, he may have retaliated. In the school's subsequent investigation of these incidents, the initial involvement of the member of staff comes to light.

Levels of reported violence

The first thing that becomes apparent when we look at the seventeen boys' approved schools which we studied is that levels of violence differ considerably between each of the age groups and between schools. Also, the number of recorded incidents do not correspond in any direct way to concern expressed by staff over boys' violence or to boys' aggressive histories. It is clear that the schools themselves greatly influence the amount of violence they get, just as they have been demonstrated to affect absconding, attainments and the success of boys after release.[16] Using material gathered during our general survey, we are able to compare three contrasting aspects of violent behaviour in these residential communities: the concern about troublesome behaviour expressed by 187 staff during interviews, the proportion of pupils defined as violent or aggressive during assessment and the number of violent incidents of all kinds recorded in school records. The correlations between all these measures can be seen in Tables A (i) and (ii) found in the Appendix.

Naturally, each of these measures are open to considerable criticism. For example, the questions we put to staff concentrated on troublesome behaviour in general and did not specifically explore violence. Secondly, there is no reason why *recorded* violence should bear any relationship to real levels of aggression as one suspects that some schools and staff recorded incidents more systematically than others. However, the evidence in Table C (ix) from a Special Secure Unit where continual scrutiny of boys and careful daily assessment of boys' behaviour is obligatory, would suggest that generally the figures we provide are close to the number of violent incidents that occur.[17]

The greatest discrepancies between the three rankings are found among the schools for junior boys. Tables A (ii) and B (i) confirm that although juniors are twice as likely as others to be labelled violent or aggressive on assessment, staff concern about their behaviour and the recorded levels of violence in junior schools are both low. But, as the boys grow older, the relationship between staff concern, incidents and an aggressive history increases. When

132

we consider the respective rankings of the twelve schools for older boys – that is the intermediate and senior schools – there are closer correlations between violence in the institutions and boys' aggressive tendencies as laid out on assessment, and this becomes especially marked if, as in Table A(iv) we exclude School F, an establishment catering for boys of an intermediate age who are educationally retarded.[18] It is clear, therefore, that the staff attached little significance to violent behaviour among younger children and many outbursts probably pass unrecorded but, as the boys grow older, their concern increases. An initial assessment or reputation for aggression leads staff to be more cautious and, consequently, more conscientious in recording violent outbursts.

Junior schools, then, are not seen by staff as violent. Very few incidents of boys attacking members of staff or of staff being violent to children are reported, although this provides an interesting reversal of the behaviour that we might have expected for more junior boys are commented on by assessment staff as being aggressive. Most outbursts at junior level are cases of boy hitting boy. In contrast, intermediate schools are more violent, particularly in incidents of staff attacking boy or boy attacking staff. Contrary to popular ideas senior boys are comparatively docile.

This evidence provides yet another example of the ways in which ideas on violence reflect people's underlying fears and insecurities rather than any reality. Anxiety seems unrelated to actual incidents. Several writers have suggested that many of our ideas on violence are maintained by folklore and fantasy which seem to have little empirical validity. Cohen has illustrated the ways in which commonly held views on aggressive offenders, such as their gang membership, their lack of motivation and their probability of recidivism, are contradicted by established findings.[19] But why people need these myths is much more difficult to determine. Within schools it is likely that anxieties define staff boundaries of authority, legitimise aspects of adult role behaviour, all of which may be threatened in time of change. But general adult concern over adolescent hedonism, such as drug taking, promiscuity, violence and laziness may reflect the difficulties and contradictory expectations adults have in classifying much youthful behaviour. A teenager's attempt at mature behaviour in sexual or some social areas we reject as presumptuous, while we dismiss his child-like spontaneity as impulsive and irresponsible.[20]

The importance of school regimes
The school's life style, too, seems to have an influence on aggressive behaviour. A glance at Table A (i) confirms that block structures

133

with strict regimes are less violent than more relaxed schools with house units and therapeutic communities have more incidents than those with more structured regimes. It does seem that the more relaxed the regime, the greater the incidence of aggressive behaviour of all sorts. But, the number of *serious* incidents is so small as to make comparisons unreliable and it certainly does not follow that violent environments are necessarily anarchic or threatening to staff. We are not alone in drawing such conclusions as these findings echo various psychological experiments in which the style of leadership has been shown to affect levels of aggression in groups, a more relaxed style of management leading to more frequent aggressive behaviour among participants.[21]

These changing patterns of violence can be clearly seen if we look more closely at four Community Homes. During the past three years these establishments have all moved towards more open flexible structures, offering care in small groups. They have all abandoned the training structure of the orthodox approved school which they had operated previously.

The first conclusion to be drawn from the evidence presented in Table C (vii) is that serious incidents of violence are few and far between. Almost three-quarters of the incidents recorded are boy-boy assaults. We can note that in the three year period in Home A, for example, boys hit staff on only eleven occasions. In those three years nearly 220 boys lived for varying periods in the institution, so the frequency of assaults on staff works out at one incident in every three months. This pattern is repeated in the other three Homes and hardly corroborates popular ideas of a surging tide of violence in residential establishments. One might also comment that assaults on staff are the most likely of all violent acts to be systematically recorded because such attacks raise serious questions about the way the aggressor should be approached in future, be it transfer to secure provision or Borstal, or may be used to engineer some change in a boy's peer group and staff relationships. Such infrequent incidents are hardly what the staff of the old approved schools had in mind when they wrote expressing concern about violence to the Home Office in 1969. More perturbing than all this and most certainly what staff did not suspect are the greater number of incidents of staff hitting boys which appears in our figures, especially as the notification of such incidents is very likely to be an underestimate of the truth.

Trends in violence
Violent behaviour in residential establishments also appears to be cyclical. Because there are so very few serious incidents it is

difficult to talk of cycles, but offences do seem to cluster, probably between home leaves as the graphs in Table C (iii) to C (vi) suggest. This contrasts with the pattern of absconding which, Clarke and Martin have shown, varies over the year, but tends to be greatest after holiday periods.[22] It is also noteworthy that the boy-boy incidents seem to cluster in senior establishments with changes in the leading group, though this is an impression gathered from living in the Homes, reading the records and is not based on accurate sociometric testing. We would suggest that when the older boys leave there is a re-arrangement of the pecking order, a feature which Polsky clearly demonstrates in one of his studies.[23] However, this is not an entirely fixed situation, for it depends on the sort of boy that arrives in the group and the strength and coherence of the boy-world at the time of change. Nevertheless, our own hypothesis and the earlier residential studies of Folkard, Schwartz and Shockley and a report on discipline by the London joint four local authorities in 1970 all suggest that the dynamics of changing relationships may well be related to cycles of violence.[24]

It is also clear from our study of four Community Homes over time that violence is increasing. The number of incidents seems to have doubled over a couple of years and, although earlier figures are less reliable, 1974 rates seem to be about three times those of 1969, even when we take into account fluctuations in their populations. It is probably this rate of increase in violence that has alarmed the principals of Community Homes rather than the actual levels but, again, it must be emphasised that very few of these incidents are serious and almost all the increase has been between the boys. We shall return later to this phenomena for it raises a number of important issues.

Characteristics of violent boys

One of the tasks we faced with the 1,120 boys in our general survey was to decide which types of boy were being admitted to each of the schools. Those schools that took second-time-round offenders or the more disturbed children could hardly be expected to be as successful as those that were taking relatively tranquil boys who were new to the residential experience. For each boy in our study 41 characteristics were relentlessly plotted, ranging from early separation from parents to aspects of personality, intelligence and educational attainments. This is a common technique when approaching such a research problem and other examples can be found in West and Farrington's study, *Who becomes Delinquent,* in Street, Vinter and Perrow's work on the American reform schools, in Clarke and Martin's study of absconding and Dunlop's recent analysis of six approved school.[25] By a process of multi-correlation, we are able to see which types of boy have a history of being actively involved in at least one violent act during their stay.

From these correlations, laid out in Table D (i), we learn that boys who are violent in their approved schools are more likely to be less intelligent than others, to have spent long periods in residential care, and to come from families which have other violent members, particularly the father from whom they will have been frequently separated in early years. We have noted elsewhere that many of the boy's fathers have been absent from home for long periods, and this situation seems to affect boys more than girls. While prolonged absence of fathers tends to make boys less aggressive when young, these circumstances increase aggressive behaviour during adolescence.[26] It has also been demonstrated that parents who condone violence, who are violent themselves or who reward aggression, are more likely to have aggressive children.[27] Parental discipline will have been fitful. The boy's father in particular will have been ambivalent in his attitude towards the boy and his brothers, a point corroborated by the fact that aggressive examples are very likely to be copied by boys if violence is seen to be rewarded or goes unpunished.[28] There is also a suggestion that institutionalised boys and those with low self-esteem are particularly prone to this sort of modelling.[29] Correlations are also clear between violence in adolescence and boys displaying difficult behaviour from an early age, many of whom have been noted as being highly aggressive during their primary education.[30] In all these areas there are strong relationships between violent behaviour during residential treatment and previous history.

What is equally interesting is that certain features do not correlate with violence. Contrary to previous findings by Morris, nuances of working class status do not seem to be significant.[31] We found that a proportion of violent boys in our population come from quite prosperous working class families, a feature noted by Farrington and West in their comparative study of aggressive with delinquent boys.[32] Nor does psychological disturbance correlate with violence. Aggressive behaviour among juveniles also seems to be much less related to other sorts of crime than researches into older offenders have implied.[33] Boys who are violent during residential treatment are not isolates, neither did they truant from day school, although they are more likely to abscond from community homes. Indeed, aggressive children seem to form a sub-

136

group, and certainly not one of low status, in both their day and residential schools.

However, it is particularly important to note that in this exercise there is a strong correlation between past and present behaviour. While such lads are clearly subject to the influence of 'labelling', it does seem that boys who have been violent before are expected by staff to be violent again, and so frequently are. Not only does such a stereotype persist over time unmoderated by a boy's passive conduct but it renders conflict as more likely and more fierce.[34] From an analysis in Table C (viii) of the incidents that occurred in School A we can see that in the 138 incidents of violence recorded, 77 boys were involved, and nearly half of these were responsible for two or more incidents in the school. Wolfgang, in his studies, is so concerned with these persistent violent offenders that he advocates that intervention should only be applied to this group,[35] but it is significant that while 34 of those 77 had previous histories of violence, as many as 43 had no such previous records, suggesting that the school also creates a fair proportion of its own violence. Unfortunately, it is not possible to trace the parallel violent histories of adults in the schools, although there is considerable evidence that certain staff are more likely to be involved in violent acts than others.[36]

Many of these observations laid out in Appendix D confirm earlier studies which sought to establish other characteristics of aggressive individuals.[37] Psychologists, such as Kolvin, Quay and Field, for example, have all established the significance of a general aggressiveness factor among institutionalised delinquents. On a more sociological level, Field has found that aggression among approved school boys is related to the size of, and position in, the family and a history of absconding, while Clarke and Sinclair related difficult *behaviour* in a community home to racial origin, history of previous difficult behaviour, absconding and home background.[38] Naturally, as aggression is expressed in a wide variety of social situations, these correlation exercises are of limited value, but they are an attempt to establish those boys who have the greatest pre-disposition towards violence in residential situations.

It is unfortunate that our data on boys' backgrounds has to come from re-working material collected during earlier research as this prevents us from testing systematically the hypotheses offered by these writers. Nevertheless, it can be seen that our findings do parallel some of these earlier studies in their stress on previous behaviour and family circumstances (but not poverty) even though our evidence is complicated by the considerable discrepancies that must exist between recorded violence and assessed aggression among boys.

Group violence

Occasionally in residential institutions, violent outbursts involve large numbers of people. We can add little to what has already been written on group violence because, thankfully, no riots marred our many visits to these institutions. However, it is worth considering Clarke and Sinclair's summary to their valuable review of available literature on violence as so much that they suggest is supported by our own work on school regimes.[2] They comment that 'the likelihood of a riot is increased by such factors as the admission of new disruptive residents or the discharging of old stabilising ones, the formation of cliques of difficult residents and the existence of grievances among them. Such patterns are accompanied by a lack of communication between residents and staff which makes it difficult for grievances to be dealt with and which grows worse as the trouble begins. The two groups, staff and inmates, grow apart in mutual hostility. The riots frequently take place during a change from a strict to a more permissive regime and may be triggered off by the staff disunity which often accompanies these changes. The disunity may increase the disturbance in a variety of ways, by making the staff more anxious, by hindering communication, and by imposing conflicting demands on residents. Anxiety levels increase in all and generally the ideas of attacking staff become more feasible to inmates. Insufficient staff or rapid changes may produce similar results. Once the riot has started, it presumably feeds on itself by a process of group contagion'.[39]

Clarke and Sinclair comment that the reports on the troubles at Carlton and Standon Farm schools revealed that the disturbances sprang from 'the existence of boredom, a wide-spread sense of grievance, the presence of a number of difficult boys, poor communications between boys and staff and among the staff themselves, the undermining of staff authority and the absence of key staff at crisis moments'.[40]

Wider perspectives on adolescent violence

A good deal more can be learned about adolescent violence than that simply afforded by the statistics we have just discussed. First of all, it is clear from a close study of staff-boy conflicts that almost all are entirely avoidable. Unfortunately, it seems that few staff have had even the simplest instructions on how to take preventive action. Frequently, they hasten into confrontation situations in which neither staff nor boy feels he can back down without significant loss of face. But incidents do not suddenly erupt, conflict is nurtured and both sides provide opportunities for the mounting aggression to be displaced, make gestures of appeasement, give chances for escape – in much the same way as a parent–child confrontation is subject to considerable negotiation, with bribery, threat and resistance mutually and lingeringly employed. But in Community homes such confrontation usually takes place in group situations where the esteem of others will be lost by backing down and, inevitably, the chances of an aggressive response are heightened.[41] We know that the presence of aggressive peers encourages aggression in others, mainly because of the prospect of help in the case of retaliation, and the presence of supporters aids the breaking down of moral inhibitions and provides a context of legitimacy.[42] Frequently adults forget that in institutions these lads have no family against which to struggle for some independent identity and hence much aggression must be visited on staff. Yet, the licence granted to our own adolescent children to be difficult and unco-operative, we rarely extend to boys in our charge.

Stress on the need for such an awareness on the part of staff is reinforced by the fact that in those incidents where staff hit boys, over half the boys involved had previous violent histories. The staff had quite clearly set up the situation in two-thirds of the incidents and were the ones who hit first.[43] Yet, people can be trained to avoid these situations, either by side-stepping the confrontation or by meeting it in much the same way as violent patients are contained in mental hospitals. It is an unfortunate fact that little of these strategies ever form part of the courses offered to students destined for posts in schools or residential homes. Indeed, instructions on things practical seem to have a very low priority. For example, how many trainee teachers are even given clear guidance on such simple things as how to do a dinner duty or to survive a playground patrol, let alone how to gracefully avoid an aggressive confrontation.

The relationships between violent participants

Particularly interesting is the whole area of the relationship between the hitter and the hit. It is not necessarily one of constant and mutual hostility. For example, in a study of a Californian police force, it was found that some policemen were repeatedly involved in violent situations although the majority were not.[44] Folkard, too, showed that certain mental hospital patients were particularly likely to be victims of attack, and suggests that the same is true

139

of staff.[45] Investigations into these aspects of staff–boy interaction would be very rewarding. It is also worth remembering that research has established that in the excited state of confrontation quite neutral behaviour can be interpreted by participants as aggression.[46] This is as true for staff as it is for children. It has also been established that frequently those who are disliked, unpopular or scapegoat figures, are more likely to be victims whether or not they are in any way provocative.[47] It is particularly important to remember in the case of young offenders, whose relationships with father or other authority figures have been turbulent, that even innocent physical resemblance to those ardently disliked can be highly provoking.[48] Much tension and the occasional violent outburst could be avoided if staff knew of these things and realised that it is not so much their authority that is threatened in confrontation so much as the more explosive and shaky masculine identity of boys particularly, many of whom have severe problems of ego development.[49] From what they say it seems that at the moment of attack the boys are highly anxious, frightened participants and subsequently feel guilty and shaken. In the same way all sorts of dress and implements which we view as threatening, indicating an aggressive intent, are protective devices, warning off potential aggressors, and are certainly not 'offensive weapons' whatever the legal nomenclature.

Equally interesting are the relationships between boy combatants. Often the fight is part of an on-going friendship, sometimes an intense relationship and only in rare cases the result of carefully nurtured hostility or indifference. We undertook a number of socio-metric studies during our approved school research to contrast the friendship patterns between block schools and those which emphasised small group settings in house units, instruction and recreation.[50] Not only did highly aggressive boys have a wider friendship network but they were more likely to be involved in conflicts with their reciprocating friends. It seems that signals between boys in a paired or triangular relationship are often misinterpreted and a fight ensues.

Violence and sexual behaviour
It can be hypothesised that, in the light of these relationships, there may be links between sexual and violent behaviour among adolescent boys. We have noted that violent lads have not only suffered from the absence of fathers but also spend a long time in institutional care. This poses them with considerable identity problems, particularly those of sexual identity. We also know that single sex communities tend to engender anxiety over masculinity,[51] and

140

this concern is aggravated in young offenders by the fact that they are bound by strong and pervasive norms on what constitutes masculine behaviour.[52] Their code of conduct allows little of the bi-sexual role play that characterizes middle-class boys faced with similar deprivations in residential settings. For working-class boys, displays of feminity, however modest, are taboo, whereas middle-class boys can dance, paint, design clothes, act and even wear drag at the school concert without arousing much stricture.[53] David Holbrook makes much of this role deprivation in numbers of his studies and A. J. Reiss, in an entirely different context, suggests that similar anxieties exist in queer/peer relationships.[54]

This should not imply that approved-school boys should hasten into earrings and keep their high-heeled shoes under the bed – indeed (the situation might be less fraught if they did) – but it does mean that they are in residential settings where their masculine self-image is constantly being threatened by what they feel about other people and by what other people feel about them. They and their schools have developed none of the mechanisms which abound in more esteemed residential settings, and which release or displace such anxieties. Consequently, young offenders will be more difficult and allay their tensions by overt masculine display, in which aggressive, violent behaviour is an immediate and unmistakable badge of courage. Institutional life poses all sorts of identity problems for boys and we have noted that frequently a small physical handicap such as a stammer, squint or even retarded sexual development can engender considerable anxieties and consequent aggressive outbursts.[55]

In a modified way some of these identity problems must affect male staff and would explain why women, on those rare occasions they are allowed to intervene, seem so much more successful in handling lads' aggressive outbursts than are men. While women may create tensions in other ways, in confrontation situations with difficult adolescents they are less threatening to boys' masculine self-image.[56] In co-educational settings it is noticeable that whatever other problems may abound the aggressive behaviour of boys and the belligerent stance of male staff is much reduced.[57]

Others have suggested that anxiety over the establishment of a masculine sexual identity seems to be widespread among working-class boys and certainly an interesting correlation does emerge between violence and sexual misdemeanour both within the residential establishment and outside.[58] Although such a correlation would be difficult to defend in a situation where violent children are subject to closer scrutiny than others, it does seem from boys' records and from conversations with them that they have a more catholic sexual appetite than others. There are also interesting parallels to be drawn between these adolescent sexual anxieties and the behaviour of certain sub-groups in the outside world. For example, much of the grotesque studded clobber of Hell's Angels, their bizarre crash helmets and roaring motor cycles suggest similar concerns.[59] Indeed, much of this group's sexual behaviour of initiation and the 'gang-bang' conceals or compensates for a deep anxiety about adequate male sexual performance.

Some of these hypotheses have been explored by looking at differing levels of violence among West Indian boys and attempting to compare the behaviour of new immigrants, many of whom have suffered paternal deprivation, with second generation coloured lads.[60] Studies of adolescents which are matriarchally dominated confirm that they are more aggressive.[61] Clarke and Sinclair certainly have found a relationship between colour and violent behaviour, but there were so few coloured children in our population of Approved School boys, indeed the total number of violent lads could be counted on one hand, that no such correlation exercise was possible.[62]

Class perspectives on violence

These links between violence and sexual behaviour begin to raise all sorts of questions about our bourgeois perspectives on aggression and crime. As a result of the considerable academic backlash against notions of social deprivation and educational deficiency which emanated mainly from the United States, we now no longer hasten to attach the label of culturally deprived or ineducable to those whose collars may be both blue and dirty.[63] But, while such value-laden perspectives may be in disarray in education, sociology and social psychology, they linger on in psychiatry and criminology. A glance at the assessment record on any young offender will provide several good illustrations of the ways in which boys' families are dismissed as inadequate. 'His father, aged 45 when Brian was committed, had not worked for 12 years previous, having been a miner who had been registered as disabled due to chronic bronchitis and associated "black outs". In spite of this, and though illiterate, he is described in reports a a sensible and kindly man.'[64]

Delinquents and their families are pejoratively measured against some fictional norm of what most families and most boys are supposed to be like. Similar unsupported attitudes are at work when we contemplate violent behaviour. Naturally, if someone hits us we feel suitably violated, but should we so readily transfer the sense of outrage, wounding and suffering to others? Physical contact plays a far more normal part in these boys' lives than in our, perhaps, over-fastidious relationships. For example, boys in special schools and community homes touch, pummel and wrestle with each other far more than middle-class children, Polsky, who also noted such behaviour in his study 'Cottage Six', suggests that this ritualised struggle constantly reasserts among the boys the inmate pecking order and certainly this is one of its many functions.[65]

Attitudes to, and definitions of, violence are very much class determined. We have spent considerable time during our research in a poor mining community. We remember one evening, as the pubs were closing, returning to a boy's home to play records. At one point during the proceedings there was a sound of much thumping and bumping overhead. 'That'll be my dad beating up my mum,' said the lad in explanation. 'It quite turns her on, and then he drags her off to bed.' How different from home life in Virginia Water! So, warming to our task, we asked each of the lads how they would set about turning on their own girl friends, remembering our own rather inconclusive adolescent attempts with low lights, white wine and Mantovani. 'Oh, you just give her a good thump,' the lad replied. 'If she hits you back, you're made!' Numerous other writers such as Patrick and Suttles have demonstrated the varying significance and the integral and cohesive nature of violence in certain geographical localities.[66] What seems in objective terms a violent action may mean something entirely different in another cultural context.

However, the problem of adolescent violence is not simply one of cultural relativism and some comment is necessary on the rate of increase of violent incidents reported in residential settings. Actual violence levels are not as yet large but if present trends continue they could become a major issue in some establishments.

Future trends in violence
Our own studies and much other research would suggest that violence increases in the institution when the stability of the inmate informal world is threatened. When radical changes in boy's roles, perceptions and relationships are demanded, considerable disruptions result. This is why moves towards a more benevolent regime, such as the introduction of pastoral staff, changes in control or the release of informal leaders, all of which may be ameliorative, can initiate unrest. It is not possible to explore here the full relationship that can exist between the formal organisation of a Home and the informal world of the adolescents it shelters, but we do know that the values of the boy world will greatly influence the incidence of violence, just as it determines absconding and other deviant activity.

143

We suspect the most violent Homes will greatly resist change, and the violence levels will persist for a considerable time.[67]

It is also clear that in times of change the many components of an institution do not necessarily change at the same rate and this can lead to a state of confusion among staff and children. For example, the norms of one sub-unit, such as the residential house, may conflict with the expectations of education facilities. The frustrations arising from this state of anomie, when the normative demands of particular sub-systems are dissonant from those of the wider institution, can provoke aggressive outbursts.[68] This means that all changes in institutions, however immediately bene-volent they may be, need very careful engineering, especially as disruptive behaviour by adolescents following liberal innovations, not only strengthens the hand of those who dismiss change as permissive, but also saps the confidence of radical staff. Critics perhaps fail to realise that it is just as likely that change in a more custodial direction would have produced similar tremors of boy dissatisfaction. Whatever the views of staff, it is clear that recent changes in the aims, administration, staffing patterns, accommo-dation and clientele of the old approved schools must be responsible for the increasing conflict that is reported.[69]

While disturbances are usually short lived, it is generally main-tained that moves towards more benign regimes in a wide variety of residential establishments, not only the community homes, have been accompanied by an increase in violence and disruptive be-haviour. Certainly our study over time in four changing community homes indicates this is the situation. A number of explanations for this offer themselves. In settings where close relationships are encouraged between children and staff and where effective displays and involvement are mutually cherished, those sharing a relation-ship will have a strong interest in knowing all the activities of each other. With such boys as those sheltered by the community homes, whose vulnerability and difficulties in relationships have been relentlessly chronicled elsewhere, the competition and jealousy over the attention of caring adults must add yet another dimension to unrest.[70]

Residential institutions differ from schools in the outside world, in that such boy–boy and boy–staff relationships are public and their development scrutinised by all. Boys become jealous of their friends' involvements with others and also of staff's affections. The widespread and successful efforts to bring about closer relationships between boys, and between staff and children in community homes, through small group living and working situations, must be related to the increase in conflict. It accounts for the frequency of violence which we have already noted as being between reciprocating friends.[71] In our experience boys are as likely to attack the erring love-object as much as they do the rival, mainly because they recognise the legitimacy of the rival's role. Girls on the other hand, usually physically attack the rival because, in spite of a good deal of verbal abuse, she accepts the legitimacy of her mate's roving eye. This, of course, raises all sorts of questions about the dominant and passive patterns in relationships and in what areas of the relationship they occur. Unfortunately, these are issues which we cannot explore here except to say that, in those situations where adolescents are kept longer under scrutiny than ever before, such as in day schools, youth clubs and residential homes, when adolescents are maturing earlier, where children are encouraged to be open and communicative about their feelings and where the adults responsible experience vicarious pleasure and jealousy as a consequence, we would hypothesise that aggressive behaviour must increase.

All this would imply that while violence to us may appear wanton, motiveless and spasmodic, it is none of these things. For the participants conflict is logical, moral and fulfilling.[72] Vandalism, apparently so senseless, hides a careful strategy through which boys balance risks of apprehension with the increased status they can achieve with peers. In the same way Goldman has established that low-status, bottom-stream boys in poor schools are those that do the most damage, seeking revenge on the institution for their constant humiliation.[73]

In fact, it is the essential logic of much adolescent violence that should give us the greatest encouragement. If it is a response to demanding social situations rather than an uncontrolled drive then youthful aggression can be checked and confrontation can be manipulated by adults.

In our discussion of violence in institutions we have suggested that serious situations are not common, that attacks on staff are rare and that as soon as we start to point an accusing finger at the disruptive lads, our own innocence is questioned. We have suggested that this is not the fault of any individual and must be expected when a large number of untrained people are faced with delicate situations for which they have no simple information on what may be at issue, or directions on how to side-step conflict situations.

We have highlighted some of the background factors of violent children and, with less systematic evidence, have hypothesised some of the interesting contexts in which we might explore the subject further: class attitudes to aggression, its sexual content, the identity problems faced by adolescents and its link with relationships in residential settings.

In conclusion, and possibly most important we have suggested that in institutional contexts with the young, we are likely to get a lot more violence and, far from shrinking from it, residential staff should be prepared for conflict. The four community homes which have provided much of the information for this paper are changing to more benign, small group settings and relationships between boys and between boys and staff are growing closer. In many conversations with staff in the community homes, in much of the writings of Balbernie and others, it is suggested that the underlying characteristic of problem children in residential homes is their very deep resentment, their sense of violation and loss.[74] These feelings are entirely justified, for we have, as a society, as caring administrators or as residential staff, done terrible things to them, often with the best of intentions.

In the old approved school structures, the violence was inherent in the process of boys' committal and release. It was made explicit in the goals and roles of everyone in the institution.[75] The only real reward for a lad was to get out. Community homes are rightly seeking something different in their new structures, searching to provide a living situation that is therapeutic.[76] Children need to feel safe to be violent and they need trained, sensitive and compassionate staff to understand, meet and explain their outbursts to them. A child's demanding, difficult behaviour in open institutions frequently improves the quality of care available to all, because it forces staff to reconsider and experiment. A lad is no threat to others when he is shipped off to some secure environment where, under the charade of treatment, he is locked up until he can be safely released to Borstal. Indeed, as we are becoming painfully aware, constant transfers create a long-term casualty.[77]

We have suggested that much adolescent violence is related to relationships and what the young offender wants is a secure relationship. When he gets one, either with other boys or with staff, he will test it out to the full. Violence, aggressive behaviour, extreme withdrawal, absconding – all sorts of maladjusted behaviour – are to be expected in community homes and staff must be given the confidence, professional support and training to meet it. Above all, we hope they have the compassion to hang on to their habitual prodigal sons. As A. S. Neill once said, 'Quiet schools are dead schools'.

SECTION A *The interrelationship between boys' background, Staff concern and recorded levels of violence*

The evidence for this correlation exercise was collected during a general survey of 17 boys' approved schools conducted between 1968 and 1972. Each individual school is represented by a letter. Schools A–E were for junior boys of ages 10–15; schools F–K for the intermediate group aged 13–17 and schools L–Q for senior boys of fifteen or over.

The ranking for the proportions of boys assessed as violent or aggressive during assessment is based on the reports prepared by the classifying schools and details can be found in the report Millham *et al.* 1972 p. 35.[78] Levels of staff concern are based on replies from 187 staff to interview questions about the problems presented by boys and the difficulties facing residential social workers. Details of these can be found in Millham *et al* 1972, pp. 290, 394, 396, 399, 409. Details of recorded violence were noted from boys' files during the research.

The list below also offers details about the structure of the school. 'House systems' mean that the school is subdivided into small, separate living units, whereas in 'Block Structures' the boys eat, live and sleep communally. The style of the regime is also suggested and readers should consult Millham *et al* 1975 for a full account of these styles.[79] Briefly, at junior level, we distinguish between the *family group style* (FG) divided into quasi family groups. These schools are federal in structure, relaxed and cosy in atmosphere, there are more women than usual with pastoral responsibilities, reduced stress on academic and work skills and little organisational activity. In contrast, the *junior training schools* are more like state boarding schools for ordinary children and some show a distinctively 'prep school' style with a stress on academic skills and activity. Here the religious stress is more marked than in other schools and the structure is more autocratic.

Among schools for older children, the *senior training style* was common with its stress on vocational training and preparation for work. These schools tend to be more closed, bureaucratic and tightly structured. Other schools, the *campus style,* had developed large structures amalgamating the better qualities of the training and family group styles and, finally, in the two so called *therapeutic communities* relationships are pursued in an atmosphere of scruffy casualness where academic and work emphasis tends to be depressed.

Table A (i) Rank orders for staff concern about boys' background of and recorded levels of violence

	Staff concern about troublesome behaviour	Proportions of boys assessed as violent or aggressive	Amounts of recorded violence	Structure style
HIGHEST RATING	Q		F	Block S. Tg.
		A – D		
	M		H	House Th. C.
	P	E	C	House F. G.
	L	J	O	Block S. Tg.
INCREASING AMOUNT ↑	N	G	G	Block S. Tg.
		C	J	House Th. C.
	O – F			
		N	M	House S. Tg.
	A	O	Q	Block S. Tg.
	G	P	B	Block J. Tg.
	E		P	Block S. Tg.
		H – K		
	D		D	Block F. G.
	B	B	N	Block S. Tg.
	H		A	Block J. Tg.
		Q – M		
	K		L	Block S. Tg.
		I	K	House Cps.
	C – J			
		F	I	Block Cps.
LOWEST RATING	I	L	E	Block J. Tg.

The above table clearly illustrates the point made in the accompanying paper that staff concern over aggression, the number of violent boys sheltered in the schools and the levels of violence recorded do not bear much relationship to each other. It also illustrates the point that the more relaxed the regime the more violence is recorded. We have not provided the figures for each school, as it is the relationship between schools that is important, not the number of incidents. These are better explored in the material provided on four schools in Section C. However, both the correlation matrix and the proportion of boys in various age groups that we assessed as aggressive are given overleaf.

A correlation matrix giving the Spearman rank order coefficients for these three ratings is as follows:

Table A (ii) All schools

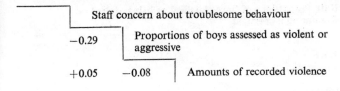

	Staff concern about troublesome behaviour	
−0.29	Proportions of boys assessed as violent or aggressive	
+0.05	−0.08	Amounts of recorded violence

Table A (iii) For intermediate and senior schools only
the matrix reads:

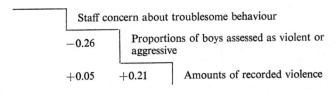

	Staff concern about troublesome behaviour	
−0.26	Proportions of boys assessed as violent or aggressive	
+0.05	+0.21	Amounts of recorded violence

Table A (iv) For intermediate and senior schools other than School F,
the matrix is:

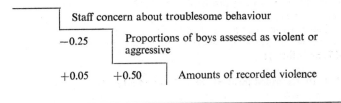

	Staff concern about troublesome behaviour	
−0.25	Proportions of boys assessed as violent or aggressive	
+0.05	+0.50	Amounts of recorded violence

(None of these coefficients are significant even at the 5 per cent level. The significance of the 0.50 figure is marginally over 5 per cent.)

Table B (i) Proportions of boys classified as being violent or aggressive during assessment

Junior boys	25%	N = 293
Intermediate boys	13	502
Senior boys	11	324
ALL BOYS	15	1119

It is clear that many more junior boys are assessed as being violent or aggressive at their classifying schools than are older boys.

SECTION C *Details of Violent Incidents in Four Schools*

In four former approved schools which we have been studying in the context of change into community homes, we have been able to explore more fully the recorded levels of violence. All of these establishments have changed in recent years from an orthodox, training structure to a more benign regime where care aims parallel the educational emphasis and where the needs of the pupil have precedence over routine and discipline. The number of violent incidents of all kinds recorded in boys files in the years 1972 to 1974 is as follows:

Table C (i) Recorded incidents of violence of all sorts

	A	B	C	D
1972	30	14	3	44
1973	47	12	11	68
1974	61	11	17	76
Mean number of boys*	120	72	64	83
Mean length of stay (months)**	19.2	15.6	13.1	16.2

* Mean numbers based on quarterly census during this period
** Calculated for boys who left during the 3 year period

It is immediately apparent that violence levels appear to have increased markedly between the years 1972 and 1974. But two of the schools, B and C, have experienced fluctuations in numbers during this period which could bias the figures and so an index of violent incidents per boy month which corrects the error was constructed. Even taking these variations into account, it was still found that violence in the schools has increased by nearly two fold in the three year period.

Table C (ii) Violent incidents per boy month

	A	B	C	D
1972	.02	.01	.01	.04
1973	.03	.02	.01	.07
1974	.04	.02	.02	.08

When these incidents are charted according to their seasonal frequency, a clear cyclical pattern is found. There are clear periods when violence is at a higher level than normal and every four months or so seems to reach a peak. The following graphs lay out the details for the numbers of recorded violent incidents in each month.

Further important evidence on patterns of violence emerges when the proportions of incidents involving staff are compared. A breakdown of each incident into categories of the groups of people involved reveals that most of the recorded violent incidents are assaults among the boys. In only one quarter were staff involved and, even then, less than a half of these cases were matters of boys attacking staff. The following table lays out the details of such an analysis. The categories are not completely exclusive as occasionally staff or boys are assaulted when trying to separate fighting boys. Hence, the totals of recorded incidents occasionally fall below the sum of the subsidiary divisions.

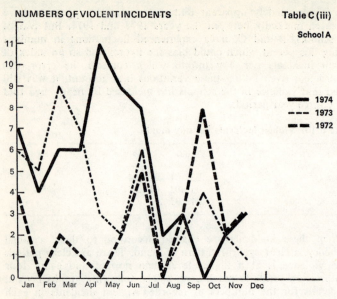

NUMBERS OF VIOLENT INCIDENTS

Table C (iii)

School A

— 1974
---- 1973
-- 1972

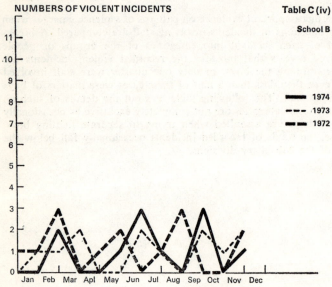

NUMBERS OF VIOLENT INCIDENTS

Table C (iv)

School B

— 1974
---- 1973
-- 1972

152

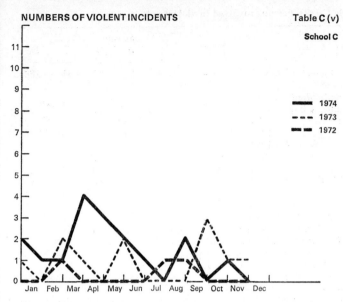

NUMBERS OF VIOLENT INCIDENTS

Table C (v)

School C

— 1974
- - - 1973
■ ■ ■ 1972

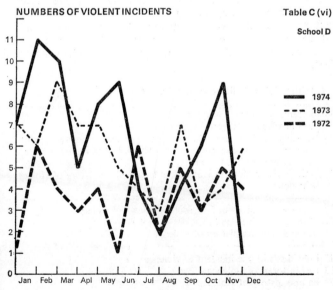

NUMBERS OF VIOLENT INCIDENTS

Table C (vi)

School D

— 1974
- - - 1973
■ ■ ■ 1972

153

Table C (vii) Persons involved in violent acts

		Schools A	B	C	D
Total number of recorded incidents 1972–74		138	37	31	188
People involved					
Boy hitting boy	1972	21	12	2	36
(in school)	1973	35	9	8	52
	1974	43	9	13	56
Boy hitting staff	1972	2	1	1	4
	1973	6	1	2	6
	1974	3	0	1	11
Staff hitting boy	1972	6	0	0	4
	1973	5	2	1	10
	1974	7	2	1	9
Total incidents involving staff		29	6	6	44
% of incidents involving staff		21%	16%	19%	23%
% of incidents involving assaults on staff		8%	5%	13%	12%
Boy–boy incidents occuring in school		99	29	21	140
Incidents involving boy in school and someone outside		13	2	4	4

The above table illustrates the point that generally the reported levels of violence are low, that most are between boys, that attacks on staff are rare, and that, if anything, staff violence to children should be as much a cause of concern as the reverse. Using evidence from School A, these patterns are more fully explored overleaf.

Table C (viii) Violent behaviour in School A

138 incidents of violence of all sorts
77 boys involved in these violence incidents
34 boys involved in these violence incidents had either records of violence or were referred to as possibly violent in reports before entering present institution
43 individuals involved in violent incidents had no history of violent behaviour

32 boys were involved in 2 or more incidents of violence
21 of the 32 involved had histories of violence
11 of the 32 had no history of violence

45 individuals in one incident of violence
13 had histories of violence
32 had no history of violence

154

STAFF/BOY
29 *incidents of violence involving staff*
- 11 incidents in which boys hit staff (7 boys involved had histories of violence before entering present institution)
- 18 incidents in which staff hit boys (11 of the boys involved had histories of violence)

Breakdown of 18 incidents (above):
a) 9 incidents in which there was a straight exchange of blows between staff and boy (4 of these boys had histories of violence)
b) 6 incidents in which staff hit boys for giving verbal abuse (5 of these boys had histories of violence)
c) 3 incidents in which staff used violence to break up fights between boys in school (all 3 boys had histories of violence)

BOY/BOY
- 99 incidents of boy/boy violence within institution
- 13 incidents of boy/boy violence outside school
- 47 of the above boys had histories of violence

Table C (ix) Violence in the special unit 1966–69

The statistics shown below of boy-boy attacks and boy-staff attacks are extremely accurate. Each boy is constantly under scrutiny by several staff, and so is each member of staff. Daily reports are written on the child and his behaviour which are extensive.

The rate is considerably higher than that given for School A and the other schools, but considering the exclusive and disruptive nature of boys sheltered in Secure Units, and the accuracy of the reporting of violent incidents, we feel the discrepancy between the sets of figures to be acceptable.

21 attacks on staff	(27%)
58 attacks of boy on boy	(73%)

79 for 714 boy months
i.e. 0.11/boy month

SECTION D *Boys' backgrounds and violent behaviour*
A detailed analysis was undertaken of the relationships between boys' backgrounds and violent behaviour. Forty-one background characteristics noted for each boy in the population of the 17 approved schools studied in the general survey were related to two other features: an assessment classification as violent or aggressive

Table D (i) Violent behaviour and boys' backgrounds

	Assessed as being violent or aggressive	Recorded as being actively involved in a violent incident in the school
	(all ages) N=174 out of a population of 1119	(Intermediate and senior boys who have been in school for eight months or longer. N=435)
Intelligence Quotient	√ √	
Previous experience of residential care	√ √	
Troublesome behaviour at day school	√ √	√ √
Bad behaviour during assessment	√ √	
History of separation from father	√	
Time boy has been at school	√	
Educational attainments	√	
Poor relations with staff during assessment	√	√ √
Ambivalent relations with parents	√	
Crimes committed with other boys	√	√
Work record of father		√
Attention seeking personality trait		√

(Coefficients significant at √ √ (1%) √ (5%) level.)

and being *actively* involved in a violent incident at school. This latter group posed methodological problems as it was difficult to take into account the length of time the boy had been there. We therefore included boys who had been at school for eight months or over and so had some time in which to display his aggression. A further difficulty stems from the lack of any relationship at Junior levels between proportions of boys with violent tendencies and recorded levels in schools. While it does not logically follow that individual junior boys with aggressive tendencies will not be involved in violent incidents, to be safe we decided to include in this exercise only boys in intermediate and senior schools. If juniors had been included any pattern that held for older offenders might well have been neutralised by a counter-acting relationship among younger boys.

The table on page 156 lays out the correlations found significant and suggests the characteristics of violent boys. We would stress that such exercises are of limited value in that violence flares in a wide variety of social situations, a point explored in the opening of our paper. But the correlations do indicate those boys that have the greatest predisposition to violence, and with whom special care should be taken.

The following factors did *not* correlate with either a violent tendency or behaviour.

Distance between school and boy's home, Boy's age on entry, Personality traits of introversion, extraversion or neuroticism, Attendance at a previous approved school, Truancy at day-school, Relations with male and female staff at day-school, Family size, Position in family, Criminal parents or siblings, absconding from home, Step-parents in home, History of separation from mother, Rejecting relationships between boy and parents, Relations between parents, Parents absent or dead, Quality of home accommodation, Criminal, care or truancy reasons for committal, Relations with boys during assessment, Assessed as in need of psychiatric attention or training for independence, Member of a large peer group at home or crimes committed alone.

References
(1) Full details of this research have been published in MILLHAM S., BULLOCK R. and CHERRETT P. (1975). *After Grace – Teeth: A Comparative Study of the Experience of Boys in Approved Schools,* Human Context Books, London.
(2) In a mimeograph, Literature Survey on Aggression, prepared in 1970 by DR R. V. G. CLARKE and DR I. A. C. SINCLAIR of the Home Office Research Unit for the Working Party on the Study of Violence in Children's Residential Establishments, the authors write (p. 1), 'Three main theories of aggression can be distinguished, one focussing on innate drives (instincts), another on frustration and a third on social learning. These theories can be combined in various ways, and even within them there are disputes about the definition of aggression and what causes it . . . The various theories of aggression are so abstract that they are consistent with almost any fashionable method of handling delinquents.'

(3) The meanings that participants give to aggressive acts has been discussed by many writers concerned with social interaction. See, for example, BECKER H. S. (ed.) (1964), *The Other Side*, Free Press, New York: COHEN S. (ed.) (1971), *Images of Deviance*, Penguin, Harmondsworth: and TAYLOR I., WALTON P. and YOUNG J. (1973), *The New Criminology: For a social Theory of Deviance*, Routledge and Kegan Paul, London. For a social psychological viewpoint, see ARGYLE M. (1969), *Social Interaction*, Methuen, London.

(4) The consequences of the various processes by which crimes are reported to the authorities have been widely discussed by official bodies such as the Streatfield Report, Report of the Inter-departmental Committee on the Business of the Criminal Courts, *Cmd 1289*, HMSO, 1961 and by writers such as WALKER N. (1969), *Sentencing in a Rational Society*, Allen Lane, London: The Penguin Press, CARTER R. M. (1967) 'The pre-sentence report and decision making process', Journal of Research in Crime and Delinquency, *IV*, pp. 203–211 and CARTER R. M. and WILKINS L. T. (1967). 'Some factors in sentencing policy' Journal of Criminal Law, Criminology and Political Science, *LVIII*, pp. 503–514. There is also a useful review of this issue in HOOD R. G. and SPARKS R. F. (1970), *Key Issues in Criminology*, Weidenfeld and Nicolson, London.

(5) See, for example, TAYLOR I. R. (1971). 'Soccer consciousness and soccer hooliganism', in S. COHEN (ed.), *Images of Deviance*, Op. Cit., pp. 134–164.

(6) A historian colleague points out that in the biography of Lord Birkenhead there is an account of the destruction of a railway carriage by the travelling Oxford University rugby team which, it is said, included two future Lord Chancellors, a future Lord Appeal in Ordinary and a future canon of the Church of England.

(7) COHEN S. (1973). *Folk Devils and Moral Panic: The Creation of the Mods and Rockers*, Paladin, Granada Publishing Company, St Albans.

(8) For a discussion of this point, see COHEN S. (1971). 'Directions for research on adolescent group violence and vandalism', *British Journal of Criminology, XI*, pp. 319–340.

(9) For a discussion of these deprivations, see LAMBERT R. and MILLHAM S. (1968). *The Hothouse Society: an Exploration of Boarding School Life through the Boys' and Girls' own Writings*, Weidenfeld and Nicolson. London: and MILLHAM S. and BULLOCK R. (1975), *The Chance of a Lifetime? A survey of Boys' and Coeducational Boarding Schools in England and Wales*, Weidenfeld and Nicolson, London.

(10) For example, in a Home Office Circular No. 224/1964 dated 23 September 1964, the Special (Secure) Unit at Kingswood School, Bristol was described as '. . . designed for the treatment and training of Approved School boys . . . who have demonstrated by their persistent absconding or disruptive behaviour, either that they will not respond to training in an open Approved School or that their behaviour in such a school is having a seriously disruptive effect on the training of other boys in the school.'

(11) The problems of extracting research material from documents not prepared for the researcher are discussed fully in MILLHAM S., et al. *After Grace – Teeth*, Op. Cit.

(12) Numerous studies have demonstrated the tendency for a self-fulfilling prophecy to operate in institutions. See, for example, HARGREAVES D. (1967). *Social Relations in a Secondary School*, Routledge and Kegan Paul, London: LACEY C. (1970), *Hightown Grammar*, University Press, Manchester: and WERTHMAN C. (1963), 'Delinquency in schools: a test case for the legitimacy of authority', Berkeley Journal of Sociology, *VIII*, pp. 39–60.

(13) For a discussion of violence inherent in the structure of the wider society, see TAYLOR I., WALTON P. and YOUNG J. (eds.), (1975), *Critical Criminology*, Routledge and Kegan Paul, London.

(14) For a discussion of the relationships between crime and social class, see MCDONALD L. (1969), *Social Class and Delinquency*, Faber and Faber, London: BOX S. and FORD J. (1971), 'The facts don't fit: on the relationship between social class and criminal behaviour', *Sociological Review, XIX*, pp. 31–52 and the rejoinder by BYTHEWAY W. R. and MAY D. R., pp. 585–607.

(15) This definition is very similar to that of SKOLNIK (1969), *The Politics of Protest*, Simon and Shuster, New York: p. 4 and discussed by Cohen in 'Directions for research on adolescent group violence and vandalism', Op. Cit.

(16) See, CLARKE R. V. G. and MARTIN D. N. (1971). *Absconding from Approved Schools*, London: HMSO, MILLHAM S., et al., *After Grace – Teeth*, Op. Cit. and DUNLOP A. (1975), *The Approved School Experience*, London: HMSO.

(17) *Red Bank Special Unit, Statistics to 31.7.69*, Mimeograph, 1969.

(18) The significance of school F to this discussion stems from a tendency among adults to interpret everyday patterns of communication among backward boys as manifestations of violence.

(19) COHEN S. 'Directions for research on adolescent group violence and vandalism'. Op. Cit.

(20) See, for a discussion of this process, SMITH D. M. (1970). 'Adolescence: a study of stereotyping', *Sociological Review, XVIII*, pp. 197–211 and SCHEFF T. J. (1968), 'Typification in rehabilitation agencies', in RUBINGTON E. and WEINBERG M. (eds.), *Deviance: Interactionist Perspective*, Macmillan, London: pp. 120–124.

159

(21) See LEWIN K., LIPPIT R. and WHITE R. K. (1939). 'Patterns of aggressive behaviour in experimentally created social climates', *Journal of Social Psychology*, X, pp. 271–299; HARTUP W. W. and HIMENO Y. (1959), 'Social isolation, its interaction with adults in relation to aggression in pre-school children', *Journal of Abnormal and Social Psychology*, pp. 17–22 and BERKOWITZ, W. C. (1962), 'Consequences of different kinds of parental discipline' in HOFFMAN M. L. and L. W. (eds.) *Review of Child Development research*, Russell Sage Foundation, New York.

(22) CLARKE R. V. G. and MARTIN D. W. *Absconding from Approved Schools*, Op. Cit.

(23) See POLSKY H. (1962). *Cottage Six: The Social System of Delinquent Boys in Residential Treatment*, Wiley, New York.

(24) See LAMBERT R., MILLHAM S. and BULLOCK R. (1973). 'The Informal social system', in BROWN R. K. (ed.), *Knowledge Education and Cultural Change*: Papers in the Sociology of Education, Tavistock, London: FOLKARD M. S. 'Aggressive Behaviour in Mental Hospitals, Nethern Monograph No. 1 Nethern Hospital, Surrey; SCHWARTZ M. S. and SHOCKLEY E. L. (1956), *The Nurse and the Mental Patient*, New York: Russell Sage Foundation, and London Joint Four (1970) *Report on Discipline*.

(25) WEST D. and FARRINGTON D. (1973). *Who Becomes Delinquent?* Heinemann, London: STREET D., VINTER R. and PERROW C. (1966), *Organisations for Treatment*, Glencoe: Free Press, CLARKE R. V. G. and MARTIN D. N. *Absconding from Approved Schools*, Op. Cit. and DUNLOP A. *The Approved School Experience*, Op. Cit.

(26) ZIGLER E. and CHILD I. L. (1969). 'Socialization' in LINDZEY G. and ARONSON E. *The Handbook of Social Psychology*, Vol. 3, Addison Wesley.

(27) BECKER W. C. 'Consequences of different kinds of parental discipline', in HOFFMAN M. L. and L. W. (*Eds.*), *Review of Child Development Research*, Op. Cit., pp. 169–208 and LESSER G. S. (1952), *Maternal Attitudes and Practices and the Aggressive Behaviour of Children*, Unpublished Doctorial Dissertation, Yale University.

(28) LESSER G. S. *Maternal Attitudes and Practices and the Aggressive Behaviour of Children*, Op. Cit. and BANDURA A. and WALTERS R. H. (1959), *Adolescent Aggression*, Ronald, New York: and *Social Learning and Personality Development*, Op. Cit.

(29) BANDURA A. and WALTERS R. H. *Social Learning and Personality Development*, Op. Cit.

(30) Research undertaken at St Christopher's Community Home by CLARKE R. V. G. and SINCLAIR I. A. C. of the Home Office Research Unit and reported in their Literature Survey on Aggression, Op. Cit.

(31) MORRIS T. and P. (1963). *Pentonville: A Sociological Study of an English Prison*, Routledge and Kegan Paul, London.

(32) FARRINGTON D. and WEST D. (1971). 'A comparison between early delinquents and young aggressives', *British Journal of Criminology*, XI, pp. 341–359.

(33) For example, MCCLINTOCK F. and AVISON N. (1968). *Crime in England and Wales*, Heinemann, London: found that the proportions of first offenders among juveniles guilty of malicious damage, violent offences and property crimes were 83 per cent, 67 per cent and 57 per cent respectively.

(34) Stereotyping has been discussed by SMITH D. M. 'Adolescence: a study in stereotyping', Op. Cit., SCHEFF T. J. 'Typification in rehabilitation agencies', Op. Cit. and GILBERT G. M. (1951), 'Stereotype persistence and change among college students', *Journal of Abnormal and Social Psychology*, CLVI, pp. 245–254. Disquieting perspectives about the impressions given in biographical and assessment material have been raised by SHEPHERD J. W. and BAGLEY A. J. (1970), 'The effects of biographical information and order of presentation on the judgement of an aggressive action', *British Journal of Social and Clinical Psychology*, IX, pp. 177–179 and the factors affecting counter attack by GEEN R. G., RAKOSKY J. J. and PIGG R. (1972), 'Awareness of arousal and its relation to aggression', *British Journal of Social and Clinical Psychology*, XI, pp. 115–121.

(35) WOLFGANG M. E. and FERRACUTI F. (1967). *The Sub-culture of Violence*, Tavistock, London.

(36) FOLKARD M. S. *Aggressive Behaviour in Mental Hospitals*, Op. Cit.

(37) KOLVIN I., OUNSTED C. and LEE D. (1967). 'Aggression in adolescent delinquents', *British Journal of Criminology*, VIII, pp. 296–314: QUAY, H. C. (1964), 'Personality dimensions of delinquent males as inferred from a factor analysis of behaviour ratings', *Journal of Research in Crime and Delinquency*, I, and FIELD, E. (1967). *A Validation Study of Hewitt and Jenkins' Hypothesis*, HMSO, London.

(38) FIELD E. *A Validation Study of Hewitt and Jenkins' Hypothesis*, Op. Cit. and research undertaken by CLARKE R. V. G. and SINCLAIR I. A. C. reported in their *Literature Survey on Aggression*, Op. Cit.

(39) CLARKE R. V. G. and SINCLAIR I. A. C. *Literature Survey on Aggression*, Op. Cit., p. 7.

(40) Ibid, p. 8.

(41) GEEN R. G. (1968). 'The effects of frustration, attack and prior training in aggressiveness upon aggressive behaviour', *Journal of Personality and Social Psychology*, IX, pp. 316–321.

161

(42) BERKOWITZ L. (1962). 'Experimental investigation of hostility catharsis', *Journal of Consulting and Clinical Psychology, XXXV*, pp. 1–; MILGRAM S. (1963, 1964, 1965), 'Behaviour study of obedience', *Journal of Abnormal and Social Psychology, LXVIII*, pp. 371–378; 'Liberating effects of group pressure', *Journal of Personality and Social Psychology, I*, pp. 127–134 and 'Group pressure and action against a person', *Journal of Abnormal and Social Psychology, LXIX*, pp. 137–143.

(43) Those whose task it is to establish the exact dynamics of violent incidents, such as lawyers or administrators in the Criminal Injuries Compensation Board, comment that it is often difficult to decide who is the assailant and who the victim when all the circumstances are reviewed.

(44) Memorandum of the Crime Analysis Section of the Oakland Police Department, quoted with other examples in TOCH H. (1972). *Violent Men: An Inquiry into the Psychology of Violence*, Penguin, Harmondsworth: p. 72.

(45) FOLKARD M. S. *Aggressive Behaviour in Mental Hospitals*, Op. Cit.

(46) SCHACHTER S. and SINGER J. F. (1962). 'Cognitive social and physiological determinants of emotional state', *Psychological Review, LXIX*, pp. 379–399.

(47) BERKOWITZ L. and HOLMES P. C. (1959) (1960). 'The generalisation of hostility to disliked objects' and 'A further investigation of hostility generalisation to disliked objects', *Journal of Personality, XXVII*, pp. 565–577 and *XXVIII*, pp. 427–442.

(48) BERKOWITZ L. and GEEN R. G. 'Stimulus qualities of the target of aggression; a further study', Op. Cit.

(49) See, DOCKAR-DRYSDALE B. E. (1968) (1973). *Therapy in Child Care*, Longmans, London, and *Consultation in Child Care*, Longmans, London, 1973, and BALBERNIE R. (1974). 'Unintegration, integration and level of ego functioning as the determinants of cover therapy, of unit task and of placement', *Journal of the Association of Workers for Maladjusted Children, II*, pp. 6–46.

(50) Full details of the sociometric test can be found in the report. MILLHAM S., BULLOCK R. and CHERRETT P. (1972). *A Comparative Study of Eighteen Approved Schools which Explores their Stylistic Variety and the Commitment of boys and staff*, Dartington Social Research Unit.

(51) This has been fully explored in LAMBERT R. and MILLHAM S., *The Hothouse Society*, Op. Cit. and LAMBERT R., MILLHAM S. and BULLOCK R., *The Chance of a Lifetime?*, Op. Cit. See for other examples, TAYLOR L. and COHEN S. (1972) *Psychological Survival: The Experience of Long-Term Imprisonment*, Penguin, Harmondsworth, and GIALLOMBARDO R. (1966) *Society of Women*, Wiley, New York.

162

(52) MILLER W. B. (1958). 'Lower class cultures, a generating milieu of gang delinquency', *Journal of Social Issues, XIV*, pp. 5–19; DOWNES D. (1966) *The Delinquent Solution*, Routledge and Kegan Paul, London; WOLFGANG M. E. and FERRACUTI F., *The Sub-culture of Violence: Towards an Integrated Theory in Criminology*, Op. Cit. and DEMBO R. (1973) 'A measure of aggression among working-class youths', *British Journal of Criminology, XIII*, pp. 245–252.

(53 Middle-class residential settings have been discussed in LAMBERT R. *et al. The Hothouse Society* and *The Chance of a Lifetime?*

(54) See the review by David Holbrook of *The Hothouse Society*, Op. Cit. in Cambridge Review, 1968 and the Birmingham Post. 5.10.68. See also, REISS A. J. 'The social integration of queers and peers', in BECKER H. S. (ed.), *The Other Side*, Op. Cit. pp. 181–210 and the similar conclusions in HARRIS M. (1973) *The Dilly Boys: Male Prostitution on Piccadilly*, Croom Helm, London.

(55) See, DAVIS F., 'Deviance disavowal: the management of strained interaction by the visibly handicapped', in BECKER H. S. (ed.), *The Other Side*, Op. Cit., pp. 119–138; examples in LAMBERT R. *et al., The Hothouse Society*, Op. Cit. and GOFFMAN E. (1968) *Stigma*, Penguin, Harmondsworth.

(56) For a discussion of the staff world in residential schools, see MILHAM S. *et al., After Grace – Teeth*, Op. Cit. Chapter XI.

(57) See MILLHAM S., BULLOCK R. and CHERRETT P. (1971). 'Coeducation in approved schools', *Child in Care, XI*, pp. 18–28 and 20–32 in issues 3 and 4.

(58) See MILLER W. B., 'Lower class culture as a generating milieu of gang delinquency', Op. Cit. and REISS A. J., 'The social integration of peers and queers', Op. Cit.

(59) See, COHEN S. 'Folk Devils and Moral Panic, Op. Cit. Also, researches undertaken by students under our supervision at an open door centre in an English city confirm this.

(60) See: CLARKE E. (1966). *My Mother who Fathered Me*, Allen and Unwin, London: SMITH M. G. (1962). *West Indian Family Structure*, University of Washington Press, Seattle: FITZHERBERT K. (1967) *West Indian Children in London*, Bell. London: HOOD C. *et al.* (1970) *Children of West Indian Immigrants*, Institute of Race Relations, London: For more specific research details see: BAGLEY C. (1972) 'Deviant behaviour in English and West Indian school children', Research in Education, *VIII*, pp. 47–55; NICOL A. R. (1971) 'Psychiatric disorders in the children of Carribean immigrants', *Journal of Child Psychology and Psychiatry, XII*, pp. 273–287 and the series of articles by RUTTER M. *et al.* (1974) 'Children of West Indian immigrants', exploring deviance, psychiatric disorder, adjustment and home circumstances, beginning in the *Journal of Child Psychology and Psychiatry, XV*, pp. 241–262 and continuing into Vol. XVI.

(61) See the discussions of the machismo syndrome and Fromm's study of the character structure of Mexican peasants in TOCH H. 'Violent Men', Op. Cit. See also, GAYFORD J. J. (1975) 'Wife battering: a preliminary survey of a 100 cases', *British Medical Journal*, No. 5951, for an exploration of the relationship between early upbringing and adult violence.

(62) CLARKE R. V. G. and SINCLAIR I. A. C. *Literature Survey on Aggression*, Op. Cit. p. 3.

(63) Criticism of the educational and cultural deprivation these can be found in KEDDIE N. (ed.), (1973). *Tinker, Tailor*, Penguin: Harmondsworth. A review of the writings of Baratz, Labov and Friedman on this matter can be found in, Social Differentiation II, Unit 10 for Course E.282, *School and Society*: The Open University, Bletchley, 1972.

(64) Collected during our researches at a community home, 1975.

(65) POLSKY H., *Cottage Six*, Op. Cit.

(66) PATRICK J. (1973). *A Glasgow Gang Observed*, Eyre Methuen, London: and SUTTLES G. (1968). *The Social Order of the Slum*, University Press, Chicago.

(67) See, LAMBERT R. et al. 'The informal social system', Op. Cit.; CLARKE R. V. G. and MARTIN D. N., *Absconding from Approved Schools*, Op. Cit. and REYNOLDS D. (1975) 'When pupils and teachers refuse a truce, the secondary school and the generation of delinquency', in PEARSON G. and MUNGHAM G. (eds.) *British Working Class Youth Culture*: Routledge and Kegan Paul, London.

(68) The term anomie occurs in the writings of the French sociologist Durkheim whose work is discussed fully in LUKES S. (1973). *Emile Durkheim: His Life and Work*, Allen Lane, London.

(69) For evidence of the increasing difficulties presented by children coming into care, see HOGHUGI M. S. *What's in a Name? Some Consequences of the 1969 Children and Young Persons Act*, Aycliffe Studies of Problem Children.

(70) See MILLHAM S. et al. *After Grace – Teeth*, Op. Cit.

(71) See, MARSDEN D. and OWENS D. (1975). 'The Jekyll and Hyde marriages', *New Society*, XXXII, 8 May.

(72) See, STRODTBECK F. and SHORT J. F. (1964). 'Aleatory risks versus short run hedonism in explanations of gang action', *Social Problems, XII*, pp. 127–140, for an illustration of the logic in seemingly impulsive acts.

(73) GOLDMAN N. (1961). 'A socio-psychological study of school vandalism', *Crime and Delinquency*, pp. 221–230.

(74) See the foreward by BALBERNIE R. to MILLHAM S. et al. *After Grace – Teeth*, Op. Cit.

(75) See MILLHAM S. et al. *After Grace – Teeth*, Op. Cit.

(76) See, for example, ADVISORY COUNCIL ON CHILD CARE (1970). *Care and Treatment in a Planned Environment*, London: HMSO and COOPER J. (1970) 'The responsible society, *Community Schools* Gazette, LXIV, pp. 253–260.

(77) See, MILLHAM S. *et al, After Grace – Teeth,* Op. Cit. and
      HOGHUGI M. and HEPTINSTALL J. (1972) 'Recommittals, a continuing
      problem', *Community Schools Gazette, LXV,* pp. 553–562,
      597–604 and 687–694, *LXVI,* pp. 23–28 and 179–183.
(78) MILLHAM S. *et al. A Comparative Study of Eighteen Approved
      Schools which Compares their Stylistic Variety and the
      Commitment of Boys and Staff,* Op. Cit.
(79) MILLHAM S. *et al. After Grace – Teeth,* Op. Cit.

Chapter IX Violence in groups
John Harrington

The present decade has been described as the age of the group, with groups hailed as being of prime importance in influencing man's behaviour. Some protagonists have gone so far as to say that an individual has no proper existence when separated from the groups that form the matrix of his life; others have taken the opposite view that the group is largely an artefact with, essentially, a mythical significance in human behaviour, and they have come to the conclusion that the formation of the group adds nothing to that which was there in the life of the individual. This polarisation of views reflects a fear that by giving primacy to man as a group animal one will degrade the individual human personality and discard free will and personal responsibility.

In the light of such a divergence of opinion one must ask why it is necessary for any distinction to be made between individual and group violence? What, if any, are the differences between the violence of the individual and mob hooliganism or gang warfare? Does the mob induce aggression of a particular kind that would not normally occur in those individuals who form the violent crowd or does it merely release latent violence? These, and similar questions, raise problems of whether the group setting changes human conduct for better or worse or to a greater or lesser extent. It has to be admitted at the outset that we are some way from knowing the answers to such important questions but there is increasing evidence that groups, both large and small, have a profound effect on the manifestation of aggresive behaviour. We cannot speak authoritatively about causes, the most that can be done in our present state of knowledge is to throw some light on those factors or circumstances which are associated with the various manifestations of group violence, leaving questions of cause and effect to later researchers.

There are many definitions of groups, most of which focus on the group as a social unit in which a number of individuals have status and role relationships with one another and who share hopes, attitudes and feelings which influence to some extent the behaviour of individual members. While such definitions may cover aspects of small group aggression, they are wholly inadequate when considering violence in large groups such as crowds.

Classification of groups in terms of the numbers involved in the conflict is simple but not very satisfactory. There is violence between individuals, violence between small and large groups; violence between larger groups and violence within small and large groups. It is clear that to try and classify violence in terms of numbers involved is inadequate and largely meaningless because it says nothing of motivation, precipitating or facilitating factors, or the psychosocial context of violence. Nevertheless some descriptive categorisation of group violence is essential whatever the shortcomings.

Another classification suggests six principle types: 1) The organised juvenile or adult gang who use violence as part of a repertoire of antisocial behaviour. 2) The periodic association of a small number of persons who may become involved in a casual and irregular way with violence. 3) The violent mob which may have a core structure of around 50 persons with leaders but with twice that number of irregular member who may be called on in an emergency, e.g. the football hooligan mob. 4) The organised group who use violence in a calculated way to further criminal, political or religious aims, e.g. criminal syndicates or extremist political or sectarian groups. 5) The violent crowd consisting of a large number of individuals who share only a fleeting relationship with each other in a spontaneous eruption of violence. 6) The violent family, perhaps best exemplified by the spirited Irish family called Hooligan, who are alleged to have enlivened the drab monotony of life in Southwark towards the end of the 19th century by their acts of violent ruffianism.

This pragmatic typology does not cover all possible forms of group violence and it must be remembered that violence is not usually the main behavioural pattern of these groups and is seldom their main raison d'etre. Even the most violent groups spend only a very small part of their time actually engaged in violence, and violence is usually but one piece of a repertoire of antisocial behaviour.

Background factors
There is no lack of general theories which are popular simplistic explanations of group violence. These theories embrace such diverse phenomena as collective violence at football matches, violence on the University campus, or riotous behaviour at pop concerts. The permissive society, parental or educational shortcomings and anything from political subversion to the abolition of conscription are among many popular whipping boys. To discard such factors as irrelevant scapegoats would be wrong but they are by their nature so general and so all embracing that they are frequently used to explain other undesirable forms of human behaviour, so by explaining everything unpleasant they explain nothing of significance. They are probably best viewed as a kind

of backdrop against which many forms of deviant behaviour can be viewed.

Studies of group violence show few areas of agreement. This is due largely to the understandable tendency of research workers to remain loyal to their own disciplines. Thus the psychiatrist is likely to emphasis the psychodynamics of group aggression, while the sociologist will perhaps stress social interactionist and labelling theory, and the anthropologist may focus on the effects of culture on group behaviour. If one accepts the assumptions on which such theories are based they seem convincing enough in isolation but they do not go far enough. The problem is not so much as to which theory can be supported at the expense of the others but how can the most cogent theories be reconciled.

The answer lies in the theory of multifactorial aetiology. This enables one to account for acts of group violence at a variety of different levels or depths which complement rather than negate each other. One may need, for example, to take into account group psychopathology, the social matrix, the cultural and subcultural determinants and the political factors that are relevant to any violent group. The many factors that may determine an act of group violence do not exert independent effects but interact with each other so that the effects are summated or neutralized. A single cause, however potent, will not result in group violence but only when combined with others will it provide threshold stimulus to violent eruption. The main value of the concept of multifactorial aetiology is that it is a corrective to all forms of reductionism which may so easily lead us to examine the matter like a newsprint picture seen through a magnifying glass when we see, quite correctly, a series of black and grey dots but fail to see the whole picture in true perspective. Any comprehensive theory of group violence must attempt to integrate those theoretical approaches that can be seen to be operant.

Group dynamics

Studies of group dynamics have done much to further the understanding of the origins and transmission of violence within groups. A group can be viewed as a closed energy system which is in psychodynamic balance but whose equilibrium can be upset by forces within or without the group. If group cohesion and identity are to be maintained, aggression must be contained within those limits which the group can tolerate or discharge in some way outside the group. At most times the forces inhibiting aggression roughly balance those facilitating it; at other times group pressures build up in such a way that tension cannot be discharged in a way acceptable to the group; then violence may erupt purely as a means of relieving pressure, the violent act having a carthartic effect, purging the group of intolerable tension. The resulting abre-action of violence leads sometimes to unexpected and unprovoked attacks. This is followed by a period in which the group is drained of its aggressive energy; a kind of latent period during which the group will not be violent unless specially provoked.

There have been many relevant experimental studies of groups but perhaps the most significant for the present purpose are the studies of group conformity initiated by Ash.[1] These show that there is a strong tendency for most individuals to conform to the opinions and behaviour of the rest of the group and the degree of conform-ity is dependent on factors such as personality and group status. The group acts as if it were a dominant authority figure, exerting pressure on members to conform to a mode of group opinion and behaviour which they might reject as individuals. Naturally there are variations with some individuals who are 'self-directed' and who will dissent, but the majority will tend to be 'group directed' and will obey violent or non-violent group dictates. Groups that do not operate on the conformity dynamic are less likely to be violent by the simple mechanism of imitation. There are also experimental studies on group obedience which overlap with those on group conformity and which suggest that the factors of conformity and obedience together exert pressure on the individuals to make them follow the group consensus. A group consensus implies the sharing of responsibilty but through sharing the individual may feel less personally responsible for what happens unless perhaps he is in a leadership role.

The method by which interpersonal relationships are ordered in the group, the manner in which group decisions are reached, and how far these accord with democratic or authoritarian practice is of great importance to the problem of group violence. Kluckhohn[2] refers to three categories of group authority and decision making; the individual, the collateral and the lineal. Individualism is an arrangement in which each member of the group has the right, indeed the obligation, to state his opinion and the group majority decision is taken by vote. In the collateral arrangement effort is directed at reaching a group consensus by decision with which most members can feel comfortable. In the lineal arrangement decisions are made by the leader and then handed down through the chain of authority. The lineal arrangement strongly emphasizes the strict dependence on the hierarchy of authority; a system of dominance and submission, leader and follower, in which each member knows his place. The lineal system is that most easily structured to instigate or inhibit displays of aggression. Kluckhohn's systems do not take into account unstructured groups where there is no definite structure—a situation often to be found in groups which exhibit marked violence.

There is good evidence to suggest that a group may influence risk-taking behaviour and that by joining a group a person may be more readily persuaded to take a gamble. Violence may involve two risks, the first of combat injuries and the second of punishment if convicted of wrongdoing. The participation of others partially removes fear of punishment from wrongdoing. Even the simpleton knows that the larger the group the less likelihood of being caught and singled out for punishment. A forbidden impulse can be expressed with a good chance of avoiding payment of the price; an individual acting alone might well have to face conviction and punishment.

The group situation also enhances the willingness to take risks of injury and death. Youths who arm themselves with knives and other weapons and use them in violent encounters may have no real understanding of the risks involved and when serious injuries result they may express surprise because this is not an outcome they had expected. They are not punters in violence for they seldom weigh up the odds for and against a tragic outcome but awareness of the risks adds a psychological kick to the situation.

The group seems to contain within it a particular capacity to encourage adventurous or daredevil behaviour. The 'I dare you' situation is much enhanced in a group and it is hard to challenge a group consensus. This applies particularly to sexual and aggressive behaviour which is repressed but seeking an excuse to express itself. Gibbens[3] sums it up very neatly, 'Nothing weakens the conscience so quickly as seeing somebody do something that you would like to do, without suffering the pangs of conscience you would expect. If you did it, you say, perhaps I would find it equally easy. The group provides explanations which, with some justification, exonerate the individual member—that he did not mean it; that he did not really hurt anyone, that everyone is picking on us, that I did not do it for myself but only out of loyalty to the group'. The group provides an easy rationalization, a way of projecting one's own difficulties on to others, a convenient scapegoat to exonerate oneself from blame. Perhaps the commonest plea in a juvenile court is 'He is not really violent; it's just that he got led astray by a group of bad lads'. This sort of statement contains only half the truth because his participation was a willing one.

Guilt and shame are potent inhibitors of violence but membership of a group helps to dispel feelings of guilt and shame by the diffusion of personal responsibilities and a shared conscience. Collective shame is quite different from that which stems from the individual conscience. This psychological sharing within the group reassures those who keep their violent fantasies as deep, guilty secrets, but finding others who share their violent feelings reassures them and paves the way for more ready expression of violence within the group.

Psychological mechanisms

Psychological mechanisms of importance to group violence are not unique to groups because they also operate individually, the difference being that because of the conformity principle group mechanisms tend to influence the majority. Freud[4] pointed to the mechanism of identification as basic to the expression of group violence. Group members identify themselves with the leader and with one another through their common ties with the leader. There are important differences between individual identity and group identity. In a group situation there is a strong tendency for group identity to have primacy. Another important difference is to be found in the varied roles that a group imposes on its members. An aggressive group will have aggressive role expectations from its members and will mould group behaviour accordingly. Freud's observations on groups leave us in no doubt about the ability of a group to release powerful aggressive forces. He saw group rivalries (a substitute for sibling rivalries) and a power struggle with the leader (who represents the father) as important. He spoke about the psychological cement responsible for group ties and saw that fundamentally the group were tied together by something which was common and shared by all the membership. Group identification giving rise to empathy between members of the group, is an important mechanism in limiting the expression of aggression within the group itself which, if it were allowed to go unchecked, would destroy the group itself.

There is a tendency for aggression to be focused on a scapegoat who can be a member of the group or an object or person outside the group. Hostilities, rivalries and other emotions that arise within the group and which cannot find ready expression within it are displaced on to external objects, in particular other groups. This is the mechanism of displacement. Groups frequently displace their aggression because they are denied the opportunity or are afraid to express their hostility directly against the source of their frustration, e.g. football fans who cannot rage at the referee, with whose decisions they disagree, may displace their anger on the railway carriage on the way home. Groups also intensify conscious or

171

unconscious desires, conflicts and fantasies within group members which are acted out in destructive behaviour when they are away from the group. This accounts for a carry-over effect so that a member of an aggressive group may only display his violence when he has gone home to his family.

Observations upon therapeutic groups suggest that while the group may help with working through emotional conflict it may stimulate acting-out solutions to problems which may be aggressive. In the author's experience this is much more likely to happen in larger than in smaller groups but the total group climate is vital so that the presence of a few aggressive personalities may create an explosive situation which may be acted out within the group or against authority. Group analysts have suggested that unconscious forces are largely responsible for group violence though some special circumstances or trigger mechanisms may be needed for these deeper forces to be activated. Much group violence that may appear on the surface to be irrational and without motive becomes meaningful only if one takes into account unconscious conflicts. The blame is often laid at the door of the ubiquitous oedipus complex which leads to hostility towards father figures and other symbols of authority. These are linked with castration fears leading to compensatory aggression; violence being the outcome of a symbolic fear of being rendered impotent. Sexual motives, particularly unconscious fears of homosexuality leading to overcompensatory masculinity, may lead to violence towards other males who constitute a homosexual threat. Mechanisms like projective identification may account for youthful groups who indulge in 'queer bashing'. They fear in others what they subconsciously fear in themselves; the resulting anxiety is dispelled through retaliatory aggression.

Esteem and reputation are no less important to the group than they are to the individual. Violence is a ready way in which a group can bolster up its own self-image and gain the respect of significant figures for whom they have respect. A lack of personal esteem may be compensated for by an infamous public reputation. Denied any positive social identity, the group reacts by adopting the opposite, namely a negative identity which, if it fails to get public respect, is not denied their hostile attention. Albert Cohen[5] noted that youthful gangs are marked by 'an explicit and wholesale repudiation of middle-class standards and the adoption of their very antithesis'. He saw vandalism as largely a group expression of a gang's rejection of the norms of respect for property.

Although many violent groups may deny they care about their reputation in the eyes of outsiders, they are certainly very sensitive about it within the group. A reputation for violence is self-perpetuating and once a group has a reputation for violent behaviour it often becomes proud of that reputation and will seek opportunities to reinforce 'Rep.' by further violence. This mechanism certainly appears to operate among some groups of violent football fans and probably helps to perpetuate violence once a group has become so labelled.

Violence is also used defensively by a group to protect its self-image against real or imagined attacks. Groups of sensitive, self-insecure youths are very likely to respond with violence against those who denigrate them. Such groups are capable of developing sensitive ideas of reference and to feel they are being sneered at or having the 'mickey' taken out of them and to misinterpret chance remarks or gestures. Those who handle groups of youths should be aware of their need to demonstrate their worth through toughness and aggression. They often have a need to deny their inferior status by non-compliance with the dictates of authority.

Adler[6] saw violence as an unsuccessful attempt to compensate for feelings of weakness or inadequacy combined in an inferiority complex. It is clear that youths who harbour feelings of inadequacy and failure of which they may be unaware tend to resolve the problem of their lack of self-esteem by joining a group of like-minded youths who may seek violent solutions. The need of such groups to prove themselves of some consequence in society is such that they may jeolousy guard their reputation for toughness. This may be expressed in graffiti like 'Hull Boot Boys Rule—OK?'.

Group violence can sometimes result when a group feels itself to be helpless and weak. Any group which finds itself cornered and in a situation from which they can see no escape, will either submit or react violently. Group ineptitude and incompetence when exposed may result in an explosive reaction. Groups are similar to individuals in that violence may sometimes be the result of frustration. Groups which are thwarted by finding things are not going the way they want or which are disappointed in their expectations may vent their frustrations in violence. In my own studies of football hooliganism this appeared to be an important factor in a group of fans whose team was being or had been defeated.

Boredom is a factor of importance within the group. Groups of small boys or older youths easily get into violence and vandalism during holiday periods when their members are largely unoccupied and when they roam the streets of our cities in small packs without specific aim or purpose. The flight from nothingness which they see as an inevitable part of their drab, monotonous lives often ends in an act of group vandalism. Violence against property or person is exciting, it arouses feelings that destroy, for the moment, the dreariness of boredom.

While group violence may result from a real threat of attack it can also be the result of imagined threat. Bettelheim[7] has pointed to the paranoid character of some groups and their leaders. Insecure groups often adopt the paranoid position before violence and defend themselves at a psychological level by mechanisms such as projection and projective identification; here others are blamed for their own violent behaviour. Violence is often rationalized as being justifiable and necessary. 'We could see they were going to get us so we got them first'; attack being considered the best form of defence. Groups who try to avoid anxiety and guilt feelings by blaming others put themselves in a position where they can justify an attack.

Sadistic violence is rarely seen in groups but there are examples of pleasurable violence towards the weak and defenceless individual by a group. Unable to handle their own fears of being attacked, such groups like to inspire terror in others and even if the victims beg for mercy, violence may be remorseless. Such bullying groups are generally inhibited by threats of retaliation but react violently to other groups who show no will to stand up to them and defend themselves.

Some groups deliberately use violence, or the threat of violence, to manipulate others to do something they want and here violent intimidation may be used to exploit others and the threat of violence used to force others to submit to their desires. In like manner groups associated with organised crime and political extremist groups, use cold-blooded instrumental violence to achieve their objectives. Hatred and violence are relatively easy to indoctrinate in a group setting and this is often exploited by political and religious sects. Evangelical fervours can convert a large group to new religious beliefs or mob violence.

Identity and manhood
One well-established fact about group violence is its tendency, admittedly shared with other forms of violence and delinquency, to be associated with youth, the male sex and a working-class background. Adolescent youths are well known for their liking for group activities of all sorts so it is not surprising that they are also violent in groups. The problem is to identify any forms of violence that are group specific or significantly influenced by the group context.

One reason why youths tend to be violent in groups is that it is only in the group context that a younger person can prove himself to his peers, and through them, himself. Alone it is impossible to show himself as cool and courageous but placed in a group he has the opportunity to prove his ability to be both daring and violent. Group violence must also be seen in the context of the adolescent search for identity. The working-class boy who has not succeeded at school and who finds himself in an unskilled or semi-skilled job becomes overwhelmed by his insignificance. Unable to establish himself individually he finds that membership of a violent group gives him a feeling of importance because violence cannot be ignored and is certain to attract attention.

Erikson[8] has stressed the identity crisis through which all adolescents must pass before reaching manhood; a crisis which may or may not be successfully resolved. In a similar vein anthropologists have pointed to the frequent occurrence of physically testing ceremonies through which young males are introduced to adult male status in primitive tribes. These ceremonies are usually carried out in groups and some observers have been tempted to compare group violence amongst youths in Western Society with these initiation rites. Group violence may be seen as an ineffectual and clumsy attempt to create their their own rites of passage to manhood into which they have not been accepted. It is quite possible that our society does not make adequate preparation for the introduction of our teenagers to adult life but it is hard to view some forms of group violence as initiation ceremonies performed spontaneously by adolescents to prove their manhood. To equate the graduation ceremony of a university student with ritualised violence on the football terraces is stretching our credulity. Nevertheless groups of working-class boys who fail in the examination system are denied the satisfaction of certificates of competence by society and must look for recognition elsewhere.

Social determinants

Group violence is never an isolated phenomenon independent of its social context. There are predictable social reactions to collective violence but how far social forces are responsible for its creation is not a subject for quick generalizations. It is clear that social conflict and the deliberate use of group violence for political aims remains important. George Sorel[9] saw group violence as socially valuable and thought people only fit to govern if they understood how to use violence properly. The intelligent use of group violence separates the elite from the corrupt and decadent bourgeoisie. Hitler and Mussolini subscribed to such a philosophy and used group violence to implement it. Group violence for political manipulation remains a reality today. Group violence is deeply embedded in political institutions and cannot be simply explained away in terms of group dynamics, as it has roots in our socio-economic systems. Group violence can sometimes be seen as a form of political statement by groups who have no obvious political affiliations. Are juvenile vandals saying in a confused sort of way, that what they are really after is more space and recreational facilities? (See Geoff Pearson, Chapter X.)

Studies of the interaction between society and violent groups has led to studies of the social determinants of group violence in which society emerges as the aggressor rather than the group. By asking the question 'Who are the victims and who are the victimisers?', supporters of social interactionist theories point to an important area of dynamic interaction between society and the violent group. Unfortunately, their case is generally overstated for political reasons and few would regard the violent group as an innocent victim of a malevolent society. No political system is free of group violence and in view of the natural biological inequalities of man it is hard to conceive of any utopian society that is not periodically polarized into minority and majority groups who use group violence against each other.

Amplification of group violence

The mass media have come in for much criticism for causing group violence, by stimulating the appetite for violence, glorifying violent displays, and making violence a commonplace occurrence that evokes no revulsion. While much of the experimental evidence on the portrayal of violence on television is equivocal, the influence of the media on group violence is more likely to be one of amplification rather than causal. The contagious effects of witnessing mob violence remains conjectural but the attention given by the media to certain forms of group violence appears to enhance the perpetration of it and amplify it. (See Stuart Hall, Chap. X1.)

Labelling theorists argue that violence may be amplified and perpetuated by first defining the form of group violence and then labelling it or the perpetrators of it as special, for example, 'Hells Angels, Mods and Rockers'. Wilkins[10] points out that once a new form of violence has been identified and labelled it is stereotyped and thereafter tends to increase. Likewise Cohen[11] referring to violence between mods and rockers says that once labelled the violence tends to be amplified by the mass media who distort the problem. My own researches[12] support the idea that the mass media focus the attention of the public in a spurious way by giving disproportionate attention to certain forms of group violence. Football hooligans have been hounded by the Press, made infamous by television and given attention far in excess of the seriousness of the crimes they commit. There is little doubt that they have, to an extent, enjoyed the special attention they have been given; it has enhanced their status, given them a social importance they long for. They know they make news and this knowledge increases their vanity and prestige or so they believe. One can easily see how the continuation of their violence is fed by publicity. It brings the group conflict sharply into public focus so that the authorities and the police feel obliged to give it special attention and may abandon the discretion they might have otherwise shown in similar circumstances. For them to turn a blind eye is impossible when the public gaze is focused upon those responsible for law and order.

Football fans certainly feel discriminated against. As one put it to me 'We were treated like a lot of criminals but we had done nothing'. This is the substance of remarks heard by the author on several occasions. The crucial importance of the reaction of those responsible for controlling violence, and factors like the interaction of the group and the police has been stressed by many observers. This aspect tends to be a rather neglected topic largely because of its delicate nature and the inference that the agencies of social control may have played a significant part in bringing about what they had sought to prevent.

Cohen has pointed to the spuriousness of the public reaction to some forms of group violence. Other forms of violence, notably violence on the roads, has attracted less avid attention and its economic consequences and costs in terms of human life and misery has been given fewer column inches in the Press. Should you injure somebody with a half-filled beer can on the football terraces you will attract far more attention by the media than if you mow him down in your motor car on the way home. This selective attention is not a direct result of bad or biased journalism but reflects a fundamental psychological need of one group to focus its hostility on to another group. The greater the distance of that group from one's own group the better, and what better than a group of young, readily identifiable troublemakers who, from time immemorial, have formed a ready focus for the hostility of their self-styled elders and betters. The battle of the generations is largely a myth but has some substance where group violence is concerned. Polarization is more natural than unification where groups are involved.

Attitudes to group violence

Attitudes to group and individual violence show demonstrable differences based on well-entrenched social stereotypes. Group violence is seen at a lower social level than individual violence, the mob is viewed as more bestial, the gang more inhuman and cowardly, the hooligan group more wanton and disreputable than the miscreant individual who tends to be accorded more sympathy whatever his motives for violence. The reasons for such different attitudes are not difficult to find. It is much simpler to identify oneself with an individual, even a homicidal one, because the potentiality for murder lies within everybody. Even acts of horrible sadism committed by individuals may be rationalized on the grounds that they must have been the acts of madmen. Individual motivation is always easier to comprehend than the aims of groups which are usually misunderstood. Affrays caused by political groups are seldom accepted for what they are; altruistic motives are dismissed and protesting groups are likely to be regarded as no better than a bunch of yobs and hooligans. Likewise, the attitudes of one group towards the violence of another group is a subject of much distortion. This applies particularly to acts of group violence committed by youths. Here the judgment made by middle-aged, middle-class groups will certainly be more harshly critical than those made by peer groups. Social class differences are evident in attitudes so that acts of group violence committed by unskilled and semi-skilled workers tend to be regarded by those of higher social status in a negatively biased way. Group violence is a sure way of polarizing attitudes between groups and once entrenched these attitudes are very difficult to change. This situation is clearly seen in Northern Ireland.

Attitudes to group violence are also influenced by individual personality factors. At one end of the scale there are the authoritarian personality types who are tough minded, particularly on the topic of group violence. They are the supporters of harsher punishment to deter the gang and the liberal use of force and instrumental violence to control the mob. To them the use of firearms against the mob may be justified on the grounds that a greater danger may thereby be averted. By contrast the tender minded call for a greater understanding of the causes of group violence and make, what seems to their tough-minded opponents to be, naive suggestions that prevention is better than retributive punishments. They tend to see the solution of the problem in radical social changes.

Studies of collective behaviour have amply demonstrated the tendency of some forms of group behaviour to show a rapid rise in popularity followed by a decline. Fads and crazes can reach near epidemic proportions but so long as fads are harmless they are tolerated. Group violence is not a craze as it never dies away completely in the way fads do but it is certainly subject to fashions which influence its frequency and patterns. Young people are particularly attracted to groups which show new styles of aggressive behaviour and fashions in dress that defy established practice (e.g. teddy boys, mods and rockers, skinheads). While violence and destruction may be important themes for such groups it is clear that many individuals who join such groups are not of the delinquent type in the accepted sense and have no intention of involving themselves in anything beyond a spot of excitement and collective brawling. Styles of group violence may be influenced by fashionable cults, e.g. the Eastern arts of Karate and Kung Fu have influenced the pattern of group violence amongst football fans.

Cultural determinants of group violence

Small groups have a powerful influence in transmitting social attitudes and moral and ethical values but they also acts as socio-cultural transmitters of violence and delinquency. Studies of group violence in primitive tribes by social anthropologists have shown significant tribal differences. These studies suggest that violence or non-violence appear as cultural traditions with a long history of transmissions from one generation to another. Group violence as a phenonmenon of primitive tribes is often quite wrongly attributed to the lack of civilization and higher culture. Many primitive cultures are far less violent than advanced industrial civilizations. Nevertheless the idea that new forms of tribalism are re-emerging in developed countries and are responsible for some patterns of group violence is worthy of discussion.

Group violence, which appears at least in part to be culturally transmitted, has been traditionally linked with places like Sicily with its Mafia and Chicago with its gangsterism. It has been said that gang violence in Glasgow is like haggis to the Scotsman and similarities have been drawn between the violent gangs of New York and the American's love for deep-baked apple pie. These analogies are clearly false for group violence is not a special appetite and it ignores the tendency for many large cities to have their own traditions of group violence which may span many generations and where socio-cultural transmission must be partly responsible.

Modern man dislikes the image of himself as mass man, as being part of a mass culture of ever-growing dimensions. Group violence is a regular feature of over-crowded urban man. The ego does not take kindly to an identity akin to a grain of sand in the vast industrial desert being swept around by forces quite outside the individual's control. There are understandable human needs to belong to a group which is small enough to have clearly defined points of reference, a group the aims of which can be easily comprehended and which provides a matrix giving the opportunity for group loyalty and identity. The working-class boy may find his group identity as a football fan, the businessman as a member of a club, both group and club provide some solution to the anomie created by a faceless industrial society. The football fan group establishes tribal membership by adopting certain distinguishing features of dress and behaviour, e.g. favours, scarves, bovver boots, etc., but their style of dress and behaviour is no less distinctive than the bowler hat, rolled umbrella and tie of the West End clubman in London. Nevertheless observations of the football fan waving his bright scarf and responding to rhythmic chanting with ritualized hand-clapping behaviour bears a striking similarity to tribal dances which are a substitute for, or a prelude to, tribal warfare. Jung might have suggested that the groups were seeking expression of a tribal archetype which had been denied them in the mass culture of modern society.

Small groups

There is virtually no dissent about the vital importance of the family in the patterning of behaviour, but it tends to be forgotten that the family is a primary group in most societies and that family dynamics have much in common with group dynamics. There are special forms of family violence recently popularized under the rubric of wife, baby and granny 'battering'. It must be remembered, too, that murder is most commonly a family affair. What is important in the present context is the relationship of family violence to other forms of group violence. In much the same way as the concept of the 'problem family' has been of value, so the concept of the 'violent family' deserves consideration. There is understandably no clear cut off point between violent and non-violent families but it is possible to identify families where violence is more than an occasional and unexpected visitor. Father is regularly violent to his wife often under the influence of drink. The children are disciplined by capricious and often brutal punishments. Family disputes are never settled by verbal arguments but by fists, and similar solutions may be used in dealing with neighbourhood conflicts. The family is here both the cradle of, and a school for, violence and a place where physical aggression is taught, imitated and becomes accepted behaviour. The transfer of violent and non-violent behaviour from the primary family group to other groups is of fundamental importance with the family acting as the facilitator or inhibitor of aggression.

180

Gangs

Any teacher of small boys will recognise a natural tendency for the formation of rival groups or gangs which indulge in fighting. While these, at best, are harmless and part of normal development, at worst they become the violent gangs of older youths who cause considerable problems for the authorities in large cities. Such gangs have been carefully studied in the United States, notably in New York by Yablonsky[13] and Thrasher[14] in Chicago, but observations in Glasgow, London and Birmingham underline many common features. A notable feature of these observations has been the linking of small group violence with under-privileged and alienated youths. Here the sociological concept of relative deprivation and status frustration are important in understanding behaviour including violence.

A tendency to distort the truth about gangs through mythology and folk-lore has been stressed by Downes.[15] Popular perceptions have been influenced by musicals like West Side Story; these and the mass media have helped to create an exaggerated folk-lore about groups of youths who may style themselves as Hells Angels or Skinheads and who are viewed fearfully by the public as spending a major part of their waking life in violent activities. Miller and his associates[16] showed that violence and vandalism was not the dominant activity of city gangs. Twenty-one gangs with some 700 members and a reputation for toughness only used violence in 17 per cent of their activities. In further observations he showed that only 17 per cent of aggressive acts by gangs consisted of physical attacks on persons or property and their aggression consisted mainly of verbal abuse. Such observations must, nevertheless, be put in perspective and even if, for example, physical violence only accounted for less than one per cent of a gang's activity it would still be significant if that violence resulted in grievous bodily harm or homicide. This does seem to happen in some gangs whose main activities are largely of nuisance value only but who suddenly come into the limelight by committing some serious act of violence.

For present purposes small groups can be divided roughly into two types, aggressive goal-orientated groups and the less aggressive socially oriented groups. The former type of group tends to be unconcerned about relationships with other groups, the latter is interested in creating good friendly relationships with other groups and is more sensitive to social and other pressures. There are also alienated groups who are poorly accepted by other persons and society in general. They develop a negative identity which is the very antithesis of the positive one of other youth groups and

181

which they proudly uphold. These groups tend to be egocentric in their behaviour, selfish in their orientation and show little interest in other groups. Such groups are likely to be socially rejected and behave violently, indulging in stupid, rowdy behaviour, causing trouble to others, resisting all adult authority and rejecting the values of other peers. These groups may try to boost their own self-esteem by trying to impress other groups or denigrating them.

One must ask the question as to how often such groups are brought together largely by the magnetic attraction of violence. Those who have studied the violent gang have sometimes suggested that the violence may be the main *raison d'être* for some youthful groups. The work of Matza[17] and Miller[18] have shown how important violence is in the status enjoyed by various members of the group and that these groups have their own value systems which emphasize strength, fighting ability, toughness, masculinity and the desire for risk. Possession by the individual of such violent potential ensures group acceptance and prestige and the absence of such qualities may lead to rejection.

The need for approval and recognition by peer groups is important. Displays of violence to prove toughness may be demanded as part of the group initiation rites or to determine group status. Failure to live up to boasts or exaggerated bragging damages status and reputation. Those who are weaklings and physically inadequate may only find group acceptance by their willingness to become scapegoats for violence. Nevertheless one sometimes finds that the most dangerous acts of violence are committed by those who are low down in the dominant scale and whose need to prove themselves is so desparate that they resort to weapons like knives rather than using their fists and boots. Non-violence is seen as weakness and may provoke an attack on a gang member who is afraid of participation.

Often violent gangs have well-marked territories which they regard as their own and any encroachment on this territory by another gang is a common reason for inter-group violence. Such gangs will also attack other young males if they are unable to prove they come from the right territory. Youths in these groups are noted for their insecurity, sensitivity and readiness to take affront. Any derogatory or disparaging remark is certain to provoke a violent reaction and even the most innocuous comment may be misinterpreted. Some psychological studies of these youths have revealed sexual conflicts and the need to demonstrate their masculinity as well as to prove their courage. (See Chap. 8.) Their apparent cool indifference to others is in contrast to the loyalties that they are said to show towards each other. They often appear to enjoy being outcasts and they enjoy the attention that violence attracts, attention boosting their self-esteem. Such a gang is often characterized by its state of flux. It lacks the true structure of a more organised group, having neither a definite number of members nor definite membership roles, nor a consensus of expected norms nor, indeed, a leader of any permanence who supplies directives for action.

Yablonsky's picture of the violence-dominated gang who resort to brutality for its own sake in order to prove themselves alive and to give their existence some validity may be true for New York but is doubtfully applicable to other situations. Peter Scott[19] in a careful study of delinquent groups and gangs in London classified them into three categories; adolescent street groups, structured gangs and loosely structured groups which might be fleeting and casual or made up of neighbours and friends. He found few proper gang members but these came from very disturbed homes and showed gross anti-social character defects. His findings do not conform with Thrasher's picture of a gang of individuals taking pride in and giving loyalty to the gang's antisocial values. This casts doubts on the social potential of the gang, a potential which has been exaggerated by some workers who feel that the gang should be retained intact and suggest all that is required is to divert misdirected energies and loyalties into more creative ones. Bettelheim makes another relevant point, namely that violence is sometimes a solution to a problem to which the group can see no alternative solution; they feel their aspirations can only be reached through violence.

Leadership and group status

Many observers have noted the fact that under conditions of charismatic leadership a group may become, as it were, hypnotised by a powerful and superior leader surrendering their individuality to him. Members, under the circumstances, begin to show marked dependency and submission; the more leader centred the group becomes the more aggressive its potential and the more prone it becomes to mechanisms like senseless imitation of violent behaviour. Many violent groups are, however, without powerful leadership.

While some youthful gangs may have a well-formed structure, many groups of youths who exhibit violent behaviour have a fluid structure with frequent changes in dominance and leadership. Some youthful mobs who are involved in violence have no discernable leadership, no real structure and no group ties or commitments. Despite this, some may stand out from the rest by their willingness to act as spokesman or by reason of their more reckless behaviour but they are in no sense leaders. They often form part of an active minority who are at the centre of events, actively participating and encouraging violence. The more passive majority tend to remain on the fringe expressing approval or ambivalence but are usually passively silent.

As previously mentioned, violence is one of the ways of establishing status in the group and while it is not always the toughest fighter who emerges as the group leader, those who adopt a leadership role in aggressive groups must prove themselves tough and courageous and be able to demonstrate a wide repertoire of violent behaviour. There is some evidence that leaders of violent gangs are more emotionally disturbed and are more likely to express their aggressive needs through the gang than are other members.

Inter-group violence

If we consider groups as human beings who interact over a period of time, the action is seldom neutral or unbiased. Such interactions may take the form of reciprocal friendship and co-operation but much more frequently inter-group relationships involve ambivalence, rivalry, mistrust, suspicion and sometimes frank hatred and aggression. These inter-group feelings distort the thinking each group has about each other.

Group violence can often be understood as a group interactionist problem so that happenings between groups have as much significance as occurrences within them. Aggression between groups has quite a different dimension from aggression between members of groups. Transactional analysis of what is happening between groups must take account of history and of current events. One of the products of establishing a separate group identity is the separation of 'them' (out group) and 'us' (in group). The 'us' delineates a number of values which have to be upheld, defended and cherished and if deviated from within or offended from without such deviations and offences are reacted to with corrective, defensive and sometimes violent measures.

Attributes which are accepted as part of group norms are seen as desirable qualities but these are seldom attributed to 'out' groups who are generally seen as possessors of less favourable traits. This attribution of favourable or unfavourable traits is not based on reality but depends on the relationship between the groups. The qualities attributed to the 'out' group are generally quite independent of obvious similarity and shared values between groups. Hence,

184

two groups, say of football fans, will seem very similar to the outside observer but will be seen by each other to be very different.

The relationship between groups and the nature of their encounters may be as much controlled by past events as by current happenings. Whenever there is a past history of inter-group tensions, these continue to play a significant part in determining later inter-group relationships long after the respective groups were in conflict. As Sherif[20] points out, the heavy hand of the past may be more difficult to bury than any current conflicts. Groups have elephantine memories about each other.

If the interests and aims of groups are integrated and harmonious the 'out' group will be pictured in a positive or favourable light by the 'in' group. If, on the other hand, the activities and goals of the interacting groups clash then the 'out' group is invariably seen in a negative or derogatory way. Each group makes the assumption that the other is in its way, interfering with its goals and vital interests. Any condition in which the two groups are competing for an objective which can only be attained by the failure or frustration of the other group is likely to give rise to violent acts.

Negative attitudes to other groups may easily lead from friendly co-operation to violence and aggression. Inter-group conflict tends to increase group solidarity and morale. Attitudes of co-operation and togetherness within the group are seldom displayed to other groups. Another important observation in inter-group dynamics is a tendency to over estimate the performance of one's own group and to under estimate the performance of the other group. These sentiments are typified in graffiti like 'Rangers—the greatest', 'Celtic—crap'.

Transitional mobs

The word mob has several connotations but it is appropriately applied to a group of moderate proportions somewhere between the size of a gang and a crowd and where the rules of crowd psychology are far less applicable. This type of group can be exemplified by the 'Quinton Mob' of which the author has some personal experience.

Quinton is a suburb of Birmingham with few facilities for its young inhabitants. The amenities available elsewhere are not readily accessible because of distance. The Quinton mob developed out of the coalescence of a number of smaller schoolboy gangs which united to defend their territory from the neighbouring mobs of Harborne and Smethwick. When this mob was studied it was found to consist of an inner core of about fifty members but the leaders estimated that they could, in an emergency, call on the support of at least 150 youths. There was an outer fringe of female members but comparing the mob size with the available young population it was clear that it remained an interest of only a minority in the area. A feature of the mob was the great pride it took in Quinton and how much better and greater the mob thought it to be compared with the neighbouring areas of Harborne and Smethwick with their rival mobs.

The Quinton mob seemed to be very much a homosexual culture of youths needing to show they were tough, aggressive and unafraid. They needed to demonstrate their masculinity not in front of girls but in front of each other and they seemed to be trying to prove that they were real men. When faced with girls they appeared shy, insecure and tried to overcome this by referring to the opposite sex as possessions rather than individuals. A trained female youth worker who tried to get close to the group was only partially successful, they accepted her only as long as she tried to bolster up their self-esteem and 'rep' but they were quick to turn their aggression on her when they felt that she had been on the side or authority or the police.

Mass violence
There is little dispute about the fact that people often behave in an entirely different way in a crowd from the way they would behave in other circumstances. What is disputed is the explanations that are given to account for what is commonly called crowd psychology. Violence in large groups, sometimes called mob violence, shares common features with small group violence but crowd psychology and group psychology are not identical. Mass violence may include phenomena such as race riots, lynch mobs, institutional riots and violent demonstrations to further political or other aims. It also embraces such phenomena as war, massacres and genocide, but these are not discussed here.

Although crowds and mobs are often unstructured, diffuse collectives, such large groups do at times contain three components which are of greater importance for violence. These are the leader, an active minority and a passive majority. The role of the leader in mass violence is much debated and is either seen as essential and all important or merely a personification of the emotional drives of the crowd. There is, in fact, a complex interaction between the crowd and its leadership, both being susceptible to each other's influence. Nevertheless leadership, however skilful will have difficulty in creating violence in a crowd that is not hungry for aggressive expression through prolonged frustration. The presence of a rabble element always inclines a crowd towards violence.

Crowd violence is best understood by considering the properties that characterize mobs. Le Bon[21] in his now classical treatise was one of the first to emphasize the mental unity of the crowd. Whatever the difference in the individuals who comprise the mob, however like or unlike their background, their jobs, their characters, etc., the fact that they have been transformed into a crowd makes them possessors of a type of collective mind. This leads to mental homogeneity and conformity of thought, belief, action and feeling. This mental unity has been explained through mechanisms like suggestion, imitation and emotional contagion. The concept of a collective conscious or group mind has come in for substantial criticism, particularly by Allport.[22] Jung was much impressed by the French concept of 'Contagion Mentale' and how any process of an emotional kind arouses a similar process in others. His concept of the collective unconscious and its archetypes have relevance for collective violence. Man's archaic past is buried in the collective unconscious and may reveal itself when exposed to appropriate crowd stimulus.

A heightened state of suggestibility is important in any explanation of mass hysteria and may involve states of mild mass hypnosis which, nevertheless, only affects a proportion of a crowd, namely the susceptible individuals. Increased suggestibility also plays an important part in imitative behaviour so frequently seen in violent crowds. There is an element of contagion so that violence can spread from a single focus in a crowd, like a fire. The witnessing of violent displays may serve as a stimulus for its spread. Homogeneity is also aided by the mechanism of temporary identification. Crowd members are bonded together by patterns of mutual identification but the identification is an ambivalent one and breaks down when fighting within the crowd develops.

In most mob situations there is a considerable potentiation of emotion in the crowd leading to a state of emotional arousal so that what might have been mild anger becomes a state of ferocity and more tender feelings like pity and compassion are inhibited. The heightened emotions of the crowd are well known to sporting spectators whose pleasure is increased by feelings that can alternate between ecstasy and extreme rage.

Although collective behaviour in crowds is usually sensible and inconspicuous, the potential stupidity, irrationality and childlike behaviour of the crowd has been noted by many observers. Under the influence of the crowd there may be a lowering of rational thought and cognitive processes that would normally inhibit aggression are discarded. In a mob the laws of logic are at a discount, abstract thought vanishes and concrete primitive thinking predominates. Omnipotent thinking easily erupts, doubts are discarded and messianic beliefs easily propagated. In such situations a mob is itself dehumanized but at the same time dehumanizes others so that remorseless violence can occur without shame or guilt feelings.

The conscience is temporarily in abeyance and forces that normally inhibit repressed violent tendencies are removed. There is a loss of personal responsibility through the anonymity of the crowd. Individual identity is lost and merged with the universe of the crowd, a fusion that leads to a feeling of omnipotence.

Many forms of violent rioting do not erupt spontaneously but are dependent on background conditions that make mass violence likely. Studies of race riots suggest that there is generally a subgroup which feels excluded from an élitist society and which struggles to improve its position against authority which resists change and which prevents the entry of the sub-group into first-class citizenship.

Sub-group members feel unfairly treated by the police and other groups who defame them and deny them social advancement. Mob violence then erupts under a variety of trigger mechanisms, usually a single and sometimes trivial incident which is exaggerated by rumour and is used by small groups of agitators to trigger mob violence.

Trigger mechanisms
Although many events, particularly rumours, may trigger off violence in a predisposed mob, the importance of verbal symbols in triggering off group violence has not received the attention it deserves. Archetypal forms of crowd violence, which are latent, appear only to need the right symbolic trigger for their release. In a study of football chants Wood[23] found there was evidence that many of these gave more or less blatant incitement to violence. Chanting increases the possibility of violence between opposing fan groups already adopting potentially hostile postures towards one another. When they chant at each other the possibility of physical violence increases and this can often be seen to follow chanting. The use of chanting to taunt the opposing fan group may be subtle or more direct. Reference may be made to previous defeats, their star players may be abused or there may be more direct threats. The singing of chants reduces fear by enhancing group solidarity and instilling group courage. The chants mirror the violence as well as provoking it. Some examples of such chants give it such perspective. Football crowd 'We want a riot, clap, clap, clap, clap,

clap'. 'I-O, I-O and off to the match we'll go, with a bottle and a brick and a walking stick I-O, I-O'; 'If you want a fight, so de we' (repeated). 'Attack! Attack! Attack! Attack! Attack! 'We're going to wreck the joint (repeat). Cheer Leader: 'What are United' Response: 'Shit'. Cheer Leader: 'What shit?' Response: 'United'. 'Do be, Do be, Do be, Do be, Do, who the F-ing hell are you? F-U, F-U-C, etc, Fuck Off.' And in a violent racist spirit with no connection with football 'They'll be running round Smethwick with the wogs (repeated), Wigger Wogger, Wigger Wogger, We hate Wogs' (repeated). Sometimes the aggressive tension is relieved by an element of humour. For example, to the tune of 'My Bonnie Lies Over The Ocean'. 'If I had the wings of a Sparrow, If I had the arse of a Crow, I'd fly over Leicester tomorrow, and shit on the bastards below.'

It is not hard to see how such rhythmic chants in a closely knit crowd can trigger off violence which might not occur in the absence of such verbal stimuli. The deliberate use of martial music and aggressive slogans is well established in military use and is a traditional precursor of the battle charge. The Japanese battle cry 'Banzai' forewarned of a ferocious attack. Slang slogans may have great importance in establishing fashionable patterns of violence in youthful groups. Skinheads provide the focus of their aggression in clichés like 'Paki Bashing' and 'Queer Bashing'. These slogans provide a definition and a focus which become a behavioural reality. The purveyors of soap powders know that once you begin to say it you buy it, and with violence once you begin to say it you may do it. Further studies of the linguistic components of group violence would help our understanding of their symbolic and deeper meaning in violence.

Mass hysteria
Mass hysteria in the form of wild enthusiasm with occasional violent features has a long history which predates the well described dance frenzies of the middle ages but violence was not a regular feature of these historical happenings. In a modern context the linking of mass hysteria and popular stars goes back to the early days of Hollywood and singers like Sinatra. There was much to suggest that the response was officially encouraged and partly staged by publicity agents who saw the opportunity to further commercial aims by prescribing the excited expectations and actions of the crowd.

The advent of 'Rock and Roll' in the early fifties had a less happy outcome as far as violence was concerned, particularly in England and Germany. The riots that became associated with

189

the showing of Bill Haley's film in 1955 were widely reported and became an expected event every time the film was shown. The group involved was young but mixed and probably contained the so-called yob element that went in search of a punch-up rather than musical entertainment. These Rock and Roll riots were to set the tone and add an important influence in determining the situation which developed in the pop cult of the 1960s and was later to become linked with the pop festival.

Although crowd disturbances were reported in connection with outbursts of Beatle-mania in the 1960s and more recently with other groups such as the Osmonds and the Bay City Rollers, the keynote has been excitement and enthusiasm with only a trivial content of violence and the only change of note being the increased involvement of very young girls in the bobbysox scene. These events showed that females are just as prone as males to crowd influences on behaviour, although the response might be different, the sex motive being more apparent than the aggressive one. Commercial considerations still apply but passive swooning has been replaced by more ardent enthusiasm and a more disorderly crowd is characteristic of the scene today. Because of the female predominance in the audience violence is accidental and usually associated with endeavours to obtain a personal souvenir of the star.

There are strong public and press expectations about the sort of behaviour to be expected with large pop concerts, namely violence and drug-taking. Drug-taking is certainly difficult to assess in any large mass but violence is more conspicuous and hard to conceal. Most observers have expressed surprise rather than satisfaction when such large pop concerts, as at Woodstock and the Isle of Wight, were largely violence free. Perhaps the commentators were disappointed that the 'copy' that they sought was not forthcoming. Nevertheless the folk-lore of pop violence was reinforced by the killing of a member of the audience by a self-styled steward of the Hell's Angels at the infamous Altmont Concert in 1969 and has been boosted by more recent events like the riotous behaviour that occurred in Windsor Great Park when an illegally organised pop concert was broken up by police intervention. In theory the excitable crowd at a pop concert has most of the ingredients for riotous violence so that the rarity of its occurrence is worthy of comment. The social group context of the pop concert is more conducive to affection than aggression. The slogan 'Make love not War' is more typical of the pop scene than in the football stadium where 'We are the Greatest' and 'We shall not be moved' are more appropriate.

References
(1) ASH S. E. (1952) *Social Psychology,* Prentice Hall, New York.
(2) KLUCKHOHN F. R. and STRODTBECK F. C. (1961) *Variations in Value Orientation,* Row Peterson, Evanston.
(3) GIBBENS T. C. N. (1970) *Aspects of Violent Criminal Behaviour.* Proceedings of the 4th National Conference on Research and Teaching in Criminology, Cambridge.
(4) FREUD S. (1953) *Group Psychology and the Analysis of the Ego,* Hogarth Press, London.
(5) COHEN A. K. (1955) *Delinquent Boys.* Free Press, New York.
(6) ADLER A. (1965) *Superiority and Social Interest,* Routledge and Kegan Paul, London.
(7) BETTLEHEIM B. (1966) *Violence: a neglected mode of behaviour,* The Annals 364.
(8) ERIKSON E. (1959) *Identity and the Life Cycle,* International University Press, New York.
(9) SOREL G. (1961) *Reflection on Violence,* Macmillan, New York.
(10) WILKINS L. T. (1964) *Social Deviance,* Tavistock, London.
(11) COHEN S. (1970) *Research into Group Violence and Vandalism among Adolescents.* Proceedings of the 4th National Conference on Research and Teaching in Criminology, Cambridge.
(12) HARRINGTON J. A. (1969) *Soccer Hooliganism,* John Wright and Son, Bristol.
(13) YABLONSKY L. (1962) *The Violent Gang,* Macmillan, New York.
(14) THRASHER F. M. (1926) *The Gang,* University of Chicago Press,
(15) DOWNES D. M. (1966) *The Delinquent Solution,* Routledge and Kegan Paul, London.
(16) MILLER W. B. (1966) *Violent crimes in city gangs,* Annals 364.
(17) MATZA D. and SYKES G. M. (1961) 'Juvenile delinquency and sub-cultural values', American Sociological Review, *26.*
(18) MILLER W. B. (1958) 'Lower class culture as generating milieu of gang delinquency', Journal of Social Issues, *14.*
(19) SCOTT P. (1956) 'Gangs and delinquent groups', British Journal of Delinquency, *7.*
(20) SHERIF M. (1966) *Group Conflict and Co-operation,* Routledge and Kegan Paul, London.
(21) LE BON G. (1922) *The Crowd* (Trans.), Unwin, London.
(22) ALLPORT F. H. (1924) *Social Psychology,* Houghton Miffin, Cambridge, Mass.
(23) WOOD C. (1968) *The Behaviour of the Football Fan Group,* Unpublished Dissertation, University of Birmingham.

Chapter X In defence of hooliganism, Social theory and violence
Geoffrey Pearson

The title is, of course, provocative. It also tries to make a point: there is a seemingly ever-growing preoccupation with the problem of violent behaviour in advanced industrial societies, but the voice of the violent deviant is never represented. Thus a state of affairs which would hardly be tolerated in a court of law, passes for normal practice in the rational discourse of the welfare professions.

I will not pretend to speak to the whole question of violence in society, but concern myself only with some aspects of violence which have been 'hitting the news' – vandalism, football hooliganism, mugging and paki-bashing, all forms of problem behaviour associated largely with young working class men.

Drawing on a growing body of critical social research, I will attempt to articulate the viewpoint and problems of the young working class hooligan, a hazardous venture which involves the risk of putting words into the mouths of other people who have chosen to act and not to speak.

Mindless hooligans and mindless theories
Much social work, criminology and psychiatry considers youthful violence as senseless and mindless. Frequently this sentiment only makes itself felt as a shadowy, background assumption; although because in the background, out of sight and out of mind, it can work in a powerful and insidious fashion. Occasionally it is expressed with full vigour, as in the following statement about vandalism:

> 'Police departments, social agencies, civic groups and organisations such as schools and churches are completely at a loss to explain their [the vandals'] meaning or purpose, and equally baffled as to how such actions can be effectively handled, controlled or prevented . . . specialists in youth problems ponder all the known theories of causation but there is no agreement. Delinquency and crime are, and have been regarded, as purposeful behaviour. But wanton and vicious destruction of property, both public and private by teen-age hoodlums reveals no purpose, no rhyme, no reason. Theories of latent aggression, paternal hostility projected against authority, frustration, rejection, lack of love – none of these can possibly furnish any reasonable clue to the meaning of such senseless and useless conduct.'[1]

This is an untypically frank expression of the assumptions built into most views of youthful hooliganism, assumptions which more commonly find their full-blooded articulation in sensational stories in the news media. In professional discourse, these assumptions are more likely to be expressed in a disguised form, as when hooligans are said to be 'sick'. This 'medical model' (or medical metaphor) of violent conduct appears, at face value, to be more compassionate, more sophisticated, and hence more likely to represent a true understanding of hooliganism. It is, however, a viewpoint which is insulated in a double sense against understanding what hooliganism represents. First, it carries the familiar enough assumption that because hooliganism is senseless, therefore hooligans must be sick. Secondly, it suggests that because the hooligan is sick, there is little point in trying to understand what he is doing. And thus, circular and pseudo-scientific reasoning does nothing more than prop up the supposedly obvious assumption that hooliganism is senseless, point-less, wanton, irrational, random, aimless, arbitrary, purposeless and mindless.

These points of view fail to understand precisely because they do not try to understand. They take the incomprehensibility of hooli-ganism as a matter of fact, and therefore see no need to look at the facts. They are viewpoints of closed minds, which sometimes seem to look on the world with closed eyes.

However, a number of loosely connected developments in sociological theory have made available the basis of an alternative stance. I will say something about these theoretical developments (as they relate to the question of deviant conduct) because they provide the foundations of my own approach. Each of them can be thought of as a reversal, and a re-working, of the assumptions of the traditional and commonsense approach to understanding deviant behaviour.

The first development concerns the extent to which people who engage in deviant conduct exercise choice and free will. Traditional theories (whether they take a biological, psychological or social form) invariably assume that deviant behaviour is entirely deter-mined by circumstances (whether these are biological, psychological or social) and that, in this sense, deviant conduct is not free. One of the major difficulties of this assumption, as described by David Matza[2] is that it depicts the delinquent as if he were chained by the forces of determinism to a predictable, and permanent, criminal career. And this, in fact, is not what happens: juvenile delinquents do not usually become adult deviants.

'Positive criminology accounts for too much delinquency.
Taken at their terms, delinquency theories seem to predicate far more delinquency than actually occurs. If delinquents were in fact radically differentiated from the rest of conventional

193

youth in that their unseemly behaviour was constrained through compulsion or commitment, then involvement in delinquency would be more permanent and less transient, more pervasive and less intermittent than is apparently the case. Theories of delinquency yield an embarrassment of riches which seemingly go unmatched in the real world.'[2]

Interestingly the controversial Home Office White Paper *Children in Trouble* 1968, stated that delinquent behaviour was a very common feature in the lives of quite ordinary and normal young people. The purpose of this essay, is to explore the social meaning of violence: and here we must be particularly emphatic, for a very large proportion of violent offenders are known to be first offenders who do not commit further offences.[3]

The implications of this vital recognition are far-reaching. In Matza's terms it involves a theoretical rejection of 'determinism' and 'positivism'. For our purposes, we can re-state this more usefully by saying that it demands a recognition that deviants are not deranged, deformed or monstrous creatures who have run out of control; that they are ordinary human beings, essentially like other people, and this recognition should be carried into any search for the motives and meanings of hooliganism.

The second theoretical development of major importance is the contribution of the 'labelling' approach.[4, 5] Deviance involves the infraction of social rules, and in traditional theories these rules are taken for granted as unquestionable facts of life. Indeed, there is a sense in which social rules become sanctified as part of the *natural* order of things, even though rules (quite obviously) are part of the *human* order – improvised, maintained, and sometimes altered, by men for intelligible human purposes.[6] In this way, the traditional approach to deviance expresses a 'reified' conception of social order; a conception, that is, which thinks of the man-made world as if it were a timeless, unchanging aspect of the natural universe.[7, 8]

The 'labelling' approach overturns this reified world-view by pointing out that social rules are man-made, and that different men (for example, different cultures, societies, classes, communities and families) live their lives according to different symbolic orders. In other words, deviants who have broken an official set of rules may well be acting according to an alternative, but equally intelligible, set of norms. Again, this insight is particularly important in relation to hooliganism which is clearly offensive to middle class culture, but much more in sympathy with some of the themes of working class life.[9, 10]

While it is true that neither of these theoretical moves is

194

without its own difficulties, blind-spots and ambiguities[7, 11, 12] they have provided the theoretical stimulus for a new approach to deviant conduct, an approach which David Matza[13] describes as 'appreciative'. Its aim is 'to comprehend and illuminate the subject's view and to interpret the world *as it appears to him*'.[13] This approach is therefore potentially a weapon of effective social criticism, for it does not take the official view of social reality as the last word. But for the same reasons, its criticism can easily fall on deaf ears; it is sometimes felt by the welfare professions that because it does not accept the official view of reality, it is an offensive, and even scandalous, point of view.[7, 8, 14, 15] For our purposes, for example, it requires us to take seriously the hooligan's viewpoint – the same hooligan who is thought by traditional deviance theories to be mindless. This critical and 'appreciative' stance, therefore, can easily offend members of the welfare professions because of the ways in which it offers a challenge to their moral authority. It can even appear to be a pointless, silly and wasteful enterprise – as senseless as the hooligan himself. But it is worth noting that in its hazardous attempt to give a voice to the deviant, critical sociology sometimes mirrors the experience of social workers and probation officers before the courts where they, too, are sometimes thought to be identified with the deviant and the underdog.

A second difficulty is that because it sides with the deviant, this critical sociology is prone to romanticism. The deviant is described as being more colourful than he is, and also less troublesome. He is rarely represented as someone who is unhappy, although some deviants (but not all) are unhappy. And because he is deviant, he is thought to be spontaneous, free of the hang-ups of the conforming citizen, living 'outside the law'. Sometimes this romantic emphasis belongs to the author; at other times, because of the potentially scandalous nature of the appreciative exercise, it is 'read in' by the audience. Whatever the case, romanticism has been a key issue in recent years in the exchange and interplay between writer and reader in the field of deviance studies.[7, 12]

This short theoretical prelude has mapped out a number of the difficulties in the area in which deviance studies operate. My method in the following pages works with the strengths, and weaknesses, of this area of study. There will be very little further theoretical reflection in this chapter, and in places the necessarily brief and sketchy outline of hooligans may leave gaps in this critical method. For all its weaknesses, however, the method of critical sociology is superior to the traditional view which is merely bewildered and confused when it confronts the 'mindless hooligan'.

The traditional perspective inevitably responds to this confusion with a 'mindless theory' which invalidates the hooligan's viewpoint as irrational, pathological, and eventually subhuman; lending itself, in fact, to methods of correction which are irrational, pathological, and eventually inhuman. Critical sociology can defend the hooligan against this invalidation; it can also point the way to how to defend the community against hooliganism.

Vandalism: broken windows and broken promises

It is becoming commonplace to say that the urban landscape is an arid desert. The peculiar metaphor 'concrete jungle' has, in fact, entered into our language as a way of capturing the no less peculiar fact that the bustling life of a modern city is often experienced as, and shrouded in, killing boredom. Critics and social commentators, in an attempt to understand this modern experience, point an accusing finger at various features of social life. The distance between the common man and the levers of power, and the rigid bureaucracies of many modern institutions, are obvious targets. Max Weber[16] was an early critic who pointed to the tendency of modern institutions to transform men into small cogs which click in precise harmony with the industrial-bureaucratic machine; and we are still without an adequate understanding of the frustrations which are generated by this state of affairs. Another frequent target for criticism (and abuse) is modern architecture which is seen to embody all the worst features of a mechanical and anonymous organisation of social life. Modern educational institutions, in the same manner, have been described as 'factories' which train children according to pre-set routines which have little to do with the aims of education in the liberal spirit. Finally, although this does not exhaust the list, the whole area of planning and urban re-development is frequently pilloried for its drab formulae which are so far removed from, and even sometimes hostile to, the rhythms of everyday life which the planning sciences are meant to support. These criticisms are intended to further our understanding of the difficulties of urban life. It is also proper to add that for many social commentators the process of criticism seems to fulfil the vital function of 'getting it off your chest'.

The awkward fact which any theory of vandalism must confront honestly is that those things which are criticised by articulate commentators also tends to be attacked by inarticulate vandals. In other words, in their utterly different fashions, social critics and vandals often appear to be making the same point against the form and organisation of urban life. I have already implied

196

that criticism is sometimes ill-tempered and cathartic – a form of intellectual brick-throwing. Can we also think of vandalism as inarticulate criticism?

Any answer to this question will be necessarily speculative, if only because we simply do not know enough about vandalism and vandals. What is known, however, shows that vandalism is quite a discriminating activity: some things are vandalised, others are not. Once again, this is an awkward and embarrassing fact for those traditional viewpoints which insist that vandalism is an indiscriminate and random destruction of property.

These general observations can be enlarged by looking at the specific findings of a number of studies on vandalism associated with housing, schools, parks and other public amenities. These studies repeatedly show up some unexpected themes in the pattern of vandalism. Howard Parker[9] remarks, for example, that houses are not as likely to be vandalised in parts of the inner-city of Liverpool where there is a strong sense of community spirit and neighbourliness. The particular area of his study, which he calls 'Roundhouse', was a downtown tenement block characterized by poor housing, low income, high unemployment and a rough reputation. Nevertheless, there was a feeling among residents that they belonged to Roundhouse (it was described by locals as 'one big family') and, significantly, vandalism was uncommon in the area which in most other respects had a very high crime rate. Parker's observations lead to the conclusion that vandalism is more effectively controlled where residents (and local youngsters) feel that they belong to their neighbourhood, and that their neighbourhood belongs to them. Tenant involvement in the planning, design, use and control of local amenities seems to be the most effective means of insulation against vandalism.[17]

Similar conclusions are forced on us by an observational study of vandalism and play in an inner-city area of Cardiff.[18] Parks and play facilities which were freely available for youngsters to play games of football, or for other activities were not damaged in any way. Youngsters, and their parents appeared to exercise effective 'community control'. During the same period, and in the same locality, a park where a fierce contest took place between local children and 'outsiders' from the neighbouring university was repeatedly vandalised. The most disturbing feature of this study, however, was undoubtedly what happened when the main park in the area (a park which was respected and undamaged) was taken over and destroyed for the purpose of building government offices. This official move seemed to puncture the sense that the park belonged to the community. Immediately, and quite

197

dramatically, vandalism and wild play began in the park and its surroundings. For the first time ever, trees were attacked and damaged. Building equipment and motor cars in the vicinity were also attacked with stones and clods of earth. The bind of 'community control' had broken down.

In these circumstances, vandalism might be best understood as a frantic attempt to re-assert control in the face of a potent demonstration of faceless, bureaucratic governmental power which had taken away the children's football pitch. James Patrick[19] in his study of Glasgow youth puts this rather well: 'The Glasgow gang boy feels that he is being pushed around, that he has no control over the social conditions which predetermine his future and yet he is expected to act like a man who is in charge of the situation'. It should not go unnoticed that the boys in my own study[18] lived in a neighbourhood which was in constant threat of take-over by the local university. The buildings of the university towered over the neighbourhood, and its voracious appetite for student accommodation, houses and land for expansion meant that it steadily advanced into neighbourhood territory. Little wonder, then, that local children in the grip of this 'territorial anxiety' scrawled graffiti on the outer perimeter of some university buildings: 'Cathay Boot Boys Rule. OK'. Vandalism in the parks was only part of a wider struggle for power and control in Cathays, and it offers a particularly disturbing example of the social effects of thoughtless planning which is imposed from above without serving the local neighbourhood.[18, 20, 21]

The foregoing example should alert us to the importance of paying attention to specific details of community life when an attempt is being made to place social problems in their correct social context. It also raises the difficulties involved in generalising from the problems of one area to those of another. Generalisation is possible in that there are many points of similarity between the problems of working class communities in different regions, and even different nations. Even so, it is probably only when hooliganism is set firmly in the context of a specific community that the real explanation for it can begin to emerge.

With these preliminary caveats, it may be useful to look briefly at the work of Oscar Newman[22] who has demonstrated the relationship between housing conditions and crime in the USA. There are many threads to Newman's research, of which only a few can be mentioned, and it should be borne in mind that because much of his work is based on statistical inference it is open to a number of divergent interpretations.

Newman's work is, without reservation, a condemnation of 'high

198

rise' housing which imposes restrictions on the growth of community in a neighbourhood, stamps much of the local territory with an impersonal and anonymous character, and is emphatically associated with high rates of vandalism and other forms of violent crime. The Pruitt-Igoe project in St. Louis has provided a dramatic example of the problem: the project was plagued by vandalism, and violence, and was rapidly losing its tenants who found conditions impossible. After only seventeen years, the public authorities grew tired of efforts at remedial action which failed repeatedly, and took the final step of destroying the high rise apartments with explosives. Newman[23] comments that, 'Pruitt-Igoe is not an isolated example; there are similar projects in almost every major city . . . Most projects are simply languishing, with 40 per cent vacancy rates, high crime and vandalism rates, and a health rating which designates them politely as "uninhabitable" '.

The connections between housing design and layout, and vandalism are complex and not always easy to trace. We are only beginning to understand, for example, that although architectural design cannot completely determine human behaviour, there are nevertheless ways in which the design of space can encourage (or discourage) peaceful human intercourse.[24] One of the central findings to emerge from Newman's work is that spaces which are open to observation are more 'defensible' and less prone to violence. This is, in some ways, a rather obvious point: where people can be seen, they are less likely to misbehave. But it also shows that residents feel less alienated from communal territories which are open to observation, and thus brings us back to the elusive (but nevertheless real) connections between estrangement from the environment and violence. A number of demonstration projects reported by Newman[23] have shown ways in which building layout and street design can have substantial effects on violence, vandalism and the deterioration of problem neighbourhoods. One such experiment is the 'closed street': streets are closed at one end to prevent through traffic, thus making the street a safe and pleasant space for children to play and residents to gather and meet. Architectural changes, of even such a slight nature, have been shown to lead to social changes, including greater communality, reduced crime, and better racial integration. These findings, particularly in the area of race, cannot be directly translated into British context. Nevertheless, it is a disturbing reflection that during the post-war period in Britain, when it is generally reckoned that youthful hooliganism became prominent, this concept of the street as 'communal space' has been systematically destroyed by the 'improvement' and 're-development' of working class neighbourhoods.[25] The crucial point is that these changes, which often went under the euphemistic title of 'slum clearance', were not always seen as improvements by local residents themselves. All too often, the planner's 'promised land' turned out to mean being decanted into an outlying council estate without friends, family or amenities; or it meant 'going up in the world' into a high-rise flat where the kids were always under your feet, and where the lifts did not work. When this post-war period of development is transcribed in terms of the actual experiences of many working class families and neighbourhoods, it is possible to begin to understand hooliganism as one aspect of a profound dislocation in everyday life.

Sometimes, of course, the houses were slums. However, the 'gentrification' of so many previously derelict houses and neighbourhoods by the middle class who transform these 'slums' into fashionable residential areas, shows that there are alternative routes for housing development. Hence the slogan of many working class tenant organisation: 'Improve us, don't remove us!'.

Finally, I will discuss some aspects of vandalism in schools, which is another area where a broken promise robs the welfare state of some of its credibility. Here, of course, it is not the promised land of tower-blocks which is failing, but of educational equality and through the equality of educational opportunity, the final promise of social equality. The relationship between educational inequality and different forms of juvenile rebellion is particularly clear. It is well established, for example, that just as schools vary in terms of the quality of education which they offer, they also vary in terms of their rates for vandalism, truancy and delinquency in general.[26, 27, 28] There is growing evidence, furthermore, that these two areas are connected, and that it is useful to think of some forms of hooliganism as a reaction to bad education.

An early piece of work by Nathan Goldman[26] for example, highlighted the fact that some schools are vandalised frequently, whereas others are not. It was to be expected that these schools often served lower working class neighbourhoods. What was less obvious was that even within this socio-economic grouping, some schools were more likely to be vandalised than others (cf. [29]). Goldman's research indicated that the distinguishing features of high-damage schools were likely to be low staff morale, poor staff-pupil ratios, obsolete school equipment, rapid staff turnover, and the all too familiar gulf between the school curriculum and the real circumstances of lives of working class people. There was also evidence[26] that the teachers in the high-damage schools were less concerned with the personal and informal aspects of education, and

200

more with administrative and impersonal factors. Goldman's conclusions were that school vandalism must be understood as a form of active protest against the school: 'The occurrence of vandalism might be an indirect but potent hint that the curriculum, school morale, or the relations between school and community need to be examined'.[26]

It is perhaps surprising that these findings from an American study in the late 1950s are echoed in a study of educational organisation and youthful misbehaviour in a working class community in South Wales in the 1970s.[28] This research looked more closely at teacher-pupil relationships, and it suggests that teachers and school administrators who recognise that formal and rigid curricula are invariably irrelevant to the educational needs of working class children, suffer less trouble in the form of delinquency, truancy and vandalism. Equally, formal systems of discipline which emphasise classroom silence, walking in straight lines, the strict observance of uniform regulations, and other petty rules, were experienced by children as quite foreign; and such notions of discipline seemed to generate trouble in schools, rather than prevent it. Truancy, in David Reynolds' research, emerges as a way in which children 'vote with their feet' against irrelevant education.

The crucial factor, to summarise, is whether or not schools serve their community. Where schools make the effort to join up education with the real experiences and needs of the community, they appear to be more successful in controlling truancy (which is, of course, associated with all sorts of other law-breaking and hooliganism) and vandalism. The same themes, which emerged in discussion of housing and planning, thus reappear in the educational sphere. Eric Midwinter[30] is not being altogether frivolous when he writes: 'When suggesting diffidently some years ago to a group of teachers that the children should be free to visit the lavatory whenever they wanted, one teacher said that, if such a ruling prevailed, Jimmy Robinson would stay there all the time. Therein lies the crux: how do we make our classrooms as attractive as our urinals?'

Scapegoating

The last section was concerned with the social contexts of vandalism; that is, 'senseless' attacks on things and property. Only rarely do people get hurt, and when this does happen it seems to be a by-product rather than the aim of vandalism. The following section deals with 'senseless' attacks on people, examining the social contexts and 'sense', of what have come to be called 'paki-bashing' and 'mugging'.

Migrant workers have become an indispensable part of the European economy.[31, 32] In Britain migrant labour has been traditionally recruited from parts of the former Empire: India, Pakistan, the West Indies and Southern Ireland. The relationship between local populations and migrants has an uneasy history of mutual suspicion which occasionally flares into open violence[33], the basis of the hostilities being quite complex. There are always uneasy tensions of culture, religion and life-style; and these have sometimes been aggravated by that sense of superiority which the British inherited as a residue from many years of imperial domination. Sometimes this is easily (sometimes too easily) summed up as 'racism'. Sometimes the migrant community (easily identified because of colour) appears to be a convenient vehicle for working off tensions: problems over housing conditions or job opportunities, for example, are displaced into 'racist' sentiments, and the migrant becomes what we call a 'scapegoat'. But to call him a 'scapegoat' is almost to miss the point, and the point is that conflicts between locals and migrants also have a basis in fact. For example, local workers often fear (with some justification) that migrant workers will depress wage levels in their industry. When jobs are scarce, locals and migrants come face to face in another very real struggle. Migrants and locals will also come into conflict over housing. Hostilities are therefore rational as well as irrational, real as well as imaginary, and any view of 'racial scapegoating' which misses this point (or refuses to acknowledge it) will sooner or later be seen as inadequate.

These general observations can be demonstrated from specific circumstances. Once more, caution in generalising from one set of circumstances to another is necessary. Different traditions in a local community, different conditions in a particular industry, different styles of housing use, overall economic, political and cultural climates: these are part of the picture of a particular community, and there will be gaps in the pattern, or unexpected developments. Nevertheless, the consistent economic relationship of the local community and a migrant labour force will be part of the pattern under this confusion of detail. The relationship is inherently violent. Young men and old people will invariably find themselves in the most vulnerable position in the conflict which is likely to be expressed through a range of experience from stubborn grumbling to open riot.

Some of the 'confusion of detail' can be seen in an outbreak of 'paki-bashing' in the summer of 1964 in Accrington, a cotton town in north east Lancashire.[34] The outbreak was sparked off by the murder of a white man by a Pakistani. These immediate circumstances can hardly explain the ferocity and persistence of the attacks on migrants which followed. After a week or so of trouble, the local newspaper described the business as 'senseless'. There was a semblance of agreement in the town (when people were prepared to talk about the matter, which was not often) that the killing had been an 'excuse' for young hooligans. What was it, an 'excuse' for; and what was it that the townspeople were reluctant to talk about?

The mill towns of Lancashire were established in the nineteenth century on a very narrow industrial base – namely, the spinning, weaving, and finishing of cotton goods. In the nineteenth and early twentieth centuries they were boom towns, but from the 1920s onwards they suffered from economic and social decay. The slump of the 1930s hit hard. The cotton industry was, in any case, already in decline and between 1929 and 1939 Accrington lost 18 per cent of its population (22 per cent of its male workers) through emigration to other areas. In the post-war years the closure of mills continued and accelerated through the 1950s, so that in the north east Lancashire connurbation (Blackburn, Burnley, Accrington, Nelson, Colne, Rawtenstall, Bacup) there was a relentless depression of wages, shortage of work, and an enormous population loss over more than 40 years. In this period the population declined by more than 100,000 people; according to some estimates[35] about 1,600 people were still leaving the region each year throughout the 1960s.

The problem came to a head in the late 1950s and early 1960s. As the collapse of the cotton industry accelerated, the labour force of the industry as a whole was reduced by nearly a third between 1958 and 1962. The industrial base of north east Lancashire had simply evaporated.

The violence of this economic reversal was matched by a profound dislocation in the community and culture of the mill towns. Here it is possible only to summarise the main points[34]: changes in family organisation and work organisation which were necessitated by the disappearance of the old routines of the mill; the decline in traditional nonconformist religious groups, their cultural life, and their institutes; the changing emphases of the co-operative movement and the labour movement; and a grave crisis in sporting institutions (i.e. football and cricket) even to the point where one club, Accrington Stanley which had been a founder member of the Football League, was forced to close down. The age structure of these towns was also markedly unbalanced by continual emigration of young people[35] and taken all together these different, but connected, developments produced a particular sensitivity to questions of stability and security.[36]

The question of race entered this economic and cultural upheaval through a series of awkward convergences. The economic crisis of the British cotton industry, for example, was brought about by competition from low-cost cotton imports – principally from the countries of the former Empire. The struggle of the British cotton industry against imported goods continues to this day, and can be traced back to the eighteenth century. It is associated with repeated trade union demands for tariff controls, and these demands reached a new peak in the 1950s exciting a great deal of local sympathy. Tippett[37] has described one aspect of this concern over tariffs: 'people in the industry had (and still have) a sense of grievance. Granted that developing countries needed help – why should all the burden fall on the Lancashire textile industry? . . . Had the Government written the industry off? No politician dared to say that this was so, but subsequent events were consistent with the view that the Government had written off a large part of it'. Seemingly cut off from the main developments in the British economy, the Lancashire industry was thus thrown into an 'unfair' competition with what was seen as 'sweated labour' in the Empire. Campaigns for tariff control have an inevitable chauvinistic and insular quality, and they easily become tinged with racist imagery.[38] And here the terrible irony of the Lancashire cotton industry was that precisely at the point of its final death throes, a new threat appeared, migrant workers from India and Pakistan. The threat of low-cost imports from the same countries had provided the economic roots of racial anxiety. The actual presence of Pakistani migrant workers in the cotton towns from the early 1960s was a bitter symbol of everything which seemed to be going wrong.

The convergences and ironies were even more terrible and direct. For example, the few mills which survived the crash were obliged to engage in capital reinvestment, and in order to secure the maximum return on capital had to introduce more intensive working arrangements – such as night shifts and double-shifts. Migrant workers readily accepted such inconvenient work, and many of them found work (in a dwindling job market) in the surviving mills. Rumour and gossip went straight to the heart of the matter: 'They're taking over the mills'. And it was within such experiences that the general conflicts between local people and migrants over jobs, wage levels, and housing arose in north east Lancashire in the early 1960s.

The outbreak of 'paki-bashing' in 1964 must be seen in the context of the peculiar role the migrant worker had come to occupy in the economic and cultural climate of the region. The incident which sparked off the outbreak was a conversation in a coffee bar between local people and Pakistanis who had got on to the delicate subject of white girls. Women and girls were another 'scarce resource' over which young working class men and migrants might come into conflict, and this aspect of the conflict should not be trivialised or joked away. The fact that migrants are effectively excluded from 'nice places' means that the struggle is all the more intense between them and the working class men and boys who hang around in 'low dives' such as coffee bars, and in Accrington this kind of minor trouble had been in the air for some time. It is also important to remember that in the early 1960s the migrant community was almost wholly composed of men; it was only much later that they began to settle with their wives and children, and earlier local gossip embellished the single sex nature of the migrant community by saying that 'they were all homosexuals'. On the afternoon of the 'paki-bashing' outbreak the edginess of the sexual conflict got out of hand, somebody flicked a match or a cigarette butt, a fight broke out, it tumbled into the street, knives were pulled, and a man died with stab wounds. That evening a large gang of youths and men attacked Pakistanis in the street. Muslim shops were attacked and vandalised. The streets in which the migrant community lived were easily identifiable and they were also attacked: windows were broken and attempts were made to set fire to some of the houses and trouble of this kind continued for a short time.

It needs to be emphasized that this hooliganism did not arise out of a vacuum. Even 'reasonable' and 'respectable' local residents harboured suspicions about the migrant community, a fact which meant that the official response to 'paki-bashing' was in some ways awkward and embarrassed.[34] A rich mythology had come to surround the Pakistani migrant: he had become what Jeremy Seabrook[36, 39] calls a 'folk ogre'. The migrant was the cause of jokes, gossip, trade union disputes, scandal, and more jokes. Many of the jokes were violent and ill-tempered – a kind of arm-chair 'paki-bashing'. It was as if the whole cultural and economic dislocation of the region was being worked through by transposing it onto the Pakistani community. And it is this complex of economic, cultural and biographical relationship which must be taken into account if we are to understand 'scapegoating' and what is rational about it; and it is this same troubled and violent experience which is so easily dismissed as 'hooliganism'. Seabrook[36] attempts to sum up this difficult area of working class experience in the following terms:

'It is an expression of their pain and powerlessness confronted by the decay and dereliction, not only of their familiar environment, but of their own lives, too – an expression for which

205

our society provides no outlet. Certainly it is something more complex and deep-rooted than what the metropolitan liberal evasively and easily dismisses as prejudice.'

When this cluster of troubled sentiments crystallises into 'paki-bashing', it may be the violent and brutal culmination of a violent and brutalising economic relationship.

From late 1969, and for twelve months or so, 'paki-bashing' was widespread in Britain. It was undoubtedly over-played in the news media during what Stanley Cohen[40] has called a period of 'moral panic', but nevertheless there was probably a real increase in 'paki-bashing', representing a fresh crystallisation (this time of a national scale) of the problems already discussed above in detail. There were obvious and important differences, however, and it is not possible to make snap generalisations from a cotton town in 1964 to the East End of London, or Birmingham, in 1969/70. Even so, what evidence there is[25, 41] suggests that disputes over housing, jobs, and territorial control were at the back of these later outbursts of 'paki-bashing'. One way in which these later experiences were crucially different was that they were linked to the skinhead life style which was beginning to dominate some working class youths over this period. The skinheads' uniform (boots, braces, cropped hair) was almost a caricature of the working dress of the model working man, and in their hooliganism and their 'aggro' the skinheads seemed to reaffirm the working class values of manliness and toughness. For the skinheads, therefore, 'paki-bashing' distinguished between Asians and West Indians. The skin-heads respected the West Indians because of their toughness, their music (reggae) which was hard and solid, and because their life-style approximated that of the British lower working class. Asians, on the other hand, were thought to aspire to respectable middle class values and, for these reasons, they represented an alien cultural style.[25, 42] Everything points in the direction that in the late 1960s 'paki-bashing' represented a class-based and discriminating cultural hostility, and not just an indiscriminate racism.

As a footnote to this discussion, another hooligan activity which became associated with skinheads was 'queer-bashing'. While this undoubtedly reflected the heterosexual chauvinism of working class culture, it also contained an affirmation of class values: 'queer', for the purposes of skinhead aggro, could include 'student weirdos' and 'hippies' who were thought to be unmanly, grossly hedonistic layabouts, drop-outs and 'wankers'.[43, 41, 44] To put all this in context, it should be remembered that the news media tend to over-portray this kind of violence and that the practice of 'rolling' homosexuals is an old game amongst working class youths, and certainly not a skinhead invention. Equally, just as in Europe the Turkish migrant workers get bashed, 'queer-bashing' is not unknown in other countries: in Germany, for example, it goes under the name of schwüle-tippen. Even so, the skinheads appeared to represent a particularly sharp crystallisation of a number of working class problems and preoccupations – including the defence of manliness, and the defence of territory. All these tendencies, of course, are defences which are displaced into scapegoating: as Phil Cohen[25] points out the traditional community of the East End was destroyed by property developers, not Pakistanis.

One final, very considerable change in Britain between 1964 and the 1970s was the sharpening of the issue of race. Increasingly strict immigration controls, the Smethwick election, the rise of the National Front, and certain wild political interventions brought the question of race into the centre of British politics in an unprecedented way. Skinheads 'putting the boot in' was, perhaps, the least worrying development on the racial front during this period: certainly when it is sited in its actual historical context it is possible to see it as no more than one moment in a period of intensifying antagonism in race and community relations.

So far it has appeared as if conflicts between local people and immigrants caused problems only for the locals, and as if the migrant community were only a passive, uncomplaining object of local violence. Neither assumption is valid. In its most unmistakable form the migrant community's unrest is expressed through the 'ghetto riot'. In a much more disguised and sporadic form, the same unrest (because there are good reasons to believe that these things have the same source) is often channelled through 'street crime': i.e. robberies, purse-snatching, 'theft from the person' offences, etc which have come to be known as 'muggings'. A 'ghetto riot' is quite clearly recognised as a kind of 'political' protest. 'Mugging', on the other hand, is inevitably categorised as 'crime'. But we must tread carefully here. As the Americans experience[45] has shown, under ghetto conditions it is extraordinarily difficult to mark off 'crime' and 'politics' into clear-cut divisions: it is difficult to say, that is, where 'theft' stops and 'looting' begins, where 'rowdyism' ends and 'rioting' starts. This is a further awkward aspect of the social and political implications of hooliganism, and one which probably finds its most vivid expression in Britain in the 1970s in the relationship between black youth and street crime.

This issue can best be stated by returning first to the critical tradition in social theory which has defied the commonsense view that juvenile delinquency is 'just crime', by pointing to the ways in which delinquency can appear as a 'solution' to many of the problems faced by working class, and particularly lower working class, youth.[46, 47, 2, 9] The problem behaviour is fairly age-specific, and the youths in question are usually living in the borderland between school and work. For many of those in the 'non-academic' streams of schools, the last couple of years of school life have become a boring irrelevance. When the boy leaves school, he joins the most vulnerable group on the job-market, and the jobs he can find will often be the lowest paid routine work with 'no prospects'. Trapped between the boredom of school and the boredom of dead-end work, such youths are under pressure to 'make things happen', to establish the fact of their manhood, and to bring themselves alive. They end up on the street – hanging around, messing about, doing nothing. Explosive action can come to be the answer, something to dispel the mood of boredom and desperation.

The experience of being black and young in Britain through the 1960s and into the 1970s intensified this mood, and for various reasons it has often been West Indian youths who are pressured and frustrated to the desperate edge of street-crime. For example, 'second generation' immigrants face quite different stresses and strains than those who first came to Britain in the 1950s. The second 'wave' of integration problems particularly introduces a shock into the parents' culture and they must adjust to their children becoming increasingly 'at home' in a foreign country. This shock may be less easily assimilated by West Indians because of the ways in which their native culture is essentially fragmented, the culture of a post-slave society[48] and does not contain the conflicts of 'second generation' youth as easily as the Asian migrant's culture. Antagonisms within the West Indian family, therefore, are more likely to spill out on to the street.[49, 50]

The West Indian community has also faced other, much more tangible, problems which can be sketched here. West Indian youths in Britain have frequently experienced educational failure, have been directly confronted with a number of the myths of equality. The black community, edged by the relentless economics of the housing market[51] into the ghetto, has experienced some of the worst conditions of housing and overcrowding. This has not infrequently been aggravated, rather than improved, by legislative squeezes on the private rented sector. In the area of employment, the black school-leaver carries an additional burden over white working class youths, a fact which is reflected in employment statistics which show that West Indian youths are at least twice as likely as white or Asian teenagers to be out of work, their unemployment rate running at 16.2 per cent in 1971.[52] In the cultural-political sphere, black youths have grown up in the period when 'race politics' have become an overt feature of British political life. The West Indian community has gone through a number of stages and transitions in its political response to these developments.[55] What has emerged, is a form of black consciousness drawing on both Caribbean influences (particularly Rasta and other 'back to Africa' traditions) and American elements ('black is beautiful', 'black power') in an assertion of a confident and aggressive identity against the hostile white world. What is called 'Babylon' (the white man's world and culture) by some West Indian cultural and political movements, is confidently expected to come tumbling down and messianic sentiments are clearly expressed in some of the protest music (reggae and its associated forms) from the West Indian ghetto (e.g., [54, 55, 56] also [57]). Finally, one result of these different developments, involving exclusion and counter-attack, has been growing mistrust between the police and some sections of the West Indian community. A lack of respect for the law (the law, maybe, of Babylon) is thus predictable from deprivation of the black community: violence can come to feel like a righteous act, righting the wrongs done to black people over many centuries; it can come to feel like politics, and a way of hitting back. Street-crime, as John Clarke and Tony Jefferson argue, can become a momentary and partial 'solution' for black youths who are members of the lower-lower class in advanced industrial societies:

'. . . he can become desperate. At this point crime can become an option since it is a "solution", at least temporary, to his problems. Mugging, given this situation, is the "perfect" crime: needing no criminal knowledge or skill to execute, it is both "instrumental" (in that it can supplement income) and "expressive", with its violence, of the felt desperation and hostility . . . It is thus comprehensible, meaningful and rational, though desperate and, ultimately, self-defeating.' [49]

These conclusions come out of an extended series of studies by the Birmingham Centre for Contemporary Cultural Studies into the moral panic which in 1972–73 produced a whirlwind of commentary and action on the question of mugging.[58, 59, 60] Allegedly, 'footpad crime' (which is another name for mugging) increased astronomically over this period. Special police squads were established, high-ranking politicians monitored progress in the 'war' against mugging, and one youth (Paul Storey) received a 20 year detention sentence for a robbery offence. It is extremely difficult to organise a clear statement of the facts of the mugging issue, because a number of factors obscure the picture. For example, mugging is not an official term and necessarily complex and arbitrary statistical juggling is required to compute a 'mugging rate' out of British criminal statistics. Also there was intense media exploitation of the subject, built around dramatic incidents and even more dramatic statistics. Finally, the mugging question became bound up in a 'law and order' campaign, just as it had in the USA under the Nixon regime.[58] Nevertheless, it seems reasonable to conclude that there was a significant increase in this type of offence in the late 1960s and early 1970s. Equally, the profile described above of the discontents of youths pushed to the edge of society, probably a more common experience for black than white, seems the most reliable indication of the social context and motives behind mugging.

We are faced with something like a mirror-image of 'paki-bashing'. The economic and cultural clashes between local and migrant populations are boiled down to a simple, violent formula: the unsuspecting 'whitey' who gets jumped by a gang of black youths is a scapegoat, a symbolic representative of a history of oppression which reaches back to the slave ships.

A report from the Community Relations Division of New Scotland Yard into mugging in the Lambeth district of South London, an area of multiple deprivation being abandoned by the middle class, gives considerable support to this kind of interpretation.[61] Lambeth has a high rate for mugging-type offences: there is also a large West Indian population, a higher than average rate of unemployment especially amongst the young, a housing stock which is inadequate in many respects, and dominated by the private rented sector which controls 48 per cent – compared with 16 per cent in England and Wales as a whole.[62] As well as establishing an emphatic connection between mugging and black youth (80–85 per cent of mugging-type offences in Brixton were committed by people identified as black) the New Scotland Yard research also establishes the likelihood of a relationship between this kind of offence and housing conditions, deteriorating police-community relations, and unemployment. Thus, when we explore what is involved in mugging we find that it is not useful to continue with the stereotyped line of thought which attributes it to 'mindless bully boys', 'witless thugs', or 'crime for fun'. On the contrary, when its social contexts are opened out, it appears as the sign of a dangerous social condition which is being allowed to push black people to the margins. And it is in the downtown margins that we can count the human cost of the violence of economics.

'We are the famous football hooligans!'

Given that violence is generally agreed to be a nasty business, **a** further awkward fact about hooliganism and rowdyism is that they can sometimes be fun. Football hooliganism is the obvious example. It offers the opportunity for feats of courage and juvenile bravado – stealing the scarves and emblems of opposing fans as trophies; or, for younger children running on to the pitch, giving the v-sign to opposition fans at the other end of the ground, and running off again under police supervision. A football crowd also offers the chance to express violent emotions and to get things off one's chest: hurling abuse at the referee, 'directing play' from the terraces, or arguing the toss over disputed goals, off-side decisions, etc. It provides a way of expressing community spirit and solidarity – linking arms, swaying in a huge crowd, chanting in unison, or even sometimes physically repelling the attempts by enemy fans to take your 'end' of the ground. Being in a football crowd is to be more than a passive viewer of an entertainment spectacle:

'A football crowd is different from a radio audience or a
conventional theatre audience, not only at the level of
emotional commitment but in the active and participatory
nature of its involvement. The crowd can not only affect what
is going on but is part of the action. The team relies on its
supporters for a psychological boost, and may be demoralised
if they turn against it.'[63]

Being at the match can offer a snatched moment of vicarious glory, invading the pitch to salute, and revel in, *your* team's victory. Finally, there are opportunities for wit, creativity and innovation, the songs and chants of football crowds reflect a rich folklore which surrounds the game.[64]

Football, as James Walvin[65] puts it in his history of the game, is the people's game: since the late nineteenth century, through to the present day, it is the thing which can keep argument and conversation alive for the whole of the working week, and make the heart race on Saturday afternoon. The violence in and around football grounds must be considered against this background, and not against the fictitious picture of a sedate Saturday afternoon outing. Undoubtedly, since wild behaviour at football matches has been glamourised by the news media, football matches now attract 'mad heads', 'divvies' and 'reputation hungry' kids who are spoiling for some aggro. Official comment and news coverage frequently puts football hooliganism down as the work of a lunatic fringe who are not 'real fans'. If the evidence is carefully weighed, however, it points to the fact that 'football hooliganism' arises directly out of the passion and ecstasy of Britain's major working class sporting entertainment, and that 'football hooligans' are amongst the staunchest and most committed supporters of the game. That is to say, they are the fans who travel up and down the country to support their team; not the casual spectators who lounge in front of a TV set and watch 'Match of the Day' at the flick of a switch.

It is possible, but by no means certain, that the attempt to reach a wider football audience (to include the middle class, women, and the uncommitted television viewer) which caused football administrators to make some effort to clean up the coarser and more vulgar aspects of the game, in turn produced an increased sensitivity to crowd behaviour and the identification, for the first time in football's rowdy history of a social problem known as 'football hooliganism'. Certainly the problem of crowd disorder came into view at the same time that the British game was emerging as part of the streamlined entertainment industry. Taylor[66] has suggested that this coincidence is an essential connection. For example, he argues that changes in the game towards professionalism internationalism and increasing commercial exploitation of soccer (changes which began to bear their full fruit in the 1960s) have forced a corresponding change in the official definition of the ideal fan. He is no longer supposed to be an active participant who is hot and blinded by club loyalty; but a cool, passive spectator – a consumer of a polished and spectacular leisure commodity. These changes in the commercial organisation of football, Taylor argues, has also altered the relationship between the local working class community, the fan, and 'his' club. Traditionally, the fan had been able to feel a close alliance with the club so that the organization of soccer felt something like a 'participatory democracy'.[66] The feeling, Taylor admits, may have been illusory. Even so, when football became big-business it was no longer possible for the fan to feel even the illusion of participation, and the shift was decisive:

'. . . the rank-and-file supporter in the 1930s *could* (however wrongly) see himself as being a member of a collective and democratically-structured enterprise. If this *was* the case, this would help explain why, for example, working class boys did not invade the pitch in the 1930s. That is, working class boys would see the ground as "theirs" (and the turf as sacred).'[66]

Commercialism breaks the spell: the sense of community gives way and the fan is alienated from the affairs of his club. Taylor's conclusion is that violent demonstrations of club solidarity, and such things as pitch invasions, can only be understood as a way in which a rump of young, working class fans resist these changes and claim back the club, players and pitch as *theirs*.

Ian Taylor's critical interpretation of football hooliganism was developed as a response to some of the earliest outbreaks in the

212

late 1960s. Since that time football rowdyism has become almost institutionalised. For example, one side-effect of news media coverage is that particular groups of fans get a particularly bad reputation and opposing fans (who want to show that they are even harder by taking on the champions) are more likely to call on them to defend their honour, or do their worst. Media coverage has in all probability escalated the trouble through a deviance-amplification effect which 'fixes' certain groups of fans with an identity as violent hoodlums; an identity which it is difficult to escape without appearing to be 'chicken'.[67] One solution is to embrace the notorious identity wholeheartedly, as when Manchester United fans taunt and intimidate the opposition with the chant: 'We are the famous football hooligans!' And if enough of you *look* hard enough, and *shout* loud enough, it is unlikely that the opposition will bother to put your claim to the test.

In an interesting study which is analysing football crowd behaviour with the use of video film, Peter March[68] has noted the ritual aspects of much of this behaviour:

'The battle sequence starts when a critical density of fans from both sides are assembled on their respective "Ends". Through songs and chants the opposition is portrayed as ignorant "wankers" who come from the worst slums where dead cats are discovered in dustbins and eaten with relish. They are told that their team is soon to be relegated to a lower division; and as that team emerges on to the pitch their goalkeeper is defined as homosexual and their forwards diagnosed as suffering from cerebral palsy. In the meantime, there have been attempts to take the away fans' territory, which usually involves a small group running down to their end, being easily repelled, and quickly running back again. During the match itself, energies are directed towards the traditional songs of group support . . . "You'll never walk alone" (or occasionally "You'll never walk again") is sung with feeling, to the accompaniment of horizontally held scarves. Unless there are any bad fouls which the referee fails to penalise, or any "unnecessary" goals are scored . . . at which point, cries of "aggro" will erupt . . . all will be tolerably amicable.'[68]

Marsh claims that if it is left to run its course, the finely balanced ritual display of loyalty and aggressions ends without physical harm. The danger, he argues, is when external agents, club officials, the police, reporters intervene and break down the balance of ritual. Then, ritual 'aggro' dissolves into real aggression and the fists and bottles fly.

Marsh attempts to argue that the ritual behaviour of football hooligans at Oxford United's ground is more or less the same as tribal warfare rituals amongst the Plains Indians: he writes, in fact, that 'battles between rival fans at football matches follow a similar pattern'. The connecting link is said to be some sort of biological 'male bonding' phenomenon[69] and while there may or may not be some substance in his claim, it hardly begins to explain a number of the facts about hooliganism of this sort: for example, its emergence in the 1960s as a cause for concern; the fact that it has a class bias; or the fact that it is associated with football and not Rugby League. Thus there are a number of gaps and weaknesses in Marsh's essentially biological theory, particularly in the way in which he does not try to site his biological emphasis socially in the subcultural meanings and contexts of youthful rowdyism: football hooliganism may well contain elements of male-bonding and ritual display, but it cannot be *reduced* to a mechanical instinctual process. The Oxford study, for all that, is full of keen observation of fan behaviour, offering a lively account of the 'larking about' which can get out of hand on Saturday afternoon at the match.

Football hooliganism, because it has been so much in the news, confronts us in a particularly sharp manner with the possibility that it is over-publicised and blown out of all proportion. This is true for each of the other areas of hooliganism discussed here, and it is a difficult question to settle in so far as we do not have the data to make a truly historical analysis. We know that the mass media present a false picture when they imply that football and football crowds were always well-behaved in the past, for the history of football is punctuated by censorious commentary (particularly from the upper and middle classes) about unruly and vulgar working class behaviour associated with football.[65] What we really do not know, however, is how unruly and vulgar crowd behaviour was in the past compared with todays' football hooligans. And therefore we do not really know what is novel about football hooliganism, or in what senses it is a continuation of old traditions.[70]

Football is popular entertainment, and popular pastimes frequently have a wide and exciting flavour, although fishing, which is also a popular working class sport in some localities, offers by contrast, serene detachment. Popular entertainments are a release from the drudgery of the working week, standing under the foreman's watchful eye and the factory clock, fitting in with external and relentless rhythms of machine production; fidgeting through the day in routine, unskilled work; becoming like a human machine through the repetitive movements of factory labour. The football

214

crowd offers a contrast. Explosive and ecstatic singing and chanting, having a go at the referee who might represent the manager, the schoolteacher or foreman who is always having a go at you, time off from factory time: these are the experiences out of which football hooliganism can arise. Simon Jacobsen[64] poses the all important question: 'If there were no football, where would this young, largely working class rebelliousness be directed?' It is the recurrent question about football hooliganism. Concerned, no doubt largely to defend 'football clubs who do their utmost to control the pests', Sir Matt Busby[71] has expressed the question in a familiar enough, and agonised, form: 'It is possible that if there were no football matches for gangs of young nuisances to go to they would be even bigger nuisances elsewhere. At least in a football ground they are penned in and not running loose in the streets'. However, the question is perhaps put in a more useful form by Charles Critcher[63]:

'The challenge of the crisis of popular culture is a political challenge, to offer a version of human life which might give people the meaning and identity they search for in sport. If we understand activities like football to be integral parts of our culture, then we may use them as indices of cultural stability. At the moment there is evidence of a crisis in which football is asked to fulfil functions and meet needs which our more general human life should encompass'.

If there is a 'crisis', then what is reflected in hooliganism is the experience of marginality and worthlessness among young, particularly lower working class men in an advanced industrial society. In a singing community of his peers he comes alive and discovers a sense of membership which is denied him elsewhere: all the more reason to embrace the slightly devilish and glamorous identity which is thrown at you by 'them' and sing along, 'We are the famous football hooligans!'

In defence of hooliganism

Throughout this essay, in which I have tried to represent something of what hooliganism is about, I have been engaged in a (largely unspoken) dialogue with the 'law and order' movement which appears to be an increasing force in British public life.[58] James Patrick[19] sums up some of the questionable aspects of this movement to 'get tough with the toughs': 'Middle-class citizens react to the situation by retreating into repugnance and repression or into indifference and inhumanity. 'Cordon off the areas and let them battle it out', is one typical comment. 'Hammer them – it's the only language they understand', is another. The very same aggression condemned in the behaviour of the gang boys is here verbalised and legitimised.

Correspondingly, the approach which I have adopted here will be described by some as being too 'soft' with the vandals, the muggers, and the football rowdies. And admittedly, in the context of appeals for stiffer detention sentences, fencing around soccer pitches, and the insistent cry to 'show them who is boss', this is so. But it is equally true that my approach demands some tough thinking and tough action from the welfare professions: particularly it requires social workers to ask how much longer they are going to put up with having problems dumped into their caseloads which they cannot possibly tackle, given the resources at their command and the nature of their work. Social work has tended to rely on, and its practice is built on, an assumption that the roots of social problems are to be found in the individual personality or in the family. It is, perhaps, somewhat unnerving to be asked to recognise that this is not always so. But there can be little doubt that whatever family influences there are on hooliganism[72] it is not useful to go on acting and thinking as if man lived in a tiny enclave of the personal sphere, somehow divorced from his wider social and cultural moorings. The roots of working class hooliganism extend back into the structure, organisation and rhythm of community and work: long term solutions will only be found by asking long term questions

This kind of questioning poses social work with a number of problems. First, to confess that many of its cherished aims have not worked, or have not been allowed to work, and that if social work is to do anything in the area of youthful violence (and other areas of concern) its efforts must be backed up by solid measures to strike out the roots of social inequality.[73] Social work is faced also with the stimulating challenge of how to connect up with, and how to guide and influence, the decisions of policymakers and planners. But to begin this, it is faced with a further problem: social work is politically immature[74] and it must learn to find a political voice, and perhaps its first message should be that it cannot solve all human misery and unhappiness and conflict; that social workers are not magicians. What social workers can do, at a day to day level, is continue to defend the weak and the oppressed against unnecessary hardship and abuse; and to give a voice to the misfits, the inarticulate, forgotten and brutalised members of society who are so easily written off as social pests.

Of course, it would be easier to defend hooligans if they were not so badly behaved. The critical question, however, is neither to condemn nor condone their behaviour: the critical question is how

216

to listen to what the hooligan seems to be saying. Blowing off steam at a football match, running riot through a shopping centre, defacing an extravagant symbol of wealth, painting your name in letters three feet high with a spray-can, or striking out recklessly at one scapegoat or another – these may be an indispensable means of expressing an unbearable alienation. Perhaps instead of simply thinking of hooligans as a pest to be eradicated, we should respect them as an invaluable 'early warning system' which alerts us to a dangerous fragmentation of social life – particularly in inner city working class districts and which strikes particularly hard at the young.

References
(1) SHALLOO J. P. (1954). 'Vandalism: whose responsibility', *Federal Probation*, vol. *18*, pp. 6–10.
(2) MATZA D. (1964). *Delinquency and Drift*, Wiley, New York.
(3) COHEN S. (1971). 'Directions for research on adolescent group violence and vandalism', *British Journal of Criminology*, vol. *11*, pp. 319–340.
(4) BECKER H. S. (1963). *Outsiders*, The Free Press, New York.
(5) SCHUR E. M. (1971). *Labelling Deviant Behaviour*, Harper and Row, London.
(6) PETERS R. S. (1960). *The Concept of Motivation*, 2nd edition, Routledge and Kegan Paul, London.
(7) PEARSON G. (1975). *The Deviant Imagination*, Macmillan, London.
(8) PEARSON G. (1975). 'Misfit sociology and the politics of socialization', in I. TAYLOR, P. WALTON and J. YOUNG eds., *Critical Criminology*, Routledge and Kegan Paul, London.
(9) PARKER H. J. (1974). *View From the Boys*, David and Charles, Newton Abbot.
(10) MILLER W. B. (1958). 'Lower class culture as a generating milieu of gang delinquency', *Journal of Social Issues*, vol. *14*, pp. 5–19.
(11) TAYLOR I., WALTON P. and YOUNG J. (1973). *The New Criminology*, Routledge and Kegan Paul, London.
(12) YOUNG J. (1975). 'Working class criminology', in TAYLOR I., WALTON P. and YOUNG J. (eds.), *Critical Criminology*, Routledge and Kegan Paul, London.
(13) MATZA D. (1969). *Becoming Deviant*, Prentice Hall, London.
(14) PEARSON G. (1975). 'The politics of uncertainty: a study in the socialization of the social worker', in H. JONES (ed.), *Towards a New Social Work*, Routledge and Kegan Paul, London.
(15) BECKER H. S. (1967). 'Whose side are we on?' *Social Problems*, vol. *14*, pp. 239–47.
(16) WEBER M. (1970). *From Max Weber* transl. and ed. H. H. GERTH and C. W. MILLS, Routledge and Kegan Paul, London.
(17) PULLEN D. (1973). 'Community involvement', in C. WARD (ed.), *Vandalism*, Architectural Press, London.

(18) PEARSON G. (1975). 'Vandals in the park', *New Society*, *34*, 679 p. 69.

(19) PATRICK J. (1973). *A Glasgow Gang Observed*, Eyre Methuen, London.

(20) WARD C. (1973). 'Planners as vandals', in C. WARD (ed.), *Vandalism*, Architectural Press, London.

(21) CRUICKSHANK D. (1973). 'Developers as vandals', in C. WARD (ed.), *Vandalism*, Architectural Press, London.

(22) NEWMAN O. (1973). *Defensible Space*, Architectural Press, London.

(23) NEWMAN O. (1974). 'Community of interest', NACRO Crime Prevention Conference on Architecture, Planning and Urban Crime, London, December 1974.

(24) SOMMER R. (1974). *Tight Spaces: Hard Architecture and How to Humanize It*, Prentice Hall, London.

(25) COHEN P. (1972). 'Subcultural conflict and working class community', *Working Papers in Cultural Studies*, no. 2, pp. 5–51.

(26) GOLDMAN N. (1961). 'A socio-psychological study of school vandalism', *Crime and Delinquency*, pp. 221–230.

(27) POWER M. J., BENN R. T. and MORRIS J. N. (1972). 'Neighbourhoods, schools and juveniles before the courts', British Journal of Criminology, vol. *12*, pp. 111–132.

(28) REYNOLDS D. (1976). 'When school breaks truce', in G. MUNGHAM and G. PEARSON (eds.), *Working Class Youth Culture*, Routledge and Kegan Paul, London.

(29) POWER M. J. (1975). 'Crime prevention: the contribution of the school', in *Children at Risk in School*, Proceedings of NACRO Crime Prevention Conference, War on Want.

(30) MIDWINTER E. (1975). 'Crime and the educative community', in *Children at Risk in School*, Proceedings of NACRO Crime Prevention Conference, War on Want.

(31) CASTLES S. and KOSACK G. (1973). *Immigrant Workers and Class Structure in Western Europe*, Oxford University Press, Oxford.

(32) BERGER J. and MOHR J. (1975). *A Seventh Man*, Penguin, London.

(33) REDFORD A. (1926). *Labour Migration in England 1800–1850*, Manchester University Press, Manchester.

(34) PEARSON G. (1976). 'Paki-bashing in a North East Lancashire cotton town: a case study and its history', in G. MUNGHAM and G. PEARSON (eds.), *Working Class Youth Culture*, Routledge and Kegan Paul, London.

(35) Department of the Environment (1971). *New Life in Old Towns*, HMSO, London.

(36) SEABROOK J. (1973). *City Close-Up*, Penguin, London.

(37) TIPPETT L. H. C. (1969). *A Portrait of the Lancashire Textile Industry*, Oxford University Press, Oxford.

(38) PRIDEAUX F. (1972). 'Of textiles and tariffs', Race Today, vol. *4*, no. 7, p. 217.

(39) SEABROOK J. (1970). 'Packie Stan', New Society, 23 April, no. *395*, **pp. 677–78.**

(40) COHEN S. (1973), *Folk Devils and Moral Panics,* Paladin, St Albans.

(41) DANIEL S. and MC GUIRE P. (eds.), (1972). *The Paint House: Words from an East End Gang,* Penguin, London.

(42) CLARKE J. and JEFFERSON T. (1976). 'Working class youth cultures' in G. MUNGHAM and G. PEARSON (eds.), *Working Class Youth Culture,* Routledge, London.

(43) CLARKE J. (1973). 'The skinheads and the study of youth culture', National Deviancy Conference, University of York, September 1973.

(44) STIMSON G. (1969). 'Skinheads and cherry reds', *Rolling Stone,* 26 July, pp. 22–23.

(45) HOROWITZ I. L. and LIEBOWITZ M. (1968). 'Social deviance and political marginality: towards a redefinition of the relation between sociology and politics', Social Problems, vol. *15,* pp. 280–96.

(46) DOWNES D. (1966). *The Delinquent Solution,* Routledge and Kegan Paul, London.

(47) COHEN A. K. (1955). *Delinquent Boys,* The Free Press, New York.

(48) HALL S. (1972). 'Black Britons', in E. BUTTERWORTH and D. WEIR (eds.), *Social Problems of Modern Britain,* Fontana.

(49) CLARKE J. and JEFFERSON T. (1973). *Down these mean streets: the meaning of mugging,* Occasional Papers, Centre for Contemporary Cultural Studies, Birmingham.

(50) HINES V. (1973). *Black Youth and the Survival Game in Britain,* Zulu Publication, London.

(51) REX J. and MOORE R. (1967). *Race, Community and Conflict,* Oxford University Press, Oxford.

(52) Community Relations Commission (1974). *Unemployment and Homelessness: A Report,* HMSO, London.

(53) HIRO D. (1973). *Black British, White British,* Penguin, London.

(54) THE WAILERS (1973). *Catch a Fire,* Island Records.

(55) THE WAILERS (1974). *Burnin',* Island Records.

(56) MARLEY B. (1974). *Natty Dread,* Island Records.

(57) HEBDIGE D. (1974). *Reggae, Rastas and Rudies: style and the subversion of form,* Occasional Papers, Centre for Contemporary Cultural Studies, Birmingham.

(58) CLARKE J., CRITCHER C., HALL S., JEFFERSON T., ROBERTS B. (1975). 'Mugging and Law and Order', National Deviancy Conference, University College, Cardiff, April 1975.

(59) HALL S. (1975). 'Newsmaking and crime', NACRO Crime Prevention Conference on Journalism, Broadcasting and Urban Crime, London, January 1975.

(60) CLARKE J., CRITCHER C., HALL S., *et al.* (Forthcoming). *The Mugging Panic 1972–73.*

(61) The report in question is 'Footpad Crime and its Community Effect in Lambeth', New Scotland Yard, November 1974. There are reports on various aspects of its contents in *The Sunday Times*, 5 January 1975, and *The Evening News*, 13, 14 and 15 January 1975.

(62) HARLOE M., *et al* (1973). 'The organisation of housing policy in inner London: The Lambeth Experience' in DONNISON D. and EVERSLEY D. (eds.), (1973). *London: Urban Patterns, Problems and Policies*, Heinemann, London.

(63) CRITCHER C. (1971). 'Football and Cultural Values', *Working Papers in Cultural Studies*, no. *1*, pp. 103–119.

(64) JACOBSEN S. (1975). 'Chelsea rule – okay', *New Society*, vol. *31*, no. 651, pp. 780–783.

(65) WALVIN J. (1975). *The People's Game: The Social History of British Football*, Allen Lane, London.

(66) TAYLOR I. (1971). 'Soccer consciousness and soccer Hooliganism', in S. COHEN (ed.), *Images of Deviance*, Penguin, London.

(67) ARMSTRONG G. and WILSON M. (1973). 'City Politics and deviancy amplification', in TAYLOR I. and TAYLOR L. (eds.), *Politics and Deviance*, Penguin, London.

(68) MARSH P. (1975). 'Understanding aggro', New Society, vol. *32*, no. 652, pp. 7–9.

(69) TIGER L. (1969). *Men in Groups*, Nelson, London.

(70) HOGGART R. (1958). *The Uses of Literacy*, Penguin, London.

(71) BUSBY M. (1974). *Soccer at the Top*, Sphere, London.

(72) KELLMER PRINGLE M. (1973). *The Roots of Violence and Vandalism*, National Children's Bureau, London.

(73) PEARSON G. (1975) 'Putting the boot in', *Community Care, 73*, 20 August.

(74) PEARSON G. (1975). 'Making social workers: bad promises and good omens', in BAILEY R. and BRAKE M. (eds.), *Radical Social Work*, Edward Arnold.

Chapter XI Violence and the media
Stuart Hall

Since the 'communications explosion', associated with the expansion of the modern mass means of communication, no single problem has excited so much attention, speculation and research, as the problem of the media and violence. Yet, in any precise sense, the problem continues to elude us. Like most other aspects of violence, the harder you look at it the more it seems to fragment and disappear into itself. The more this particular relationship – the media and violence – has been isolated and studied, the less confident we are that the questions we have been led to pose are the correct ones.

However, before we try to push back the frontier of our ignorance a little, at least to the extent of rephrasing some of the questions, we ought to try to take the measure of what has been discovered about this relationship through the application to it of the normal social-scientific methods of inquiry. The latest in a succession of expensively funded research into this problem was completed in 1972. This is the Report to the American Surgeon-General, initiated by a request to the Department of Health, Education and Welfare by Senator Pastore, and published under the general title, Television and Growing Up: The impact of Televised Violence.[1] The findings, which for convenience I summarise here, as representing the results of the most comprehensive recent survey of the problem, are neither startling nor conclusive nor significantly out of line with what was already known. Not startling, because though the final report and its accompanying five volumes of research reports raise many interesting and important points, it cannot show any straight-forward correlation with a significance higher than 0.20 to 0.30 between exposure to television violence and aggressive tendencies in those young people who view. Even the cautious attempt of the Committee to convert this finding into a 'modest relationship' provoked a storm of controversy in the American social scientific community. Not conclusive because, above all, even in terms of this modest correlation, the Report is quite unable to say how the two are related. Viewing of violence may lead to aggression among some: or, aggression may lead to a propensity to view violence, for some: or both may be the products of a third, unspecified condition. This is really where we have been for nearly twenty years. It has been established by this sort of research for some time that children and young people are impressionable and imitative creatures. In the short-term, they learn a great deal, in an irregular sort of way, and may imitate and mimic what they see and hear from almost any and every significant educational force they come into contact with; parents, peers, school, the media, significant others in the community. Television is among the sources of this kind of imitative learning, especially for the younger age groups, but its influence does not appear to be either strikingly strong nor deep and long-lasting, nor anywhere nearly as significant as, say, school or parents. We know that the impact of televised violence is much sharper for a very small proportion of the younger audience, but they appear to be the vulnerable group, already predisposed by a host of other circumstantial factors to 'act out' aggressively, and if television provides the necessary 'trigger' almost any television will do the trick; and so might almost any other violent or vigorous stimulus. Under limited circumstances, the research suggests, television may have the effect of stimulating aggressive behaviour, either through imitation or instigation. The trouble here is precisely 'what conditions'? Unfortunately, most of the clear cut evidence comes from the highly controlled social-psychological experiment, conducted under extraordinarily well-controlled laboratory environments (thus meeting what is thought to be 'scientific' requirements), so unlike the conditions of normal viewing, and so crude in their symbolic conception as to be virtually useless for extrapolating to wider, more normal, social settings. The famous Bobo doll experiments, where children are exposed to filmed aggressive behaviour (adults on film punching stuffed dolls, to the accompaniment of cries like 'Pow!' and 'Bang!' and then allowed to play with similar dolls, and deliberately frustrated: whereupon they smash the dolls heads in, with accompanying whoops of 'Pow!' and 'Bang!') tell us more about what passes for science in contemporary social scientific research than about real life responses to real violence or, indeed, violence on real-life television. Once the experiments are brought out into a world more closely resembling the one in which we and the children actually inhabit, the clarity of the results, as we might expect, fade away. The moment context, reality-testing, the real world intrude, the vulnerable few isolate themselves out, and the rest – the rest of *us* drop out of the bottom of the computer programmes. In one of the clearest, most succinct and least alarmist recent reviews of the evidence Grant Noble observes that 'The limited evidence from naturalistic studies, including my own, suggest that the effects of televised aggression are less marked [than the kind of evidence referred to above would suggest] and can even be beneficial . . . My own view of the effects of televised violence is that nine times out of ten it has no effect on the viewer. In the remaining 10 per cent of cases the effects depend first on the type

222

of televised violence and secondly on how aggressive the viewer feels.'[2]

Grant Noble's book is worth reading for the soberness of the judgements he makes and the hypotheses he advances. In a limited way he has tried to test, in field studies, the findings of the two major figures in the imitative or aggression-stimulating schools of social-psychological research which dominated the field in the 1960s, and found them, on the whole wanting. If anything, he suggests, anxiety rather than aggressive-imitation is a more likely end-product of exposure to violent television material. Most importantly, his studies seem to point to a relation between what children view and what they do which is far more complex, subtle and indirect than the hard-edged research normally proposes. This relationship may structure, in ways which are hard to define, young people's definitions of the reality of the real world: it may shape the nature of their fantasy life; it may contribute to 'contiguous learning' – i.e. 'give children ideas both what to play with and how to play'; it may operate, as play does, to help us 'work out' or work through problems, relations and solutions hypothetically. Like myths the relationship may provide 'charters for social action' or 'metaphoric expressions of prevailing social values'. These are all important, indeed crucial, social influences, but they are hard to prove; even harder to isolate and attribute to television as against other factors; and they are certainly not of the dramatic order such as should provoke a moral panic, a traditionalist backlash, or provide the raw materials for a clean-up-television-and-end-moral-pollution-on-our-screens crusade. Yet, concerning television and violence, we continue to have all three.

This may be the point at which to step back and ask, not how much violence does television or the media cause, but rather, why are we so preoccupied with violence? Why are we so convinced that the media must be a 'school for violence' and one of its principal causes? Why are we so preoccupied with this particular way of framing the question? What – to put it another way – is the social history of this social problem?

This is a dangerous step to take, because it tends to make the first problem disappear (perhaps too easily and quickly); but also it plunges us, instead, into what used to be called the 'sociology of knowledge' and what ought to be called the social history of social problems, or the sociology of contemporary ideologies. We cannot begin to offer a definitive answer here, but we can begin to indicate the elements of an account, and even this modest attempt has the effect of more or less totally restructuring the field of inquiry and the sorts of questions to which we need answers.

223

Some of the false trails seem to arise because of the way we think about both violence and the media. We think of violence – which is, of course, an extremely complex and general category – principally in terms of aggressive behaviour: aggressive behaviour is by definition bad, bad for the individual, and for the society in which it appears. The sort of aggressive behaviour which we associate with violence is usually located within the individual's psychological make-up. Of course, our beliefs about violence are also projected outwards into society: but here society is the victim, the object of violence – that which prevents us from being 'naturally' violent, and hence what violence undermines or attacks. The concept of social violence or of institutional violence has been extremely difficult to put across, and has hardly penetrated what we might call normal, everyday moral and political discourse. Collective violence is thus understood as the sum or the aggregate of violent individuals, letting their natural aggression free to roam and practice against society. Above all, violence is a behavioural category; it consists, primarily, of violent acts.

Much the same kind of behaviourism seems to dominate the way we think about violence in the media. Indeed, this is not a matter only of everyday beliefs and lay ideology; the behavioural image seems to have penetrated deep into so-called scientific thinking and research, not only about the violent effects of the media, but about media effects in general. In the earlier phases of mass communications research, violent messages were thought of and researched as if they were propaganda messages or commands. However and wherever they appeared, they were researched as if they directly propositioned us to behave and act in certain ways, straight recommendations to behave violently, much in the same way as presidential election campaign messages were instructions to vote for a certain candidate, or 'Buy Whiter Than White' was a proposition to go straight out from the radio or television set to the supermarket and obey the instruction. 'Effects', in other words, were immediate, short-term: they worked like commands, they could be seen and shown in terms of the number of people who directly behaved in the ways shown or recommended, and the key test of their effectiveness was to be measured principally by behavioural response. Very large numbers of the early experiments were, therefore, structured in terms of 'before/after' effects: before, we were nice, harmless, law-abiding citizens; then along come the violent images and propositions; and, lo, out we go, our aggressive instincts aroused and unsatisfied until we had expressed ourselves in violent action, our instinct for imitation unappeased until we had 'acted out' what we had seen on the screen.

In the later stages, as this narrow interpretation of 'effects' applied through the general survey methods produced negligible or insignificant results, the research strategy which replaced it did not abandon or modify the original hypothesis, but tightened it up. The 'controls' were not strict enough: the variables not sufficiently tightly tested. The second phase was thus dominated by the laboratory experiment: what had previously been seen to be the 'effect' of the media in providing models for social behaviour in ordinary life settings, was narrowed down into what the 'subjects' of the experiment would do in the immediate aftermath of being subjected to violent filmed material. Now the 'effect' of violence was expected to show up in the immediate forms of play following the exposure. What is more, the nature of the message (hitherto understood on the quite inadequate model of the campaign or advertising slogan) was even further reduced to a straight behavioural impulse. The content, form or structure of the message was accorded little or no status in these experiments. Virtually any piece of 'filmed aggression' would do. The subjects were conceived of as ready and willing to 'read' any violent stimulus off and immediately transfer the stimulus into an imitative or aggressive response. Gradually the limited applicability of the results gained by this type of social-psychological investigation has been more and more widely acknowledged: and though the recent American reports – the Surgeon-General's study referred to above, and its distinguished predecessor, the Eisenhower Report on the Causes and Prevention of Violence[3], which gave considerable attention to the effects of the media – still rely heavily on experimental findings of this type, their highly unnatural nature has fallen into disrepute. However, even in the best and most sophisticated parts of these studies (for example, the contributions by George Gerbner of the Annenberg School to the sophistication of research strategies in the studies of the media and violence, reported in both American studies: and the BBC and Leicester Centre for Mass Communications Research studies which draw heavily on Gerbner's departures) are still not altogether free of what I am calling the 'behavioural' interpretation. Gerbner has introduced the quite critical point that violence on television is not real violence but a 'message about violence' (a very different thing): that is to say, it is gradually being recognised that messages are symbolic, not natural or behavioural forms, operating under the rule of language and signs, and not under the rubric of a 'stimulus'. This is a welcome departure, but still most of the

225

studies of violence on television assume that what is called 'the violent episode' – that is, the sequence of the film, play or serial which is likely to have an 'effect', the one which actually shows an individual being aggressively violent towards another individual – is the scene which, on its own, had an effect: and that, for purposes of research, it can be isolated from the rest of the programme in which it appears, its social characteristics (who hits whom, where and when) and its behavioural impact studied on their own.

Now, however else the complex messages of the mass media 'work' it seems fairly certain that they do not work like that. It is a considerable time, and a multitude of research programmes, since Himmelweit and her colleagues,[4] in their study of Television and the Child, confirmed by socio-psychological study what most critics and all aficionados of the 'Western' long ago assumed: that, though violence was intrinsic to the Western genre it was unlikely to be the actual episodes of violence in isolation which explained either their deep hold over the imagination of the modern cinema (and later television) audience, or the reactions of viewers to them. Himmelweit and others have convincingly shown that the stylization and codification which is characteristic of this form is crucial to its meaning: and that conventionalization of narrative, situation and character also have an effect on how children respond to it and what they learn from it. Not only do children 'learn' the conventions of the simple-structure Western, like the rules of a game, but the very conventionalization of its elements serves to 'background' the actual violent content, displacing the focus of interest on to other elements. In another paper I argued, following Himmelweit, Warshow and others, that we learn more about styles of masculine conduct, how to 'keep one's cool' in difficult situations, how to 'come on strong and silent', and a variety of other similar moral and social 'cues' from the stylized nature of the Western genre than we ever learn about how to imitate actual techniques of inflicting violence or injury on others.[5] The violence of course, is intrinsic to the form, as it is with most of the action and adventure narratives with which the fictions of our culture are packed. But we learn other things about violence in the context of a whole structure of other themes: e.g. it is impossible to abstract the violence from the struggle between law and nature which is also an intrinsic theme of the Western form, and the other social myths about which, in its simplified way, the Western speaks. All the scenes of violence in this and the other adventure genres in film and television, which have been the source of so much public disquiet and the focus of so many research programmes, are embedded in a moral structure, however simple or rudimentary. Westerns, indeed, have a strikingly clear, though often skeletal and over-simplified moral structure – a moral economy, to which they strictly adhere. However strange it may seem, few violent actions are wholly gratuitous, meaningless or unexplained: they are always motivated in some way or another. Further, they are enacted by figures with transparent moral identities but complex personal and social characteristics. Everything which the research suggests about the nature of the identification of the young, in fantasy, with the heroes of these adventures, points to and supports the proposition that their violent acts are seen and understood as part of a wider complex of moral structures, and that it is these complexes as a whole which exert their mythic value and force over our imaginations. This is certainly not to argue that these perennial modern myths are 'simply entertainment': that we learn nothing, take no social messages, derive no meaning from them except in whiling away the time. But it seems clear that our engagement with them is a complex, imaginative and symbolic one: that their impact is not immediately behavioural or imitative, but indirect and cognitive – they serve, as myths have always done, to reproduce certain crucial social meanings and values, to provide imaginative 'charters for action'. Effects of this kind may be harder to prove, harder to separate out from other social influences which help to produce social individuals; harder to slot into grand hypotheses about the 'causes for the rising tide of violence': but we do not get any closer to an understanding of the relation between the media and violence by simplifying it in the service of clear hypothesis-testing. Basically, the approach to the study of media content which has tried to evade or dispense with the category of meaning, treating the language and form of the representations of the world we see (real and fictional) as if they were meaningless, contentless impulses – blips on the screens of our nervous system – and the approach to the study of 'effects' which reduces meaning to behavioural effect, in the short term, have done immense damage to our way of conceptualising the problem, without in any way advancing the field or contributing to our social knowledge about the media and violence. Both have led us down the behaviourist trap.

But we have all – researchers and ordinary citizens – been willingly led down blind alleys, partly because our notion of how social science produces useful knowledge about the real world is deeply tinged with positivism; but even more because there are few areas of social action where we think so 'positivistically' as the area of violence itself. If, as we have argued, the media do

227

not work and cannot be understood by a simple behaviourism, it seems true that violence does not work and cannot be explained in that way either. The tendency to think of violence as a single, simple category given in nature not culture, and reducible to a set of propositions about 'natural human behaviour' is a pronounced one, by no means only within scientific research, but also – perhaps most of all – in our everyday thinking and language, and in what passes as common-sense wisdom.

In a proper sense, we ought not to talk of 'violence' at all, but of violences. In our society there is a whole culture of violence – a complex set of ideas, vocabularies, lexicons of violence which classify out the world of social behaviours. The 'culture' or languages of violence serve, like all of our complex vocabularies, to classify and order the chaos of experience into meaningful clusters, each domain of which carries different moral weights, different associations, different feelings and value. Like all social vocabularies, they render certain clusters of actions highly visible and salient to us, actions which arouse strong positive or negative feelings: but they also serve to render other natural acts culturally invisible. You can tell something important about the historical development of a society simply by noting how the 'vocabulary of violence' changes through historical time. For example, the 'violence' which so preoccupied the early media researchers and moralists in the United States was, overwhelmingly, fictional violence (after the model of the movies). After the mid-1960's with the rise of the black movement, the ghetto rebellions, the student and anti-war movements and the growth of the American New Left and of political dissent, the violence about which moralists, researchers and officials were most concerned was real-life violence, actuality violence, the violence of the news, the documentary, the violence of social conflict. Some recent work done by Alan Shuttleworth and others at Birmingham[6] shows very clearly how differently the British press describes different kinds of violence: the routine, distanced, impersonal language of some of the 'routine' reports of violence: the dramatic, sensational, emotive language used to describe other, more unusual or extraordinary kinds of violence. These cannot be explained by looking for such 'natural' categories as the size or scale of the violence involved. Just as one small scene of violence in a Western film which does not obey the old conventions (like the Wild Bunch) has a far greater emotional kick than watching hundreds of Indians ride to their deaths in the old-style two-dimensional Western film, so our popular press can describe death by war or starvation of thousands of human beings who happen, geographically or historically to be far away from us in a distanced and impersonal rhetoric, whilst employing richly loaded and intensified rhetorics to describe single violent incidents which are close at hand, physically or psychologically, relevant or salient to the life-situation and experience of its readers. The public language of journalism (on which, since so few of us ever experience great violence at first hand, we depend for our descriptions and ideas of violence) has a very different rhetoric for the My Lai massacres in Vietnam, the Sahara or Bangla Desh starvations, or the Biafran war than it does for the description of a single child molester closer at hand. So the natural register, which suggests that violence is ordered along a simple quantitative scale, is massively inflected and over-determined by our cultural vocabularies, our classifying schemes of interpretation. When we are dealing, not with directly experienced violence but with secondary accounts and descriptions of violence – the source from which most of our general ideas about violence originate – it is the mapping and ordering effects of these cultural vocabularies of feeling and value – to which the media massively contribute – which matter, not the natural fact of physical injury. It is not simply a matter of the media telling us what to feel and think about different kinds of violence – though they do indeed have this selective cognitive reinforcing effect. To some degree, the media reflect as well as selectively strengthen the maps of meanings about violence which are already at work in culture, and which order and help us to make sense of the experienced social world. These changing vocabularies of the media, therefore, reflect the changing patterns of perception, the shifting map of social concerns, about violence in the society. This, too, is a cultural not a natural development. There may be societies which seem to us particularly prone to violence, as a result of their peculiar historical trajectories, but there is also a 'social history' of violence, a social history of the concerns about violences.

We might try to make this point more concrete by looking at some of the different feelings and attitudes attributed in our own culture to different kinds of violent crime. It has been recently suggested[7] that in common-sense ideology, different kinds of violent crime – about which there has been, in recent years, something very nearly approaching a moral panic – are differently conceived and arouse different kinds of social sentiment. Murder, for example, one of the most violent kinds of crime, arouses considerable public feeling, often of a morbidly collective kind especially if accompanied by sexual assault. Since murder is statistically rare and quite out-of-the-ordinary, people seem to be fascinated by it, but not to relate or translate it into their own personal universes. People feel very differently about organised violent crime – again few of us live and work in situations where we expect to encounter its effects at first hand. When we look, directly, or through the use of photographs, into the face of someone accused of murder, we feel ourselves looking at someone who is 'other' and alien as a person from ourselves and others we know: however, what we feel about organized criminal violence is that there is a conspiracy somewhere, an 'invisible society', loose and practising on society. This is a powerful but abstract fear, different from our response to murder, but very powerful and recurring: i.e. throughout the 1950's and 1960's a speculative news story continually appeared suggesting that the 'Mafia are moving into Britain', though in any organized sense, such an eventuality has failed to materialize.

Now take two other kinds of crime (street crime and theft) both of which are lower in the scale of violence than either murder or organized violent crime but which nevertheless are experienced in a far more charged and personal way. When described in the rhetoric of popular journalism, street crime and theft generate sensational and stereotyped uses of vocabulary. They are markedly different from murder or violent crime in that although street crime involves perhaps sudden attack, including physical jostling in the course of a theft or snatching, burglary involves no physical contact at all, indeed, the whole process is one of undetected stealth. Yet the fact seems to be that we experience both, and use a rather similar emotive vocabulary to describe them, as if they involved similar types of violation. But what is it which has been violated? In the first instance, our physical persons; in the second, our homes and property but not ourselves. What unites them, in terms of the vocabulary of violence and violation we use, is the sense of intrusion into sacred, private space: in the first instance the intimate space of our bodies; but certainly also the intimate public spaces – doorways, street corners, sidewalks, playgrounds, parks, shortcuts, etc – which we have come to think of as perfectly secure. In the second instance, it is the personal, private space of our home and intimate possessions which awakens the sense of violation – strangers breaking and entering, handling our things, rifling through our possessions, the objects which define us as individuals. What is violated is in fact a social and historical construction, not a physical entity: it is ourselves as persons, to which the whole historical development of safety, of the spread of the rule of law and order, have contributed: or our public-communal spaces. And indeed, this history which has made these things possible as cultural constructs for us, is embedded in our reactions to both kinds of 'violence'. For we are not only 'violated' but morally indignant about both kinds of crime, in part because the idea of each kind of crime is structured by a vivid contrast: what it used to be like/what it is like now. Time and again in the personal or public descriptions of these kinds of crime, we will come across this other idea which is held in powerful association with it: the idea that what was once safe is safe no longer. When we say we are 'concerned about violence' or concerned about the way the media might contribute to violence, we never have in the forefront of our minds this effect: the rhetoric of moral and social discourse on violence always seems to occur, not isolated on its own, but as part of an extremely complex, historically dense, cluster of meanings. Yet this is how we actually use language in our culture to talk about and to express our feelings and concerns about violence: and this is the set of discourses about violence from which the mass media continually feed.

It is worth spending a little more time on these discourses about violence in our culture, especially where they occur, not as part of an official or scientific or theoretical discourse but as part and parcel of 'common-sense ideas'; and particularly in what we might call the more traditional of common-sense ideas, the more traditionally inclined social strata in our population, where the preoccupation with violence and crime seem to be so pronounced. If we try to speculate a little about the underlying premises in the traditional common-sense ideas about violence, we will find that, embedded in the so-called 'natural' idea of violence are an extremely complex set of premises and notions, a set of powerful social images, which may not be coherently held, consistently expressed or theoretically clarified, but which are no less powerful in the way they help us to classify our 'problematic social reality'.

Within common-sense ideas about violence there appear to be two large, loose structure of ideas, which we might think of, conveniently, if roughly, as 'conservative' and 'liberal'. In conservative ideas about violence (where traditional thinking is at its strongest), the origin of violence is thought of as inside individuals. It is located, either as a psychological or as a spiritual impulse: that is, it arises either from the 'bad' or from the 'evil' in us. Some might argue that the former, the psychological 'explanation' for the origin of violence, is really only a secular version of the latter, the spiritual explanation. Both are grounded in the natural (which is why, in this area, behaviourism exerts such a powerful sway over our thinking)—they are aspects of an irreversible, permanent, unchanging 'human nature'. 'Naturally', our natures

231

are violent and aggressive; or 'naturally' we are all tainted with evil – original sin – of which violence is a tangible outward expression. It follows that, if we were simply left to our own devices, we would all behave violently and aggressively towards one another. Hence, this notion of violence is very closely associated with its opposite, restraint. Only the establishment of effective restraints prevent us from giving free expression to the 'evil which is within'. Both conceptions of violence, therefore, tend to produce as their opposite their necessary complement, ideas of order and constraint. Psychological impulses to violence like the impulses to crime, unregulated competition, and irrationalism (there seems to be a very close link between them) can be tutored out of existence, or rather, held in check, kept in control, either by the application of strong external disciplines, or by the creation of strong internal regimes of psychological discipline. In this view it is the disciplined society and the structures of an ordered society which impose an externally constraining discipline over our natural tendencies, which ensures a stable and civilised life, free of irrational play of violence. Hence, there is a strong preoccupation here with the institutions which exert discipline—the church, the state, the family and the school: and in general with a hierarchically ordered society, which gives a continuous public expression of, and recognition to, the need for 'the orderly life', the ordered society'. Because the two ideas are so deeply intertwined the social equation which strikes the necessary balance between them is finely established, and a change of magnitude on one side suggests a change of magnitude on the other. Hence, any perceived upsurge in violence and aggression is interpreted either as a threat to the stability, order and discipline of society: or a token that the institutions which exert restraint are not doing their job properly – the crisis of the family and the school, which is so intrinsic a part of our vocabularies of moral concern nowadays: or both. There are good historical reasons why, under certain specific conditions, this general concern with the effectiveness of the social restraints over violence should precipitate into specific cycles of moral concern, a specific sense of 'crisis' in the disciplining institutions of society, a specific kind of moral panic.

Of course, in this view external constraint alone will not suffice. It is far more effective if the violence which is a natural propensity within each of us is tutored and regulated by a strict regime of internal self-discipline. If we take a more psychological view, then it is the self-discipline of the internalised morals of society in the form of the forces of psychological repression – the super-ego; if we take a more religious view then it is the self-regulation by morality and conscience. In this respect, England is a peculiarly well-ordered, highly self-disciplined society; what Reich would have called the 'character-armour' of the puritan conscience[8] and the rigorous taboo on spontaneous pleasure, which begins in the earliest years with the regulation of the emotions, of the sexual life and learning the 'hard lesson' of the postponement of gratifications.

This cluster of attitudes and concepts which we have called the 'conservative' or traditionalist common-sense ideology about violence is really an extremely strong 'structure of feeling' in our society. It has a very distinctive place, and is continually echoed and re-echoed in certain parts of the media. Unless you bear in mind the hidden connections which I have tried to unravel a little above, it is hard to make sense of the contributions to, say, 'Any Answers' or 'Any Questions': or to understand precisely from what level of thinking and feeling come those deeply concerned and deeply conventional 'letters to the press', both popular, and, even more, the local press, or many of the 'grass-roots', 'silent majority' contributors to 'phone-in programmes on radio. Without wanting to treat social classes as single agents who enter history with number plates on their backs, I think of this as a peculiarly lower-middle or what used to be called 'petit-bourgeois' voice: or the voice of the traditional, as compared with the progressive, more cosmopolitan, middle classes. It is from this stratum that the moral crusaders, the populist guardians which have deepened the preoccupation with social violence and spear-headed the moral backlash in recent years have been drawn.

This attitude, and the precise historical conjuncture which has precipitated it in the form of a distinct and organised 'social movement' may become clearer if we think of the second great cluster of ideas about violence, not wholly dissimilar or distinct from the first, and on which many of the same currents of feeling are drawing. This is what we might call the 'liberal' structure of feeling about violence. Here, violence is conceived of more as the product of social forces and conditions than of individuals; though individuals who are not 'fully formed'; un- or under-socialised, who are 'weak' or 'sick' or 'disorganised' may also reveal a proneness to expressing their weakness or their under-socialization in expressive and irrational bouts of violence. Here, violence is often seen as the accompaniment of social conflict; as arising from social conditions, from poverty or destitu-tion; from low or bad education, from impoverished home and family life; unstable social relationships; an insufficiently caring or self-supportive community. On the face of it, this more 'liberal' notion, though often treating the individual as largely the object of determining forces acting upon him, ought to be more amenable to the idea of the progressive 'reform' of violence by the improvement of social and community conditions. And, indeed, the reforming impulses, moderating violence with care (as in the rise of the professions and the professional ideology of social work) or moderating violence by steady, gradual improvement (giving rise to Fabian and 'labourist' measures of social reform) have been one by-product of this structure of feelings about how to prevent, or better, cut off at its source, the impulse to violence which appears in society. Again, the media intersect directly with this structure of feeling: in what we might call 'social problem' television and radio, in the investigation of social conditions through the investigative documentary: and with the immediate consideration of practical, pragmatic measures to 'improve things' in much of current-affairs coverage and debate, as well as in the social problem side of feature journalism.

The media not only play a part in constructing violence into a social issue, they also have a role to play in the orchestration of the concern which they have helped to create. For, without fail, sections of the press and spokesmen on radio and television will use these causes for concern as the basis for stimulating the public into a moral panic, or for organizing a public crusade and expressing public moral indignation. The popular daily and Sunday press, especially, with its ideological roots deep in the traditionalist structure of feeling described above, and its social roots deep in the traditional heartland of those voices of local residents, the silent majorities who are the bearers and articulators of this moral indignation on behalf of the whole nation, frequently then assume the 'public voice', adopt the 'moral watchdog' rule and thunder, in the name of the people, for vengeance. Elsewhere we have tried to describe this process in greater detail; how the face-to-face agents of social control employ the media, where they have natural access to the topics for which they have administrative responsibility, to air the social interpretations of the indicators they produce; how then the press assumes the public voice and, by incorporating the administratively 'neutral' accounts into more fullsome and vigorous accounts and explanations of its own, calls in the name of the nation for measures of constraint and control, frequently bringing in another distinguished spokesman from some other area, who reads the social signs in the same way just to close the circle.[7] The orchestration of public crusades and moral panics about violent events is worth examination, e.g. the critical years of polarization between the mid-1960's and the present in certain of the populist papers.

The media are one of the principal agencies continually exploring society's normative boundaries; what are the breaking-points and limits of social tolerance? This deconstruction and reconstruction of consensus is compounded by two other aspects of media work. The first is news value, that structure of professional ideas and practices, of routine and know-how which organize the routine work of news-selection and construction. For news values, tied both to the professional requirements of journalists and the competitive requirements of the media, will always prefer the sensational, unpredictable, unexpected, dramatic, conflict, and extreme contrast over what is normal and predictable. In Jock Young's phrase the media 'select events which are atypical, present them in a stereotypical fashion, and contrast them against a backcloth of normality which is overtypical'.[9] (See also [10]). This is further compounded in television by visual news values, and the choice of dramatic or sensational pictures as a way of making an impact compared with almost any other way of relaying information or analysing situations. The operation of news values through the media, and particularly the operation of visual news values in television, has the effect of representing every event at its most dramatic moment, which almost by definition, is its most violent moment. Thus strikes are represented at the moment when pickets and police come to blows and the Northern Ireland conflict is represented by the millionth of a second picture of a bomb exploding. This displacement to the dramatic aspect of a story has the effect of foreshortening events, since on the whole it is easier to show the results of an explosion on the screen than to explain the complex causes which led to it in the first place. It also has the result of testing out the normative boundaries of society through the exploration of its violent aspect. In the general search for the dramatic the press is inclined to select (as representing or standing for the rest) the most illegal aspect of something which is morally disapproved; the most subversive side of something which is illegal; and the most violent side of something which is subversive. But, as I argued earlier, these are also the very normative contours of society itself. Acts, people and events which are morally unconventional represent a threat to society's values and moral cohesion; but those who are morally deviant and acting illegally are challenging the law (e.g. a hippy who smokes cannabis); and someone who acts illegally and on that basis tries to change society is subverting society (e.g. drug taking, pot smoking, student militants); but subversives who employ

235

violence are the enemies of law and order, the disciples of anarchy. Thus, society's self appointed moral guardians who desire greater social control, more authority, discipline and restraint and who because of the progressive polarization of society feel that things are slipping from bad to worse (i.e. up to the threshold of violence) may have their worst fears daily and nightly confirmed by the relatively independent processes of the media, who find it convenient to classify problematic or threatening events into and through these widening circles of disturbance. The effect of both working to reinforce each other is to promote a tightening circle of social control, a solidifying of the tradionalist world view, a moral backlash and populist crusades – all in the form of an escalating moral panic about violence.

In this paper I have deliberately played down the common sense way of trying to think about the relation between violence and the media: first because the common sense view is based on a wholly inadequate conceptualization of the problem; and second because it has, as a consequence of its inability to conceptualize, failed to produce any clear-cut or convincing evidence or proof for the relation it is seeking to demonstrate. But I have also deliberately tilted the balance because I believe the common sense view, often backed up by quite inadequate research masquerading in the guise of science, has the effect of rendering invisible certain other, different aspects of the relation of the media to violence which seem to me both far more important and far more tangible. I hope what I have said will not be taken as representing a sanguine view of the question of violence. I am simply not convinced that the use of this catch-all category, with its great over-simplifying power and its horrendous connotations is at all helpful in our attempt to answer questions which seem to me more significant. It is violences, not violence, that we need to understand; violences as embedded in the structures of our ideas and perceptions, in our classifications and categories, in our discourse about society and our ideologies. And then, whose violence? For what purpose? Directed against whom? But that is another Pandora's box.

References
(1) Report to the American Surgeon-General (1972).
    Television and Growing Up: The impact of televised violence.
(2) NOBLE G. (1975). *Children in Front of the Small Screen,*
    Constable, London.
(3) EISENHOWER. *Report on the Causes and Prevention of Violence*
    (1959).
(4) HIMMELWEIT, H. T., *et al* (1958). Television and the Child.
    Oxford University Press: Oxford.

236

(5) HALL S. (1974). 'Encoding and Decoding', *Education and Culture,*
26, Council of Europe.

(6) SHUTTLEWORTH A., *et al* (1975). *Television, Violence and the
Crime Drama Series.* Unpublished report, Centre for
Contemporary Cultural Studies. University of Birmingham.

(7) CLARKE J., CRITCHER C., HALL S., JEFFERSON T., ROBERTS B.
(Forthcoming). *The Mugging Panic 1972–73.*

(8) REICH W. (1970). *The Mass Psychology of Fascism,*
Souvenir Press, London.

(9) YOUNG J. (1974). 'Mass Media, Drugs and Deviance', in ROCK P.
and MACINTOSH M. (Eds.) *Deviance and Social Control,*
Tavistock, London.

(10) HALL S. (1974). *Deviance, Politics and Media,* in ROCK P. and
MACINTOSH M. (Eds.) *Deviance and Social Control,*
Tavistock, London.

237

Chapter XII **The violence within**
Tom Douglas

'A tragedy is the imitation of an action that is serious and also, as having magnitude, complete in itself . . . with incidents arousing pity and fear, wherewith to accomplish its purgation of such emotions.'
Aristotle, Poetics 6

1 Introduction

The basis of sociodrama is as old as man himself. In terms of recorded history the concept of 'catharsis' through the medium of drama is to be found in Aristotle. However most modern users of the technique are dependent to a large measure upon the work of J. L. Moreno and his formulation of the theory of 'spontaneous' learning. In fact, modern sociodrama combines the cathartic effect noted by Aristotle which was the purgation of emotion by the audience while watching the play, with the development of insight in the actor while playing the part of another person.

Bennett[1] says: 'Moreno's premise is that a significant aspect of the learning process is learning through active responses – as differentiated from "content" learning, in which the learner is a relatively passive recipient, taking in what is taught and feeding it back on request. He contends that the most valuable aspects of learning, in terms of total-life application, occur in the field of human relations; and in this area, the individual will function at his best if he learns to act and react with spontaneity, free of blocks, capable of working through his frustrations, evaluating each situation in terms of its actual components rather than in terms of preconceived stereotypes'.

It would seem to follow then, that in the complex area of human violence, 'content' learning, i.e. the informational aspects, lectures, seminars and discussion groups, while supplying a basis of knowledge would perhaps do little about the lifelong habit patterns of the learners. In the context of the Development Group's seminars on violence in particular this would tend to show in the selective nature of the perception of the seminar participants.

Litwak[2] writing about the effect of group processes on communication, stresses the fact that to conceive of human beings as rational, i.e. able to accept communication and to interpret it with complete objectivity, is obviously false as witness the use of techniques of repetition and reinforcement which are frequently used to enhance the take-up of informational inputs. He writes, 'Three findings seemed to occur in a universal enough form to dash any hope that communications theory might rest on the assumption of the rational man. These findings were:

(1) Self-selectivity in listening.
(2) Self-selectivity in interpretation.
(3) No necessary relationship between knowledge and action'.

Quite simply (1) implies that people will very rarely listen to any piece of information which is slanted to a viewpoint they do not hold. (2) implies that even if they should listen they are seldom convinced because they select from the offering only those parts which are consistent with and reinforce their previously held opinions. Finally, even when reached and partially convinced Litwak maintains that 'there is some evidence indicating that people who are exposed to and accept facts which conflict with those they originally held will not necessarily act on these facts'.

Given that the intention of imparting facts in the first instance was to modify people's behaviour, then Litwak's findings offer small hope of success where the facts offered run somewhat counter to the view of those it is desired to inform.

The seminars on violence were originally specifically designed to enhance the knowledge of all aspects of human violence amongst groups of people who were responsible for the daily handling of people in residential situations in which violence of some sort was a constant factor; constant, that is, in being ever present in some form or other, not in a steadily maintained level. It was hoped that increased understanding of the nature of human violence could result in enhanced performance by the members of the groups in coping with their every day routine situations which as the seminars developed included a wide range of services including some which were not residential.

With this end in view it was decided to attempt to bypass some of the selectivity blocks referred to earlier by the use of the experimental learning device of socio-drama. This device is a development of role play. It takes a social situation which is fairly explicit and members of a group select roles within the situation, rehearse and finally play them before an audience of their peers. The performance is followed by discussion. 'Follow-up studies of role-playing have repeatedly shown that the procedure is more effective if there is feedback afterwards.' [Argyle [3]].

What developed over several seminars was a tightly keyed scheme designed to lead the seminar participants to become aware of their own violence and of the nature of their emotional responses to incidents of violence. Bennett[1] lists the following contributions to the learning process that such a constricted experience can have.

'(1) It commits people to act out their true feelings with reference to a situation in a permissive atmosphere, and thus effects catharsis.

(2) It develops flexibility in handling situations and enlists the resources of the individual in facing unanticipated circumstances.

(3) It enables the individual to make mistakes and to experience failure in a sheltered situation, without fear of consequences, and thus enables him to try himself out in situations without being damaged in the process.

(4) (omitted as irrelevant to the current discussion).

(5) It develops understanding of our own motives, aims and drives and those of other people, points up, through direct, spontaneous, creative experience, what happens when these elements interact and how both the situation and the persons are re-shaped by the interaction; and demonstrates how deeper insights *commonly experienced,* aid in effective and constructive human relations.'

2 The design of the exercises

The seminars were held in two parts separated by two–three weeks. The first week was concerned with informational input and discussion, the second with discussion of case material, some additional information and the exercises. Thus the seminar members had worked together in small and large groups, in formal and informal settings for some days before they came to the exercises. They had had some opportunity to establish contact and to set up working and friendship groups and individual relationships. Each small group had grown accustomed to its designated leader, an individual chosen by the organizers, briefed by them and whose name was listed on the course programme as a group leader. The Exercise usually occupied the best part of two whole days and was programmed as follows:

Briefing meeting for observers, planners and group trainer

Session 1   Introduction of the whole group to the concept of 'experiential' learning and to the idea that the exercises were designed to enhance understanding of all kinds of violence. Re-allocation of seminar group members to a smaller number of groups. Some group leaders were then appointed by the group trainer as 'observers' and their change of role explained.

Each newly constituted group was then sent off to its own room and asked to formulate a document on 'violence'. No leaders were appointed and little

	guidance given as to how to complete this task. Observers were asked to watch and record the behaviour of members.
Session 2	Feedback from the small groups. Each group was asked to remain identifiable, i.e. the members being close together to present their material. The observer in each group was asked to contribute his more objective report not only on the 'content' of the document but also on the 'process' by which it was arrived at. Each group and its observer reported in turn, before all the seminar members.
Session 3	Introduction of the whole group to socio-drama techniques. Each small group was given its drama task and the observers required to record, after the large group has been split and sent off to group rooms. This meant that originally each small group was unaware of the drama task of the others.
Sessions 4–6	Were concerned with the playback of each group's drama before the remaining members. This was followed in each case by discussion of the content and process elements with constant reference to the observers for comment on the behavioural patterns displayed.
Section 7	Small groups were asked to formulate a feedback document based on their experiences. Group leaders were then reinstated as leaders.
Session 8	Feedback documents from each small group were discussed in the total group. There was then a summing up process and the exercise concluded.

This was followed by a report-back meeting of observers, planners and group trainer. The number of sessions in an exercise depended upon the number of seminar members present and hence the number of groups.

Equally the timing of sessions was flexible to account for factors like distance to rooms, meal times etc.

3 Detailed analysis of the exercise

The briefing meeting was solely designed to convey information to the group leaders about the possible effects of the proposed change in their roles and to reassure them about the consequences.

The introduction to the large group contained all the rational explanations for the exercise and the possible learning outcomes, but no effort was made to allay anxiety about what would actually happen. Originally it was felt necessary to generate some hostility about such an intellectual and authoritarian approach, but such provocation was found to be unnecessary and dropped. Few people in the seminar group recognized that they were experiencing being handled in an authoritarian manner until at a later stage they were asked how they had felt about it. The culminating points of the first session were the arbitrary re-selection of the groups, the allocation of the group leaders to the role of observers and the imposition of a near impossible task, the 'thesis' on violence.

During the feedback in session two after some ninety minutes in the small groups, the hostility of the seminar members to the group trainer became quite apparent. By using the observers, by freely admitting the autocratic nature of the decision making, seminar members were gradually made aware of how angry they had become, how abusive in their language and how far this had gone before they became conscious of it. These feelings were then immediately related to their back-home experience. In this session much attention was given to the struggles for power which took place in the leaderless groups, the kind of reception given to new members allocated to established groups and the disruptive effects of having a task which is almost impossible and not a great deal of time in which to complete it. Some time was given to the consideration of why people actually do what they are asked and an attempt was made to analyse the pressures involved.

At the end of this session seminar members were much more aware that they themselves are violent people and that little provocation is needed to precipitate a violent response. They become aware of how easily they too can generate situations, unwittingly, which promote violent responses in others who are in their care. There is a dawning realisation; that violent behaviour in others is outside and separated from oneself and easy to talk about, but that one's own violence and violent nature are usually hidden away and not taken into account. Some anxiety about the need to control one's own violence is usually expressed at this point.

The socio-drama now offers the opportunity to act out for five minutes that personal violence in a supportive and creative atmosphere. The drama tasks have an inherently violent nature, but the safety valve lies in each group's acceptance of the level of portrayal and any member's ability to opt out. Some of the tasks used are listed below:

(1) You are a group of citizens in the street near a bar which has just been bombed by a group of terrorists.

(2) You are a group of parents demanding road safety measures

on your estate where the third child in a month has been run over.

(3) You are a group of hostages held by extremists who are surrounded by the police and army – one hostage has been shot – others expect to be.

(4) A group of squatters is being evicted.

(5) A group of young parents are protesting about babies being snatched from prams.

Any area of possible human conflict can be used. From the bare bones, seminar members using ingenuity and acting ability of a high order perform some of the most humanly stirring dramas it is possible to see.

Once again the way in which the exercise was set up, who took decisions, how people got their particular role becomes very important. Group members become aware of their dominant or passive roles, how they manipulate and are manipulated by others. In the drama itself the freedom to act out is very liberating and group members become aware of their response to violence in a situation real enough for real emotions and real behaviour to show. The comments of the audience group clearly give feedback to the drama participants about those areas of their behaviour of which they were unaware. The feeling and experiencing in a supportive atmosphere has bypassed rational control and in most instances has provided a widening and unforgettable experience quite outside most people's ability to conceive intellectually.

The remaining sessions of the exercise were devoted to integrating the experience and enabling participants to talk about it and share it with others. The techniques used are therefore designed to reduce tension, to reinforce learning and to re-establish old links e.g. reinstating the observers as group leaders. If these feedback and integrative procedures are successful seminar members take away an enhanced understanding not only of violence in the abstract but of their own violent natures and needs.

4 Interpretation of the exercise

Above all else the function of this exercise was to produce 'spontaneous' learning as defined by Moreno and to attempt to integrate that learning in each individual member of the seminar. The consciously used selection mechanisms have to be bypassed so that not only does content learning take place but the blocks to other areas of content learning become revealed for what they are.

In socio-drama, and in being confronted with an independent and numerically superior witness to his behaviour, each participant is presented with the opportunity to reassess his habitual image of himself. This opportunity occurs in the exercise in several ways.

Firstly each member becomes aware of the violence of his reaction to the authoritarian approach of the trainer. Logical, rational and verbally explanatory though this approach may be, and drawn directly from the kind of situation/change explanation so commonly used and expected to be effective in everyday life, it is demonstrably unsatisfying and ineffective in a situation where uncertainty, anxiety and an element of threat exist. The learning here is quite simple. Each member discovers for himself that reactions which he has been wont to label as violent, aggressive or hostile and thus indirectly to condemn, may well be truly appropriate responses from people in situations which appear to them as threatening. In other words the member learns through his own reactions that the interpretation of a situation is largely conditioned by where you stand in relation to it and to what sense of power and influence you feel you have to control the situation.

Then the leaders and their groups are faced with a change of relationship. Whatever leadership style the group leaders have used prior to the exercise they abandon it in favour of the passive role of observer. On many occasions this proved a very difficult change and observers were pressurized by group members to resume their original role. From being regarded as helpful and enabling people they came to be regarded as agents of authority and of confront-ation and members grew suspicious of them. However as the exercise proceeded people recognized that they too frequently changed roles with or without explanation and some awareness of what this can do to people whose security is already slight, began to form.

At this point many seminar members are ready to accept that as far as emotional states are concerned non-verbal communication of what is done, the behavioural acts, carry much more weight than what is said. Members become increasingly aware that behavioural cues which conflict with verbal cues create a state of tension with the almost inevitable result that the behavioural cues are responded to and the verbal cues ignored. They realize that this creates a discrepancy in expectations, a credibility gap as the behavioural cues have not been consciously offered and responses are usually expected to the consciously used verbal cues.

It is significant also that members become aware of the dis-parate reaction caused by a communication cue feeding directly into an already existing emotional state. If for example, the Seminar group as a whole have been experiencing conflict with authority in the 'back-home' situation and the authoritarian approach of the group trainer feeds directly into this, then the hostile response can be many times more intense than could have been expected from such a rational approach. Phrases such as 'It would be administratively convenient' and direct verbal appeals such as 'I must ask you to trust me!' can produce disproportionately aggressive responses. No one seems aware of this gross exaggeration at the time, but later some feelings of guilt and anxiety are apparent and learning about this kind of response has been made. Unusual and unexpected responses to fairly routine situations in ordinary life are usually met punitively especially by people in authority who tend to describe such outbursts as 'quite unprovoked'.

The setting up of the drama situations rather than the drama itself eventually becomes a focus of interest. When it is pointed out that a fairly elaborate piece of rehearsed behaviour has been created from a single sentence suggestion, the prospective element and the decision-making factors start to become appreciated. How the scene was decided, the characters chosen and the action focused upon, are all areas of interpretation which must come from experience. Some people habitually take charge of situations, other habitually follow. In a situation where the delegated leader has visibly been withdrawn to the passive role of observer these habitual behaviour patterns of members must emerge.

At this point it is crucial to remember that every member of the seminar is professionally responsible for the care, guidance and control of others. It now becomes clear that habitual behaviour patterns have not the same interpreted meaning for others as they have for their perpetrators. Many times in the exercise members have their behaviour reflected back to them by the observer, by the group, by the total group and can be nonplussed. Some even recognize instantly with great clarity that the disparity between what they believed they were doing, how they believed they were acting and what others actually saw, accounted for a great deal of the disparity in the responses they perceived. Statements like, 'Oh well! If that is how you saw me coming across, I can quite understand why you got angry. But I didn't mean to be like that !!' abound. How like the kind of mis-communication with which Laing deals in his book 'Knots'.[4]

In the drama itself, five minutes of acting appears to be a very small and easily encompassable period of time. Verbally this is true, but in terms of action it is, or can be an age. No scripts of any length have ever been produced during the exercises, but this has never caused a drying-up. Quite the contrary; rehearsals have only led to the bare bones of the action being hammered out and plans for any properties being outlined. The spontaneity so engendered has several very effective uses.

In the first place time has to be filled and the pressure, before an audience, to fill it is very great indeed. However there are only two resources available. One is the character and situation of the drama itself and the other is the experience, knowledge and feelings of the actor.

Thus at one level each member/player can take refuge in the character of the part he is playing and the responses he gets from the other players. From this situation he can learn something of what it is like to be someone else, the kind of learning most of us are not very prone to undertake. Even our advice to others tends to be egocentric 'If I were you . . .' a straight refusal to accept that others could even want to see anything in any way different from ourselves.

However the material for the character is often slight, usually being based upon someone that the player remembers, and this brings into play all the back-up material which derives from the player's own personality. Conscious blocks do not operate too well in this kind of situation and players tend 'to get carried away' with their role. Afterwards players comment on how easy it became to behave in ways that they had not believed possible. 'I had no idea that I could enjoy being involved in violent physical activity', or 'I actually wanted to hurt!'

Clearly seminar members are faced with the fact that the control they exercise over their own feelings may be bypassed and that certainly large areas of those feelings are off-loaded in otherwise innocent situations. The situation in which the drama is enacted is supportive enough for this kind of learning to take place with maximum effect.

The final scenes of the exercise revert to an intellectualisation of the processes which have been experienced and a restoration of equilibrium. In terms of group training the participants having unfrozen, thus allowing learning and insight to take place, now re-freeze at a more authentic level of adjustment. This does not mean that the intensity of the experience is reduced or forgotten but that it is integrated into the individual's personality and provides a basis for a potentially more effective level of operation.

Each stage of learning has been self-effected and achieved in conjunction with peers. Obviously this cuts out the possibility of conflicting ideas which can then be selected out, because what is happening *is* the learning process. Factual and theoretical data are only offered by the group trainer as and when this is relevant. In other words information is only given when it becomes apparent to group members that they need information in order to proceed.

246

In this manner such information as is offered becomes the possession of the group member because it is immediately relevant to his current needs.

Finally there are many escape outlets if pressure becomes unacceptable. At all stages seminar members were aware that they can opt out. Group pressure makes this fairly difficult to do, but the greater the need the more likely that group pressure will be resisted. Less involved roles can frequently be found for those who need to opt out e.g. that of Prologue or Commentator with such prepared material as will make the function easy to perform. The part of non-acting director is another possibility. In any case such is the size of the total group that it is possible for anyone who so chooses to participate at a very moderate level. Each individual member thus has great potential to control his own investment in the exercise.

Nevertheless it remains constantly surprising to see how involved many people become, showing great enthusiasm, and judging by the subsequent feedback, a high level of learning takes place. This may well be caused by the totality of the learning situation. For two days an atmosphere is created in which members find it increasingly possible to expose their behaviour to critical scrutiny. For example in the early stages of the exercise where members have been arbitrarily allocated to new groups, most groups have maintained a large part of their original membership. All groups, however, have been faced with accepting members who while having had similar experience in their own groups have not *shared* that experience with the members of the group they now join.

This advent of a newcomer to an established group is a commonplace of residential life and theoretically the seminar members are rationally aware of the inherent dangers. Nevertheless in the exercises it was remarkable to watch the ways in which the newcomers were dealt with in a situation in which some degree of stress for all members existed. Members were accepted and then forgotten, or allocated menial tasks and generally left to fend for themselves.

Confronted with this behaviour and with the resentment that it engendered, members were immediately aware of the discrepancy between their knowledge and understanding of such a situation and their actual behaviour within it. It becomes clear once more that appropriate action and behaviour is not an automatic product of adequate knowledge and understanding, and that the 'blind' area of behaviour is capable of producing unexpected and unanticipated responses in others which are frequently rejecting, hostile or aggressive based upon perceived hurt, or slight.

247

A great deal of the time not actually taken up by planned exercises was used by seminar members to discuss what occurred in the socio dramas and the planning periods which preceded them. The seminars were held in a residential situation and it is very likely that the main integration of learning takes place in informal discussions over meals and in spare time. The stimulus is great because personal involvement is great. There is also an element of strangeness about the situation although such exercises are being used much more frequently for all kinds of groups of people.

5 Discussion

Socio-drama can increase insight into human relations situations. Participants are offered an opportunity to transcend their own private views. Acting the part of another and feeling the response of other participants to oneself in that role, clearly offers the possibility of learning more about what such a person in real life must be like. What kind of problems does he have? How does he solve them? What kind of restraints and pressures does he experience?

Miles[5] lists the uses of role playing as follows:

(1) Increasing insight into a human relations situation.
(2) Diagnosing situations.
(3) Pre-testing problems solutions.
(4) Practising needed skills.

When a person is spontaneously acting the role of another person he is in great measure exempt from criticism either from himself or from others; he is after all just play acting. But the behaviour is real enough to ensure that learning can take place.

The programme then of the exercises in the Development Group's seminars on violence was designed to bring some element of violence into the 'here and now' where it could not be comfortably disposed of by the use of words as if it were something which always occurred in other people but never in oneself. Our society is verbally oriented and great store is placed upon the value of words. But words can serve the purpose of obfuscating equally as well as that of clarifying. Violence is a distasteful social manifestation and one which arouses fear about the individual's ability to main control as well as fear about personal suffering.

It was rewarding in the exercises to see that the ability of ordinary people to assume the roles of others is very great and evidence of the straight through link between behaviour and feeling is very easily obtained. As group members tentatively engage in aggressive or violent behaviour, the very behavioural acts generate the appropriate emotions. Thus a man who shouts abuse and insults at another very soon begins to feel the animosity to the other appropriate to his behaviour. It is a sobering thought that this link is so strong.

The drama sessions allow the acting-out of violent scenes in comparative safety. They also allow the audience to witness violent behaviour at close quarters and to be much more objective about it than is normally possible. It is true that the 'observer sees most of the game' and a learning experience of great potency is created because of the immediate relationship between the behaviour observed and each observer's own experience.

In Miles' terms insights have been created and understanding of the nature of human relations has been enhanced; members have been offered several opportunities of analysing situations containing violence in the safety of the group situation; they have also been able to test out their own responses to violence and may well have realised that some of their fears of control and of involvement are unwarranted or at least overdeveloped. They have also had an opportunity to be involved in and to practice their behavioural response in a relatively 'safe' situation.

References
(1) BENNETT M. E. (1963). *Guidance and Counselling in Groups,* McGraw & Hill, New York.
(2) LITWAK E. (1967). *Community Theory and Group Factors in Behavioural Science for Social Workers,* E. THOMAS (ed.), Free Press, New York.
(3) ARGYLE M. (1967). *The Psychology of Interpersonal Behaviour,* Penguin Books, London.
(4) LAING R. D. (1970). *Knots,* Penguin Books, London.
(5) MILES M. B. (1971). *Learning to Work in Groups,* Teachers College Press, Columbia University.

Each of the members attending the Seminars on Violence described in the foreword was asked to record an incident of violence in which he or she had been personally involved or had witnessed and where possible to obtain an account of the same incident from another person who had been a witness or involved. The participants of the seminars came from many services and occupations and their experiences spanned a wide range of situations and problems. The task they were given was interpreted in many ways, some people recorded incidents in which they themselves had been violent, others incidents in which they had been violated. Some recorded an individual violently abusing himself, others incidents in which an individual was abused by 'the system'. Some chose to stand back from violence and ask their client to write about violence; some produced fascinating reports of one incident recorded by all the participants, showing the marked variations in perception between attacked and attacker.

In this chapter a selection of these case studies is presented; some have been edited, others remain untouched. In all cases the style, grammar and spelling of the original is retained. Each incident is presented without comment other than an occasional sub-heading which seemed appropriate. It is hoped the reader will be able to identify some causative factors in the incidents and thereby gain a greater understanding of the nature of violence and why it occurs in certain situations. One thing is certain, no one can remain unmoved by these incidents, nor is it easy to apportion blame. Both the violent and the violated suffer, locked in a complex labyrinth of interpersonal relationships from which the only exit is usually violent.

Whilst the balance of their minds . . .
During the two weeks following Mrs E's suicide attempt, I visited frequently, on a Saturday morning at the end of this period, my Area Officer knocked at my flat door and told me that Mrs E. had successfully committed suicide.

The story was that Mrs E. had been out with B. and in the pub, there had been a big argument when B. was heard to reject Mrs E. This was the third such occasion that week. In a very distressed state, Mrs E. had gone home. From the things found in the downstairs rooms, Mrs E. had gone through many photographs of the children and her ex-husbands, writing comments

on the back of them. She had then scribbled an apparently obscene note which the Police retained but which had repeatedly said that all men are bad, evil, etc, and they cause women's destruction. She then went to bed putting a polythene bag over her head, wrapping the plastic bathroom curtain over the top and tying it round with ribbon. Next morning, 13 year old T. arrived as usual. When he got no answer, he got into the hous through the hole in the backdoor. He saw all the mess downstairs and then found Mrs E. in her room. He went to the telephone box and rang the Police and then returned to the house and stayed with the two little boys who had been locked in their bedroom. When the milkman arrived, he had found his mother's purse and paid him off. He had also apparently freed his mother's head and tried to revive her.
Field Social Worker

The night patrol officer walked past the table-tennis room. It was 10 pm and all was dark. He heard a noise as if a chair had been knocked over. He went into the darkened room and, switching on the lights was startled to see a body suspended by the neck from an overhead girder. With commendable speed of action he ran forward and took the weight of the body while he reached into his pocket for a knife to cut through the belt which encircled the boy's throat. An ambulance was called and the boy was rushed to the local hospital where, fortunately, his life was saved.
Housemaster, Community Home

This account concerns a mental hospital admission. I was on emergency standby duty in an advisory capacity and was contacted at approximately 11.30 pm by the female duty fieldworker. She informed me that a 35 year old engineer had that evening suffered a breakdown of sorts and had been admitted into hospital. The patient was depressed, suicidal and had behaved at times aggressively towards hospital staff. Arrangements had been made for a mental hospital admission under Section 29, of the 1959 Mental Health Act. The female social worker requested assistance with the admission and I arranged to meet her at the hospital at midnight.

When I arrived I found that the patient had been sedated and was quite placid. In the circumstances, we decided to undertake the 40 mile journey by car. There were in fact no difficulties during the journey which I spent as escort talking and reassuring the client concerning the admission and his family who lived in England. When we reached the hospital in the early hours, there was, for some unknown reason, no receptionist immediately available and in the circumstances we sat in the reception area. The patient, who had to some extent recovered from his sedation, suddenly indicated that he needed a 'toilet' and was told of one only some 20 yards away. I made to accompany the client and was surprised but not unduly startled when he began to run in the direction of the 'toilet'. I hurried behind and became a little concerned when he shouted 'I don't need assistance'. When we arrived at the door, he leapt inside and attempted to slam the door shut – being obstructed by my foot, which I had quickly thrust forward. I was at this stage attempting to force the door open against extreme resistance. I was also trying to inform the client that I had to stay with him for a little while longer or words to that effect. At the same time I was becoming extremely alarmed because I knew that there was a lock on the inside of the door and restricted space inside. I pushed harder and managed to thrust my head and shoulder around the door. I was horrified to see in the half-light that the client had an open knife and was very determinedly cutting deep into his wrist. I immediately shouted to my colleague to get help, forced the door and entered. I had no immediate thoughts other than to get the knife away from the client. In order to accomplish this I was compelled to grapple with the client who had turned on me to some extent and forced the door shut. I was at this stage anxious about the consequences – but was strangely not particularly frightened in any way. It seemed necessary to be fairly decisive in an unlit restricted area; grappling with an armed mentally ill client who had become violent towards himself and those who interfered. I managed to hold his hand which held the knife away from both of us during the ensuing struggle in which I consciously tried not to hurt him. I opened the door and tried to pull him out into the light of the hospital passageway. Suddenly as if realising the hopelessness of his position and possibly because of the after-effects of sedation, his strength left him and he fell heavily dropping the knife to the floor. I retrieved the knife and dragged him into the passageway, put my coat under his head and began trying to effect treatment. At this moment my colleague, an ex-nurse arrived and helped until further assistance arrived shortly afterwards.

My colleague always believed that I had knocked out the client and to some extent a myth generated in the department concerning this incident. I have subsequently found that other officers tend to seek my assistance when involved with aggressive or violent clients believing undoubtedly that I would be capable of containing any unpleasant situation. I find it interesting to reflect that if social work skills fail, social workers would appear prepared to accept violence as a means of restraint or defence regardless of

causation factors. By assisting with these cases I find it interesting to consider that I may be colluding in creating the possibility of violence although I tend, like most social workers, to prefer the the belief that this is a part of a helpful and necessary process.
Senior Field Social Worker

The control of a community home shall be maintained on the basis of good personal and professional relationships between the staff and the children resident therein.
The Community Homes Regulations 1972 (1)(1)

The problem of writing about a certain incident during a working day is, where do I start?

You could say it started when I saw this boy out in the sports field, on top of the goal posts. Having myself, with two other working boys, spent three days re-making and erecting them, you can well imagine I was rather annoyed as I had previously told this lad on two other occasions during the day to stop hanging on them. I called from the door of the house saying that I wanted him to come in pretty sharp. He took very little notice of me, clambered down, and casually walked over to where I was standing, just outside the door. This made me very angry and as he went in through the door I kicked his backside.

When I got inside, he turned towards me and told me that if I did that again he was going to 'fucking well hammer me'. At this point I saw red, but at the same time I did remember reading in his report that he had previous history of violence, so I thought – the chips are down, I will find out if he means business or not. So I told him if that was how he felt, to come on and have a go. With that I went up to him and gave him the opportunity to have a go at me. I still thought that I could dodge anything that he could throw at me. SURPRISE . . . SURPRISE – Bang, he caught me with a good punch on the side of my jaw. With this I gave him one back with the flat of my hand. He then picked up the games board which was by the wall and threatened to belt me over the head with it. At this point one of the boys jumped in between us, and this gave me the opportunity to grab the lad round the neck and lead him towards the door and into the Quiet Room. (While this incident was going on I was getting quite a bit of verbal abuse from or two of the other boys).

When we got into the Quiet Room, away from the other boys, he started to cry – at the same time he said that he was sorry for what he did. I told him that it was no good being sorry now, as it would not do any good, and in any case it was as much my fault as his. He then told me he was being led on by some of the other boys who thought it was a good bit of fun playing up to the Housemasters. This I believed to be true as I knew there was a couple of boys in the house that did use the other lads in this way.

I told him to remain in the Quiet Room for a time and calm down, which he did. I then returned to the House where I was greeted with more verbal abuse from the same two lads. With this I got the rest of the group together and we all sat round and had a discussion about the incident. I thought this did a power of good as it eased the tension tremendously, and it made the boys realise that we are all human and can be pushed a little bit too far from time to time. I also found that we all got to understand each other a lot better, especially with the lad concerned.

Summing up this particular incident I would say that it has taught me a great deal, and I know now that I would never get involved in a situation like that in front of the other boys again. I think that I would take him to one side and discuss it with him on his own.

I say this now, but when you have had a particularly bad day with some of the lads, it can become rather frustrating, especially when you have a very difficult group, with one boy in particular who would do anything in his power to stir up the other boys against the Housemasters.
Housemaster, Boys Community Home

T. goes to a school for malajusted. He had recently been in trouble with the law, having been involved with other children from his home in theft and malicious damage. One might say that whoever he comes into contact with is used as a means of working through his own problems.

On the day in question, he left the breakfast table to get ready for school before anyone else and was closely followed by one of his peer group. After a few minutes there was a lot of banging, shouting and obvious horse-play, of a rough nature going on.

I made my way upstairs to stop the noise. A young lad was in bed, having suffered from a rough night with an asthmatic attack. A housemother was in bed on her day off. The time was only 7.10 am.

I found T. and his friend fooling about with a cupboard door. Neither of the boys heard me approach but by this time T. was doing all the banging and laughing. I took hold of his arm and quickly guided him downstairs. He did not struggle.

254

Once downstairs and out of earshot, I spoke to him in a loud voice. I was annoyed. He had been taking advantage of everyone over the past few days and with me it had suddenly come to a head. 'Weren't the people around him suffering?' He pleaded that it wasn't his fault that all the noise was going on – doesn't it take two to make an argument? – Why always him just lately? He became offensive and I told him not to speak that way and how dare he use that kind of talk to me? I felt compelled to stop him and the obvious way was to take hold of him. I took a step towards him and at this he encouraged me to 'Go on then and hit me'. I had committed myself and by this time was in view of his friend and also audible to everyone else in the house. I became frustrated and knew it was wrong to strike. I pushed instead – a good hard push that sent him against a door, which gave and broke his fall. I pushed his head down between his knees and immobilised him, at the same time verbally enforced his undignified and immobilised state as being consistent with one of a youth who does not know how to conduct or control himself in the presence of an adult, who has to put up with his behaviour day in and day out. I told him I could flatten him there and then but had thought better of it.

I then turned my attention to his friend who had gone very quiet and pale. I think this halved the burden of humiliation I had just placed on T. I then swung my attention to the boys' appearances, which were none too good for school.

The situation then became one of subservience on their part and of frustration of having to turn to physical aggression on mine.
Deputy Superintendent, Long Stay Childrens Home

When I reflect, I find it surprising how few and far between have been violent occurrences of which I have direct knowledge or had direct involvement. The train of circumstances which is related below is not notable for the degree of violence involved but there are one or two features which are of particular interest.

I was contacted by telephone on arrival at my office by a residential officer (P.) who was working as a relief homefather in a Children's Home. P. is a young man, a qualified teacher and a graduate in psychology. We had caught him, as it were, at a loose end between permanent appointments and were glad to use him in a relief capacity. I must confess that it was with the idea of modifying the attitude of some of the more staid and inflexible staff members that I particularly arranged his placement. I was therefore very surprised when he telephoned and said, 'Look, I'd better tell you first thing but last night I clouted one of the boys. I know its against the rules so what do you want me to do'?

I asked for a resume of the circumstances. It appeared that the boy concerned, S. aged 15 years, had been most objectionable in the dining-room at tea-time and when corrected had sworn at the housemother at his table. P. had told him to behave himself and get on with his tea but the boy had thereupon upset some food over the floor and stormed from the room. P. followed the boy out of the house, ordered him back to clean up the mess he had made and thereupon received considerable abuse. P. thought that the boy made as if to strike him and slapped S. around the face. S. then ran off.

Subsequently, the boy was missing for most of the evening. At 9.30 pm P. went to the boy's bedroom and found him in bed and apparently asleep. S. had evaded the search and retired to bed unseen! The following morning S. arose and went to school in the usual way appearing his normal self.

I told P. on the telephone that I would visit the Home later in the day but meanwhile to carry on as usual. When I visited, P. was looking annoyed, he said he was; with himself. S. he said, was a cheerful lad, not given to such outbursts and he thought he had handled the whole thing badly. He said that he was not even sure now that the lad had intended to strike him but wondered if he had used the possibility in order to slap the lad.

I told P. that I thought he was making altogether too much of the whole episode. Yes, it was regrettable but we needed to know how S. had reacted and what he felt about it. S. came home from school at the usual time. He knows me and has a vague idea of my role. He said, 'Hallo, Mr H., come to tell me off?' He is a likeable lad with an engaging grin and was certainly not worried whether I had come to tell him off or not. I decided it was no time for casework niceties. I said 'I think Mr P. dealt with that at the time didn't he?' 'Yes' said S. 'and you should have seen his face'. He was much more worried I was'. He then went on to tell me how he overheard P. in the office talking to another member of staff and blaming himself for losing his temper! S. said 'If I hadn't been broke I would have brought him a packet of fags today to show there's no hard feelings!'

He shared the joke with two or three of his friends who were amused but quickly forgot it. He also told his visiting Social Worker Mrs B. who wasn't amused and didn't forget it.

The Social Worker came to the office a few days following her visit to S. and said that she was surprised that I allowed P. to continue working in that particular Home and that he should have been dismissed without notice. When I told her that I had no intention of telling P. to go she was extremely angry with me. She eventually calmed down but only the realization that S. had seen the whole thing as a 'bit of a giggle' and that to make much of the incident would do him no good, stopped Mrs B. from going to the Director to complain. In vain did I talk about the stresses and strains of residential work; that residential officers were people and sometimes made mistakes and that sometimes ones reactions were not entirely rational. To her I was (and remain) a reactionary who would bring back the birch given half a chance. But there is a footnote.

On the 5th November, I attended at one of the large Homes where a large bonfire and firework display was laid on for children and staff. Mrs B. was there with one of her children, a boy of about 6 or 7. I was standing quite nearby when this child, who had been plaguing her for something or other, quite accidentally tripped her and she stumbled. I moved forward to assist as I thought Mrs B. would fall. She didn't; she recovered her footing and dealt the little boy an almighty swipe round his head, knocking him to the ground. She looked up to see me watching her. I know I must have looked a bit shocked.

She looked back at me for about five seconds and then hissed at me, 'If you can't see the difference then you're in the wrong job. I LOVE my child', and so saying, she wrenched at the arm of the still crying child and without a backward glance, hauled him from the scene.

Chief Assistant, Residential Services, Department of Social Services

My hate came out . . .

D. an eleven year old Nigerian followed his parents to England when he was eight years old. He was left in Nigeria as a baby with grand-parents. D. found certain difficulties at home. Relationships with parents and other children born to them in England were not good, and they suffered because of this and it showed in his behaviour. D. came to us for assessment.

For the first two or three weeks we found D. conversing freely, friendly and anxious to learn and also to display his talents. He was a keen reader and found himself among a group of non-readers who enjoyed any sort of disruption. D. during this period frowned on this – therefore he was not always very popular with them.

On the evening of 19th May 1973, D. left the house with this group of boys and a housefather for a game of football in a nearby park. Within half an hour he was returned to me, the housefather announcing that he was causing trouble and he could not control him. The housefather left and D. shouted after him 'It is not fair'. His eyes was flashing and he was breathing heavily. He proceeded to kick at the furniture, kicked all the chairs over and got books from shelves hurling them about the room. Two younger girls in the room attempted to pick up the books he then kicked them and threatened more if they interfered. I then intervened and held him. I tried to sit him on the settee but he fought and kicked. He would not answer me as to what had happened in the park. I told him I could only help him if I knew all the facts. I was holding him still but he continued his struggle shouting 'It was not fair – leave me, I want to go'. I asked him if he would sit down and tell me all if I let him go. I was then feeling worse for wear as he was strong for such a small frame. I took a chance and let him go. He darted over to the dining-room table and picked up a knife, saying he was going to kill someone if he was not allowed out of the room. I sent the two younger girls to the cook asking her to give them supper for me. This request would bring her as it is not normal for me to ask this and she would sense that something was wrong if the girls did not say. It did, for soon after I disarmed D. and held him as she came in. He became even more frantic when he had an audience. Cook left with the girls and in a couple of minutes the Superintendent came in, I was glad of a second person so that I could withdraw from actually restraining D.

Together we talked to him, both of us. He was still kicking, I took off his shoes, he did not protest. He asked us to let him go. I had already let go and the Superintendent said he would, as long as he was sensible and sat quietly. When he let D. go he walked over to the sideboard and picked up two coffee mugs, saying that he was going to smash the television. He aimed one of the mugs at the television and it shattered against the wall. The Superintendent told him that he had now shown us how angry he could be and told him to put the other mug down. He did so and came back to us without invitation.

We talked to him of Nigeria and asked if little boys there were expected to fend for themselves and also to defend themselves as well. We told him that here he would find that the folk were willing to share his problems if he would let us. This irritated him. He said he could take care of himself and that we were nosey. Gradually D. moved closer and sat in a position where he could be held. The Superintendent somehow got him into his arms. At first he struggled but allowed himself to relax enough to curl up there and be held. We talked on and on getting no answer but he was listening and then the sobs were audible.

258

I had earlier that day suggested a visit to a new Wimpy Bar. I now asked whether he would like to go. I got no answer and he did not seem enthusiastic but soon came round to the idea that he was taking me out and not me taking him. He smartened himself up while I put my two small girls to bed.

Out we went, it was walking distance but D. wanted a bus ride so we rode on the bus.

We ate at Wimpy's in silence. I was too tired to talk and D. possibly felt the same way.

On our way home there was a shining moon in a very clear sky. D. drew my attention to the moon saying 'In Nigeria the moon made people do terrible things'.

We were back on our old relationship. Conversation was renewed and my education on things Nigerian was about to continue.

Housemother, Childrens Home

Even working in a long established structured environment, where violence is almost non-existent, there are at times occassional outbursts, usually brought about by a chain of mistakes which at a certain point in time may join together to bring about a flashpoint, or temper outburst sometimes ending in violence. This is a recap into how one of these incidents did occur.

The assessment centre, having received the papers and a request that the child be admitted for assessment, contacted the office of the Social Worker, who unfortunately was not available. However, her senior was, and all the details were given to her to pass on. Later in the evening the Social Worker rang to confirm that she would be bringing the girl at the arranged time. Next day at the appointed time the Social Worker duly arrived with the girl and all the girl's personal effects, which we had asked them not to bring. We had requested that all the girl should have was just a few personal effects which she might like to have whilst she was with us. On entering the building the girl was obviously very apprehensive and was even more upset when she saw the door being locked after her. When asked to pick a few of her most personal things from her cases she started to become slightly verbally aggressive and unco-operative. At this time the home's pet dog chose to arrive on the scene and unfortunately the girl was frightened of dogs, which did not help matters at all, and I think that was the last straw for the girl. She now became physically and verbally aggressive towards the staff present and had to be restrained and removed to the separation room. After a short cooling off period the girl soon quietened and after being reassured she was far more co-operative.

Thinking after the incident it was easy to see that it was a series of small things that had built up into a crisis for the girl, causing her to lose her temper. These problems perhaps should have been avoided, however, they were not and what should and usually was a straight forward admittance procedure turned into a nasty experience for all concerned.

As one can see it was a series of small incidents which caused the problem, namely;

a) Failure on the Social Worker's part to pass the correct message.
b) Failure on our part to check with the Social Worker that she had all the revelant information when she phoned.
c) Not informing the girl as to what kind of an establishment she was being brought.
d) Not allowing the girl to keep all her belongings, once she had brought them.
e) The dog, perhaps the most significant thing.
f) The feelings of a girl who perhaps had been moved several times this year.

Senior Residential Officer, Assessment Centre

I sat alone in my little cell, I heard strange footsteps on the stairs, the keys in the door. My head turned quickly as I looked to see who was there. My heart stopped beating as I saw Sister C., she told me that I had a phone call. I went to the phone and it was my Brother in Law. When I had finished Sister C. said I had to go back in the cell, I said 'No, why should I'. My hate began to come out. I didn't mean to be rude to her but I don't know what came over me. Then Sister asked me to clean out the detention room, but I refused. The detention room was really messed up, she wanted me to clean it out because someone was going to be put in there. But I didn't believe her when she said someone else was going to be put in there, and I told her that she was just saying that because she wanted me to do it. But I soon found out that she wasn't telling a lie because J. came out of the bathroom soon after. I broke a chair just because I wanted Sister to lose her temper but she was so calm about everything I did. So I began to swear but she still didn't lose her temper. We was up there from 7.30 to 9.30 just standing there arguing to myself I suppose because Sister wasn't taking any notice of me. I was trying to get past Sister, but she was so strong, because I thought she was very weak, I was talking to J. for about ½ an hour and then Sister say to me that the girls will be up to bed soon, so if I could just pick up the papers for her sake. I wanted to and in another way I didn't. So I told her that if she let me go in the bedroom, I will clean up the mess after, but instead of clearing up the mess I had a wash and put my nightdress on. I thought at that moment Sister would go and get some more of the staff to put me in detention but instead she just stand there calm, I wanted to cry but I wouldn't let her see that I was worried. I asked Sister about 10 times if did she want a chair because she would soon get tired but instead she told me it was against her religion. So I told her it was against my religion to pick up paper after 7 o'clock. I was sitting on the bed and Sister was just stand and she looked so tired. I thought she was going to cry. I felt really selfish, but I still wouldn't clear up the mess, because I wanted her to think I very spiteful. Sister didn't go to bed until about twelve all because of me and that was because, Sister B. who think she is so great came and was pulling me about. So I ran downstairs and went into the bathroom, then sweet little Sister C. came down and told me to come out, I was crying because I knew that Sister B. was going to put me in detention. I got out of the bathroom and ran upstairs and clear the mess up, but after I had clear up everything I ran and locked myself in the bathroom again so Sister C. came down and tell me to come upstairs to my bed. I wouldn't because I felt so ashamed of myself. When I finally went up Sister stand there on the stairs. She looked so concerned. I went to bed and she cover me over and then turn the lights off, but when she went out I burst out crying, and I was crying for at least 1½ hours and then the night staff came in, and she asked me if I wanted something to drink but I say not, and she stayed with me for a bit and I suppose I fell asleep.

M., a West Indian girl aged 15 years

M. had been unco-operative over the weekend, refusing to do any work or participate in the group activities. At one stage she was placed in detention, or rather went in of her own accord as she refused to go in when this was suggested – ten minutes later she went in when I left her.

Some time later she was wanted for a telephone call and I went up to get her. Afterwards she again refused to go to detention and as she had left the room in an untidy and dirty condition with torn books, dirty cups, etc, I asked her to remedy this, but she was not keen to comply with my wish. Eventually she went up in a half-hearted way and proceeded to remove the books and utensils with her foot, and in fact the last state was worse than the first.

I told M. that I expected her to pick up the items as otherwise everyone would have to walk over them. She refused on grounds that this was against her religion, namely that she could not pick up any dirt after 7.00 pm and added, with a twinkle; 'You

261

wouldn't want me to go against my religion'. I agreed that I would not like her to go against her conscience and then we discussed her religion for a time and she held her views and refused to change her tactics. She said that she would like to go to bed and I said this would be in order when she had lifted the debris.

She tried to push me aside but I told her that I was determined that she would do as I told her and she was equally determined to hold her ground. She was angry and swore and ran to the bathroom where proceeded to break a chair and slammed the door (probably in the reverse order!)

She came out and changed her tactics saying; 'Please let me go down as otherwise I shall hurt you and I don't want to do that because you are only weak'. I replied that I would let her down when she had done as I said and then I used a coaxing voice. M. was relenting a little and she agreed to pick them up but she needed something from her room. She promised faithfully to come back up if I would let her collect 'something'.

M. went to her dormitory and immediately set about getting ready for bed, washing, undressing and getting into bed. I reminded her of her promise but she replied: 'Didn't you know I was a liar?' I replied in the negative but added that I was prepared to wait until she performed the task.

By this time two hours had elapsed and the other girls had gone to bed. M. suggested that I also should go to bed but I explained that I would gladly go to bed if she would do the simple task. At this point she offered to make up a bed for me in the dormitory or get a chair, but I declined these alternatives and on being asked why I laughingly replied that perhaps this would be against my religion. M. was very talkative now and asked many questions about my background and about her own family in the West Indies and in Birmingham. She was ashamed of her mother and would not have her to the school saying; 'She would show me up'. Her married sister had been allowed to come as had her brother-in-law. M. spoke about her behaviour of the preceeding days and about her wish for a transfer to another establishment and her reasons for leaving previous establishments. She remarked that she wanted a strict school or preferably Holloway where she would be punished.

Quite suddenly M. jumped out of her bed and declared that she might as well do the task because she wasn't enjoying her bed while I stood up. Unfortunately she met another member of staff on the stairs and instead of continuing up she ran down to the bottom floor and went into the bathroom. She was not wearing slippers and I was worried about her catching cold and I said this.

After about ten minutes she went up, picked up the items, and instead of returning to her bed she again descended to the ground floor.

I followed M. and again coaxed her to go upstairs to bed. With some more persuasion M. went up and got into bed. I had a few words with her to the effect that I was glad we were both able to go to bed and that the incident was over and done with. M. was very near to tears as I tucked her in and bid her goodnight.

I met the night staff on her rounds and explained the situation and she promised to look in on her and make sure that she was alright. The following day brought a note of apology from M. and I made it my business to go and see M. that day.

Our relationship had not suffered from the incident, and perhaps to some extent I played on the fact that a good relationship existed between us. I had felt that once the request to tidy up had been expressed I must see it through. M. has these sort of blow-ups every month and it is felt there is some connection with her menstrual cycle. During this time M. appears to change in her physical appearance and takes on a kind of 'catatonic' position. She will not conform to any request, and will sooner or later manage to provoke an aggressive reaction from the staff. She holds no ill-feelings towards the staff in question in spite of threats to knife either herself or the person involved. The incident is over and for another three weeks we have a pleasant, attractive and impeccably dressed young lady.

Head of a Girls Community Home

The following incident occurred not long after I started work in an adolescent unit accommodating 20 severely emotionally disturbed teenage boys and girls. It happened at a time when I was still unsure of myself in the role that I was playing in that establishment and lacked confidence in my ability to cope with situations which might arise there, this may have precipitated the event or at least have directed its somewhat unsatisfactory conclusion.

J. was a large girl of nearly 16 with red hair and a fiery temper. She was an extremely disturbed girl coming from a family with a dominant yet very neurotic mother and a submissive, over anxious father. She had a history of numerous acts of violence inflicted on others and on herself – she had made serious suicide attempts on three occasions and had thick deep scars on both her wrists as reminders of this. She also found herself attracted to young female members of staff and usually 'fell in love' with the latest arrival, who at this time happened to be me.

One evening I was alone in one of the sitting rooms when J. came in in an unusually quiet mood and, without saying anything, came over and started stroking my hair. Having been forewarned about J. I became very tense with her and my anxiety about the situation became obvious to J., who, sensing my apparent rejection of her stormed out of the room and it transpired out of the unit. Outside the unit she was seen poking at her wrists with bits of stone, a thing she would often do when frustrated in some way. Eventually the tension in her rose to a level where it had to be released in something and I was the obvious target. She returned to the sitting room this time with a somewhat vacant stare on her face and a glazed look in her eyes. She walked over to me, shook me hard and then put her hands round my neck and started to squeeze. I tried to push her away this time for good reasons, but she was much stronger than I was and she held me tight. After only a few seconds, however, another member of staff appeared on the scene. He had seen J. outside the unit, had realized the mood she was in and had come to make sure that everything was alright. J., who was in quite a hysterical state by this time, hardly resisted removal from the situation by the other member of staff and was taken to one of the single rooms to calm down. For a while there was a great deal of tension between J. and myself – to J. the incident was perhaps a reminder that she was unable to control her emotions enough to stop herself from damaging something or someone she liked, and I was both anxious in case this sort of attack might reoccur and also worried that I was in part to blame for the whole incident. Because of my inexperience it was quite a while before J. and I were able to talk about what had happened and to a certain extent to establish why it had happened and what our feelings about it were. After this had been done J. began to relate to me in a much more meaningful way and there was never any recurrence of J's violent behaviour – which still persisted and probably will always persist—being directed towards myself.

Residential Social Worker, Unit for Disturbed Adolescents

A Menace to Society . . .
To describe one's reactions to physical violence of any specific nature is a very complicated and hard thing to do, as the reactions to certain violent happenings differ according to the place and the mood one is in. For example one could be watching the TV and some silly idiot could tap your shoulder and when you turn round you are not sure who's to blame. After 4–5 interruptions the anxiety and violent feelings mount up so as to put one in a very

264

temperamental position where you would beat hell out of the person concerned, not just belt him once or twice but just keep belting him with whatever came into reach, and once he was down just keep belting him so he will not do it again.

Everyone has a certain amount of aggressiveness in themselves but some show it more than anyone else, and usually the ones with all the mouth are just what it says 'all mouth', and the quiet refined type are the ones that a straight challenge or fight is not what they would want to accept, but on the other hand if they were subjected to a very large amount of interference or provocation then I am certain that they would retaliate and not just hit out, but they would keep on belting him with a chair or bottle or anything heavy that would cause a large amount of damage so as not to give the opponent any other opportunity to have another chance to seek revenge or, to simplify it, 'have another go'.

On certain occasions I have been the subject of physical threatening, not violence or assault, just that a certain person has threatened me, and to a certain extent kept on provoking and taking the piss out of me, for example:

I went to a Secondary Modern School and I did not get on very well due to family problems, and I left when I was about 13½, and went to Approved School. While I was there I met a boy called G. who was the same age. I did not like being away from home and I used to cry and get very upset about it. He lived in the same town as I did and we knew each other very well, my Mum and Dad knew him and when they visited me they used to team up with his parents and we would all go out together and have a good day out. It used to break my heart when they had to leave me and go home and I would get very upset and cling to my mother as though I was really going to never see her again, and she was just the same and we were very close at that stage, but it gradually wore off as I became hardened and a bit aggressive. I used to be very shy and frightened but then I learnt that if you hit someone first with a fist or bottle they won't do it again and you learn by others mistakes. Well G. used to go back to the Approved School and tell them all about me and my Mum and Dad and how I used to cry and snivel and say how I didn't want them to leave me there and I wanted to go home.

All the other boys, or a few, used to laugh and torment me and say my Mum and Dad were snobs and stuck up and all other sorts of abuse were thrown at me and generally my life was made Hell.

Every day I was the victim for poking about and to be thrown in the swimming pool. If a joke was to be played then I was the scapegoat, or I was the person they all looked for, I cannot explain it all but there are much more details, but I give just a rough picture of what I mean.

Anyway I would be pushed around, victimised, turned out of bed and made to suffer at their enjoyment, and mainly G. was to blame. By the time I left 15 months later I was changed and I had already warned them off, and I told him that if I ever saw him again I would kill him and I meant it. I hated that person and I would of had the greatest pleasure by making him suffer unbearable tortures that even the wildest nightmares and horrors don't exhibit.

Anyway I left the school and I went home to my parents, I didn't say anything to them and I found a nice girl friend and I tried to settle down and I forgot all about the troubles and hate and vengence I held against Society for locking me up and I got a job.

One day about eight months later I went to a youth club as usual on a Friday night and all my mates were there, they were all about the same age 15/16/17, you know all teenagers, and in a way I got on with them all. They were always wanting a laugh and I have seen them smash a kid's teeth out and beat him across the face and body with an iron bar, and I never thought I could do that to anyone. Anyway that night my mates H. and D. came down to the club. H. was about 17 and D. 18, they are both 21/22 now, anyway they came in and they told me that they had nicked a car and it was outside. So I went out and they had a 1600 E and I didn't know much about cars then but it really looked something to me, so we went for a drive and H. suggested we go to look for some greasers to pick on and burn them off the road, but I said I didn't want to so they took me back to the club. They said they would be back at 8 o'clock. So I went in and they left with a hectic wheelspin and earsplitting screech of tyres on tarmac. I went in and I didn't notice it so much then but a lot of people were staring and laughing, but I didn't catch on until I saw him, G., talking to them as he knew them, but they didn't like him much as he was a big mouth and showed off, he was telling them how I used to cry my eyes out when my Mum left me after a visit and how I was the weakling of the place. I felt a right fool, and he was saying to me 'Alright Snoopy', this had been my nickname. Then the worst bit came, he had the DJ, or club owner who was only 24/25, put on the record 'I've lost my mummy', that record that has a little kid screaming his heart out in a shop.

Well this was the lot and I told him what I thought, sort of 'Why don't you . . . off', and he said 'What you gonna do?' and

I said 'One day I'll get even' and I walked out and my girlfriend ran after me. As I was walking out of the door I saw H. and D. go past and pull up in the pub car park so I went over and told them what had happened and I said he was a big bloke and a razor fanatic. Anyway we planned to get him after the club at 9.30. We went into the pub and I had my first drink a vodka and black-currant, after about three or four I felt on top of the world and D. had some tablets which we all had some (I found out later were Blues or speed) and we waited for the club to close. As it got towards 9–9.15 G. came out with some bloke who was at the home school after I left and they both got onto a Lambretta scooter and drove off. We followed them and they went up to a place in Middlesex, about 12 miles from where we lived, we followed and after about ½ hour G. turned onto a housing estate and his mate got off, had a few words and G. pulled away and drove back towards the town area. We followed and D., who was driving, asked what we should do, stop him and get him in the car and take him somewhere and beat him up, or what, but I didn't want him to know who it was who was going to get him so D. said 'Let's just knock him off his bike' and I really thought that it was a good idea, and H. said 'Make sure you get him good, and don't let him get on that old tin heap any more, after we're finished he won't push anyone around for quite a while'.

We tailed him for about five or so minutes and he passed through town and onto the main road which has no lights on it and it is very dark and D. really booted the car and we shot off across the road and after him. .

We turned a sharp bend and came through to Middle Lane in town where the road is about 8–9 foot wide and two lanes of traffic is a very tight squeeze indeed. D. came alongside G. on his bike at about 60 mph and as he came up on his rear he spun the wheel left and then right and the car swerved across the road smashed G's bike which forced him off the road and the bike just went wild, fell on its side, skidded for a few feet and smashed into a wall, and G. just lay there, his face was all bloodied and cut and he was out, or fainted, but he really looked a right mess and I can truly say I was really satisfied and pleased with it. I swore and spat on him and we got in the motor and drove off. I felt really happy and I was at last revenged, call me a *sadist* but I really enjoyed seeing him bleed and suffer. Just because I hated him for what he had done in the past, but it was all forgotten until I saw him. And I can truly say that if I hated someone enough in here, who was treating me bad and pushing me around, if I ever saw them on the outside I think I would do it on my own.

There are not many times I have been the victim of violence but if there were I would not antagonise or provoke, but I mount all these things up until such a time that I know I can pay back and give a lot more to that person when I find them on their own and in a quiet place, but otherwise I am quiet and keen to get on and settle down, but just a few big headed people, especially here, really annoy me to the brink of devastation and I really would love to make them suffer as much as I can, and I'd like to see this on certain occasions come true.

But otherwise I am just a normal person, a bit quick tempered, and temperamental but I wouldn't wish harm on anyone unless they really offended me, and I mean really went out of their way to slag me down, as my Probation officer says 'there is a very aggressive side to me, as I know, and I must learn to control my anxiety and feelings and not store them all up', and slowly I am achieving this and I hope to *soon* leave and settle down with my brother and just forget the past and plan the future without any more trouble.

Borstal Boy, 19 years.

T. (15) had been at M. for three months, he came to us on a Care Order. Although T. could be extremely difficult at times he was popular with the staff and children.

One afternoon recently while I was on duty T. left the schoolroom and came over to the house, when I saw him he was crying and shaking, I asked what was wrong and he replied 'You'd better get over to the schoolroom, I've just stabbed the new kid'. I called to another member of staff to see to T. while I went to see the injured boy. He had been stabbed twice in his head and once in his back with a small kitchen knife.

The fight

T. and P. (12) were in the same classroom, the fight had been arranged by all the senior children (about eight) to take place sometime that day. The 'gang' wanted T. to win so a couple of them were quite willing to help, one of them went to the kitchen and got a knife which T. hid down his sock. Not long after school had started that afternoon P. kicked T. while T. was at his desk, T. jumped up and P. hit him knocking him on the floor, T. then produced the knife, P's only weapon against that was a very sharp pencil which he thrust into T's face. T. then used the knife stabbing him twice in his head and once in his back. The school teacher was unable to separate them so called to the other teacher for help. Although the teacher saw blood she didn't realise P.

had been stabbed until she heard P. shouting for someone to take it out. Once they had been separated T. ran out of the door.

After the fight
After seeing P's injuries I phoned for an ambulance, within minutes the police arrived, shortly after, the ambulance. T. was immediately put into one room to await CID officers to start a very long interview. I went with P. to the hospital where it was discovered he had a punctured lung. A CID officer collected me from the hospital and we went to the police station. T. had also been taken to the station by this time. He spent a long time being interviewed and making his statement and was later charged with 'wounding with intent' and was detained at the station until the next morning.

Attitude of the gang
All were very shocked when I told them what had happened to T., they were obviously upset and concerned at the thought of him being locked in a cell. The only feeling shown towards P. was resentment, they semed to be blaming him for everything and hoped he wouldn't return to us when discharged from hospital. The fight didn't appear to be just between T. and P. P. was the new boy and although only twelve behaved a lot older and he threatened T.'s position as 'top dog', they all lent a helping hand in stirring up both boys into a fight. Two of the gang had very obvious reactions, one boy went very red and held one hand over his face all the time I was talking to them, another burst into a very nervous laugh and later cried himself to sleep.

T. and P.
P. is now out of hospital. After having eleven stitches in his head and spending a week resting his punctured lung. He seems to think he might get sympathy from the gang as he was the injured party, he will probably be shocked when he doesn't.

T. is now in a Remand centre. Immediately after the fight he was upset, probably from shock. He realised very quickly the seriousness of what he had done and showed great concern for his mother. He had expected to be locked up but was upset when he knew his mother would have to know the whole truth. He was very confused about the future, he thought he would be able to go to court the next morning and have his punishment decided, and was worried when told that decision could take up to two months.

Senior Housemother, Assessment Centre

269

Words leave something behind . . .

This is an example where I think that the formal system of training in the Social Services Department had a violating effect upon an employee.

The employee came to the department following a period of two years service elsewhere. He was taken on as an untrained worker with the assurance of secondment for training.

After two years service he was (a most healthy person of 50 years) seconded for a two year Polytechnic course. It was clear at the time that he was going to need help coping academically and with management of particular casework aspects of the work. It is also clear that he did not get special help in either of these areas and was doomed to be failed by the system. There were no explicit early warning signs given to him that he was not functioning at a level expected by the college standards. He personally felt that his performance was passable and his ongoing evaluation gave no untoward signs. After the first year he was given indications that he could not succeed in the course and ought to ease himself out.

As a practitioner who could not pass the fitness test he returned to the department retaining the position of untrained worker and the experience itself of, to him, rejection created severe problems. In the writer's view poor selection and even poorer methods of rejection caused this worker much sorrow that he returned to the department with a broken spirit. It is not insignificant that he did from this point develop blood pressure problems and within a short spell collapsed suddenly and died.

Anonymous

If you have gone through life and you have either seen or experienced violence it can have many different effects on you.

You can have many experiences of violence like I have and it can leave a pretty bad effect on you, it makes me look back and think what was the lesson I have learnt?

It has taught me in many ways not to be violent to my children, it is not necessary to hurt a child, instead of violence understanding is what a child needs not hitting. By hitting you are knocking all the love out of the child. Violence is not necessary in any form. The worse form of violence in my mind is not ordinary physical violence but mental violence. By mental violence you hurt yourself more than by hurting and hitting someone.

I have learnt by my experiences.

My name is M. J. I am a mother of two children, two boys M. aged $5\frac{1}{2}$ and G. aged 2. They are two wonderful, lovable boys but can be very trying at times and my shouting and swearing at them does not make things easier for them, if anything it makes it harder for both of them.

I come from a very strict and good family background. When I was at home my brother and myself never went without food and we also had clothes to our backs.

I was the oldest of the two but my father and mother were more strict on me I could never understand why, but when I think back through the years I realise why, because I was the only girl and they were protecting my interests, but at that time I thought they were being mean and depriving me of things that other girls had, but now I understood they were doing it for my own good.

My parents were good parents but my mother seemed to care for my brother and my father for me, the atmosphere between our family was sometimes very strenuous, my father used to shout at my mother and I sometimes felt like killing him. He was very cruel to her, not hitting her but shouting, and words can hurt far more than being hit. Words leave something behind. I would sooner have seen my father hit my mother than hear him say cruel words which she and myself will never forget. I remember when I was 16 years old I came home from work and my father turned round and shouted to my mother 'here comes your bastard'. I was stunned and eventually broke down and ran to my father and was kicking and hitting him, telling him how I hated him and wished he was dead. He just laughed. The more he laughed the more I shouted 'I hate you, I hate you'.

My mother was heartbroken, and I knelt down beside her telling her that if I wasn't wanted in the house I would leave home. My mother said 'no' and eventually when all the shouting was over my mother took me to one side and explained to me how she became pregnant, and my father was sent back to England, after one year my father sent my mother the money to come to England, then they were married. I was born in Germany and then when I was about $1\frac{1}{2}$ years my mother brought me over here.

The most horriblest experience I can remember was when I was 17 years old and I was still a virgin, my father one night came into my bedroom and had no pants on. He got into my bed. I woke up and screamed. He ran out. I stayed awake all night absolutely petrified, every time I thought about it I felt sick and hated my father. After that I couldn't bear to be near him. If he was in the sitting room I would go and help my mother with whatever she was doing. I really hated him because he had cheated my mother.

I started courting at the age of 17, not long after the incident with my father, with a boy called M. He was working at a paint company, we were courting for 6 months and up to August I was still a virgin but I had sexual intercourse with my boyfriend which was very painful, often I felt disgusted and ashamed of what we had done. I became pregnant but never told anyone until I was nearly 3 months, then I told my mother I was going to have a baby. She called me a disgusting girl and said I ought to be ashamed of myself. I replied I was glad and she said I wasn't to tell my father. She said he would kill me and I said he couldn't touch me for something that was only part of nature, and that she and my father had done the same, so there was nothing disgusting about it.

I was fed up about the attitude my mother was taking, so I went up to my father and said M. was coming to see him about us getting married. M. came up to the house and asked my father if we could get married, to my utmost surprise my father said yes, and said if we needed any help we knew where to come. Then my mother piped in and said 'do you know that she is pregnant?' I went white expecting him to hit me, he sat there for a bit and asked M. and me if we knew what we were doing, of course we said yes, after I kept thinking how nice to get away from my father.

I was married in January 1967, and lived with my mother-in-law. What a cow she was. Life wasn't too bad. I went out to work and so did my husband. I was working up to my being 7 months pregnant, then began to drag. I used to get up at 5 o'clock in the morning. I made my husband his breakfast and took it up to him, then I would clean his shoes and get his sandwiches ready, when he went to work I would lie down on the settee for an hour, then my fun started. I used to take all the curtains down wash and iron them, clean the windows, and paintwork, then I would polish all the furniture and the nicest job of all was scrubbing the carpet. I really enjoyed doing it. I felt very proud of what I had done, it was a great achievement.

In March 1967 we went to look at a beautiful house that a nurse and her husband were selling for £500. We were extremely excited thinking how nice it would be to have a house of our own. We asked them how much deposit they wanted, they said £25 and £3 a week. Well, we hadn't got the money so we asked my father for the deposit and we said we would pay it back at £2 a week. Well we went back to see the people and they told us that someone had paid cash for it. We went home very upset and disappointed. We then began to think we would never have a home of our own and we never did.

My son was born in July 1967, and I was thrilled to bits, when I came home our troubles started. M. my son was a very bad sleeper and I was awake for two weeks and was really ill. I had no patience, my nerves were that bad that one night he was crying constantly that I picked him up and threw him on the bed and was shouting 'for God's sake shut up'. I really wanted to hit him and felt so violent, I suddenly stopped and realised what would have happened if I had hit him. What kind of a mother was I to start on my baby. I thought I was a mad woman, it really frightened me.

After a few days my son slept without any trouble and after that he was a wonderful baby. I used to bath him every night in front of the fire. My husband used to watch television and never really took any interest in him. If he was playing and I was talking to him he would tell me to shut up. After a while I was that upset that I used to take M. into the front room and bath and play with him, just so we wouldn't get shouted at, I hardly left my son and preferred to be on my own with him.

In January 1968 my husband came home and told me he was leaving us as he had found another woman. I was stunned and the cup of tea I had in my hand I threw at him and ran upstairs. He came upstairs and grabbed my hand and threw me from the top right down to the bottom. All I remember was knocking my head and then hearing my husband crying and saying 'are you alright, please answer me I'm sorry'. We sat down on the settee and he said he wouldn't leave me and he would go and tell her it was over. I never really believed he would. He went out and didn't come home for two days. We never got on very well when he came back, he was very distant. Eventually we decided to sleep in separate beds, he moved out of the big room and slept in the back room, so my son and I slept in the same room.

By the end of January things got worse and worse. he gave me £4 a week to keep us, that was two adults and one child. I couldn't manage, so I bought the food for M., enough Cow and Gate and solids to last him for a week. He never went without food, with the money that was left I bought food for us, but I never had any as there was never enough after he had his meal. I used to have bread and jam.

I remember one incident when I had no money left, after my husband had his tea I said 'Please could I have some money for some food', he gave me 2p for a bag of crisps. I bought the crisps and made myself a crisp sandwich, I was literally starving.

A few days after my nerves were really bad, and I went to see a Solicitor about a separation. When I came home I told him we were leaving him. He went beserk and went and got his shotgun and filled it up with a cartridge. He went into the room where the baby was and stood over him with the gun. I rushed past him, picked the baby up and all the colour ran out of me. I begged and pleaded him not to shoot us. He just said 'I'll kill the pair of you'. I screamed and ran out with the baby wrapped up in a blanket, we ran all the way down the street, my only concern was for the safety of M.

After a few hours we went back, my heart was in my mouth wondering what will he do? Anyway we went in and he wasn't there, what a relief, I undressed M. and fed him, got him ready for bed, then I got ready for bed myself and locked the door so he wouldn't touch me.

The following day I went to my Solicitor and told him of the incident of the previous night. He advised me to leave him as soon as possible. I arrived home and started packing. I took M's cot down and got a taxi. Well I got M. ready and my husband arrived home. I was really scared, anyway I told him we were leaving, the next thing was I had my arms round my son to protect him from my husband's evil blows which ended up with my face covered in blood, two black eyes and my husband's boots going into my stomach. I felt so sick and gave the baby to his mother. The next thing I remember was waking up in my mother's bed apparently someone had driven me up to my Mum's.

I never saw my husband until September, when he asked me to go back to him. I agreed thinking I would be alright and he had finally changed. How wrong I was. I became pregnant and he left me. I got a corporation flat and was very lonely and frightened, not daring to tell my parents I was pregnant. I never even told them till I had my baby, a beautiful girl called S. I was very proud I had got a boy and a girl, M. was very helpful, he used to get her nappies and help me feed her, he was marvellous. My daughter was born in May 1969 and my parents reaction was to me one of resentment. They never came near, but one day I received a letter saying I could come up to visit them with M., but would I not bring S. up as the neighbours would be talking. I replied to the letter saying if I could not bring S. then none of us would come. I really felt horrified at the way they were acting to us.

In November 1969 S. died of Bacteria Enteritis. I was broken hearted and hated everyone. I didn't even believe in God any more. I thought he was punishing me but couldn't understand why he was punishing me. It left a terrible mark on me when we buried my daughter. The only thing that was on my mind was 'Please

God please let me die with her and end this torment'. I must have been a very selfish mother not to think about M. What kind of a person was I? Mad perhaps. No, just heartbroken that after six months of living, God took my only daughter away. He did it for a reason. He does everything for a purpose. Maybe he thought she was too good to live here on this unpleasant earth, anyway she is never forgotten, she was never, and always will be on my mind.

At the time of my daughter's death I was living with a man called S. who was very good to me until she died, then he went to pieces just like I did. He refused to work and then my troubles started. We used to argue and I often ended up seeing stars. M. was very frightened of S. and clung to me like glue.

One night I told him I was finishing with him. During the night he came in the bedroom, dragged me out of bed by the hair and started to thump me. I got M. and hid him under the bed. S. dragged me into the front room and knocked holy hell out of me. Little M. came in screaming. I got off the floor and ran to pick him up. The next thing I knew he took M. off me, put him in a chair and got the kitchen knife in his hand. He shoved me on the floor and held the knife on my stomach. I was petrified and started screaming 'you bastard, I can't help myself why are you doing this to me'. He replied 'If I can't have you, you can't have this baby'.

Eventually he let go of me and I got up and when his back was turned I ran out with M. screaming. My neighbour phoned the police. They came and I told them to get him out. He kept saying 'I'm sorry C. I didn't mean it'. I refused to answer him and they told him he had to leave. What a relief. Well they got him out and M. and myself went back to bed. I didn't sleep, I was worried in case he came back.

The following day he walked in as I was ready for going out. He turned round and said 'If you don't take me back I will do something stupid'. I just laughed. In the afternoon when I came back from town, the police were at my door. They asked me if I knew S. . . . I said yes, they then told me he had had a crash and was in hospital and was asking for me. Well, we went up to see him and he had written on a piece of toilet paper, begging me to take him back. I had a good laugh. The matron of the hospital asked me if I would have him back. I refused and walked out. He was discharged and directly came looking for me. I refused to see him but he wouldn't give up, so in the end for the safety of M. I just left my flat and went to B Hostel which is a home for mothers and children.

I left and got a house with four rooms. It wasn't bad but at least it was a roof over my son's head.

I started to live with a boy aged 29 called T. and life was great for quite a bit. Until he wouldn't work, so I got fed up with it. So one night I put the children into bed and waited for him coming in. He arrived home late. I let him in and gave him his supper, and then I told him I wanted him to go. He just sat there, so I got the plate and threw it at him. He got up and I was numb in case he would hit me. He never touched me. He asked me if I wanted him to go. I said yes. I went in the front room and got his suitcase and threw it right through the glass door. He went and I was really upset at what I had done, and thought I was going mad. After he left I was ever so ill, and my hair started to drop out.

About two months after my gas and electric was turned off, so I brought the bed downstairs and we lived in one room, and I had to cook on the fire. In the end I couldn't stand it. I left and went to stop with my friends. I thought they were a happy couple, but I found out different. He used to knock her about and one particular night he came in and asked her for her family allowance. She was so frightened because she couldn't find it. She told him and he flew at her, knocked her head on the wall and then turned round and belted me because I told him he was a bully. I waited till morning and then got M. and G. dressed and left. I went to my Probation Officer to tell her what had happened. Anyway I asked her when I could go to the rehabilitation centre. She said just before Christmas. I went to stop at my friends who lived on her own with her children. I went into hospital on the Thursday for a termination. I came out on the Saturday. I again approached her about F House, she told me I couldn't go till January as they had a measles outbreak.

At the beginning of January I was to appear at Court to go to F House, and I had second thoughts and didn't go. I felt so guilty that I had let down so many people who wanted to help me, that I went to Court and apologised, and really did want to come to the rehabilitation centre. I am very happy that I did because so many people show that they do care and do want to help me. My whole attitude to various things in life has changed. The most important thing to me is my being able to understand my children which to me is a great accomplishment.

This is the turning point of my life and I shall never look back into the past. It is the future I am looking at now, I am never going to be like I was. Being here at F. House has taught me that.

During my 4 months rehabilitation period things have changed completely the most important change of my life is my ability to *love* and *understand* both my children, before I came I had a great tendency to hurt my oldest boy M. both mental and physically, mentally I hurt him by saying 'You are stupid I think you should see a doctor' that must have hurt him as much as it hurt me to say it. I was still like this up to one month ago when I realized how much damage I must have been doing to him.

I feel differently towards my children. I love and understand them and my being at F. House has taught me that someone does care about me and their caring about me makes me feel they are interested in my problems and my feelings.

As I know they care for me I hand over my love and warm feelings to my two lovely children, I realize my mistakes and at one time I thought I had a Juvenile Delinquent as a son but now it is out of my mind about that so I know he cares and loves me as I love and care for him.

I shall never regret me learning about how to understand my children I thought it was impossible for anyone to tell you how to bring your children up but it is a good job someone can help you.

M., aged 24 *years*

Epilogue . . .

At approximately 9.20 am on Monday 22 February, I was called from the kitchen to M. House where S. was the cause of much disturbance. As I arrived I heard S. screaming threats and abuse which was directed towards staff. I saw her remove her left shoe and strike Miss F. across the head and face. S. was restrained from further violence by myself and Mr. E., whose spectacles were knocked to the floor. S. calmed a little, but continued to threaten and abuse staff. She eventually climbed through the window and ran into the grounds still shouting abuse. As I approached the front door of M. House in order to seek S., the door was opened by her and she flung clods of earth into the house, some of which struck me on the face and shoulders. S. shortly returned to the house and prowled the building seeking Miss F. and threatening further violence. I spoke firmly to S., but at this point she was unable to accept help, advice or reprimand.

S. did not attend school that morning but did return in the afternoon. However, her mood was such that the general atmosphere was an uneasy one. Throughout the evening S. attempted to disrupt activities, bullied younger girls and was a constant threat to the stability of the group.

I feel that, as this incident is only one of many, S. presents a persistent threat to staff and younger children. I would commend the tolerance and patience of the staff who are almost constantly subjected to provocation which progresses beyond the bounds of human endurance.

(extract from Head's Day Book)
18.2.71. S. had to be excluded from the Dining Room for disruptive and violent behaviour. She threw food and plates at staff and children and had to be ejected by two male members of staff. A short while after the incident S. was seen by myself, she said that she could not talk about what had happened so I gave her paper and pencil and asked her to write it. The following was produced:

'On February 18th I did not want anything to eat. I did not go over to the dining room. Nobody came to bring me over so I went and caused trouble. I was taken to the playroom and I sat and think how naughty I have been, I am because I was sent out of the dining room. I did not do as Aunt told me and I was banned from the dining room. I do not belong in a house I belong in the rain and cold, but if I was a good girl I would not be in a home right now. I am here now so I will have to stay in here and behave myself. I could try to behave, I could if I wanted to.

Life is dead for me I am no use for anybody. In my life I am just a silly little girl. My mother never kiss me, I always had to kiss her. If I did not kiss her I would feel very sad for myself.

Aunt J. left cold dinner for me, but I refuse to eat it. I do not come from a pig sty I come from my mother's vagina . . . I hope you know that.'

|-||

Printed in England for Her Majesty's Stationery Office
By Burrup, Mathieson & Co., Ltd., SE1 0NX
S964656 LE   Dd 290460   K32   3/76